ETHICAL VALUES
IN THE AGE OF SCIENCE

ETHICAL VALUES IN THE AGE OF SCIENCE

By PAUL ROUBICZEK

CAMBRIDGE
AT THE UNIVERSITY PRESS
1969

Published by the Syndics of the Cambridge University Press
Bentley House, 200 Euston Road, London N.W.1
American Branch: 32 East 57th Street, New York, N.Y.10022

© Cambridge University Press 1969

Library of Congress Catalogue Card Number: 72–85737
Standard Book Numbers:
521 07619 6 clothbound
521 09592 1 paperback

Printed in Great Britain
at the University Printing House, Cambridge
(Brooke Crutchley, University Printer)

CONTENTS

To

WERNER HEISENBERG

PREFACE

My original intention in this book was to concentrate entirely on the theory of ethics. But I soon realized that my attempt was based on an assumption which can hardly be made at the present time—that the need for ethics is generally felt and that its importance is acknowledged by everyone interested in moral problems. In fact, however, the significance of ethics (as a separate discipline in the traditional sense) is very often either questioned or denied; more and more people come to believe that, in this field as in others, the philosophical method has been—or should be—replaced by a scientific one. Morality in particular is frequently seen as determined by non-moral factors which can be scientifically ascertained, and this would either make ethics superfluous or confine it to purely practical considerations.

I therefore changed my original plans. The first part of this book tries to prove that there is both room and need for ethics. This is done with the help of an investigation into the relevant claims of history, psycho-analysis, sociology, and some aspects of natural science. Only after thus testing the foundations of ethics in terms of the situation in which we find ourselves, do I proceed in the second part to a discussion of different ethical teachings. I pay particular attention to the relationship of values and value-judgments with morality and ethics, because this approach (as it seems to me) has been unduly neglected. The last chapter also tries to clarify the connection and difference between ethics and religious faith.

I have much pleasure in acknowledging my great indebtedness to Douglas Hewitt and Allan Keeling; I am more grateful than I can say for the time and care they devoted to helping me to clarify difficult problems and to find the right form of presentation for my thoughts. I am equally grateful to Hilde Keeling for her patience and the trouble she took in the preparation of the typescript.

My thanks are also due to my previous publisher, Darwen Finlayson, London, for permission to quote short passages from my book, *Thinking towards Religion*.

P.R.

Clare College, Cambridge
May 1969

PART I

CHAPTER I

PHILOSOPHY AND ETHICS

Moral law, taken for granted for centuries, has become increasingly problematical. So long as it was accepted unquestioningly, hardly anybody doubted that it was an absolute law; everyone believed either that it was part of God's will, or that it was self-evident and self-sufficient, and therefore in no need of further justification. This absoluteness, however, seems to have become unacceptable. It might indeed be best to reserve the concept solely for the past, since in present-day thinking morality is looked upon more and more (at least outside theology) as the product of biological, psychological or social factors. Yet some uneasiness still accompanies this process of making all morality dependent on apparently more fundamental facts; for instance, few people, if any, can be fully satisfied with any teaching which is bound to diminish the feeling of personal responsibility. Nor, to give another example, does the problem of good and evil appear obsolete, despite scientific explanations of human behaviour. Therefore, the claim that there is a moral law which gives to morality an ultimate sanction, a basis which is absolute because it is independent of any further causation, cannot—or should not—be denied without a thorough investigation. It is to this investigation that this book attempts to make a contribution.

Some of the difficulties of the present situation are shown by our use of the word 'morality' itself. Sometimes it is simply equated with prevalent social customs; more often, perhaps, it is used whenever personal problems are touched upon, and then it is applied to problems of the most diverse kind, such as the choice between different ways of making money, the punishment of children or of criminals, or chastity and marriage. In a sense this is justified, because there are few personal problems which have no moral implications, but, obviously, these implications should

3

be clearly stated to give to the word 'moral' a meaning of its own.

Once we try to restrict the use of the word, however, we meet another difficulty—the commonly neglected need to distinguish between fundamental moral law or basic morality and its application in particular circumstances. Marriage, for instance, is often spoken of uncritically and without reference to its personal aspects, as if the fact that marriage takes different forms in different societies were one of the essential problems faced by those who assert the existence of a moral law. It is then argued that, since for the Christian monogamy alone is moral, while in some other religions polygamy is permitted, morality is obviously entirely dependent on external circumstances. In fact the forms of marriage constitute a problem which only arises when morality has to be applied within the framework of society; the fundamental moral question in marriage (as elsewhere) has to do with the human relationship between the persons involved, with their motives, attitudes and actions, with love and trust.

Moral codes may differ as to whether a man may have one wife or four; all are agreed that a man may not have any woman that he likes whenever he likes. Moral codes may differ again where lying is the lesser of two evils, but all are agreed that ordinarily speaking the truth is the right course of action. Such variety as there is in moral codes can often be explained by the fact that these codes are not statements of ultimate moral principles but are applications of such principles to the actual conditions of a particular society ... There are certain factors which prevent us from seeing the fundamental resemblances in the different moral codes.*

It is true that moral considerations may convince us that monogamy is a more adequate way of acting according to moral principles; whether or not this is so should be the essential point in any discussion of the moral value of monogamy in our society. But only the principles themselves ought to be called moral, despite the undeniable importance of the existing laws and customs, and even though a proper description of these can help us to come to a moral decision.

To arrive at a clear concept of this basic morality, one could

* W. Lillie, *An Introduction to Ethics* (London, 1948), pp. 113–14.

4

perhaps adopt the following definition: that it is a pattern of behaviour based on the absolute value of the good. But even this raises more problems than it solves. What is the meaning of the term 'good'? Is there anything which we can legitimately call an 'absolute value' and is there anything absolutely reliable on which to base our behaviour? What is the exact meaning of the term 'absolute'? All these problems must be discussed at length, before any definition can be accepted. For the time being I just state that in what follows I use the word 'morality' to mean 'fundamental morality' and, whenever necessary, pay due regard to the need to distinguish it from any special application of moral concepts, which will also be discussed.

This book, however, is concerned, not with morality alone but with ethics, and this makes it easier to postpone the question of definition until later. Ethics includes morality, but is wider in scope; as well as the foundations and implications of morality, it includes the question of how far we can know for certain and speak about an absolute value at all—that is, the epistomological problem of the limitations of knowledge. We shall therefore investigate the presuppositions of any definition.

The subject-matter of ethics is traditionally circumscribed by the following three questions:

1. What ought we to do?
2. What is the meaning of 'good'?
3. Are we able to do what we ought to do?*

The first two questions are moral ones, but in their ethical sense they also lead to the investigation of how it may be possible to arrive at an answer, why any answer is valid, and if so, on what grounds we are under the obligation to observe any rules or laws

---

* See for the first two questions G. E. Moore, *Principia Ethica* (Cambridge, 1959), (Paperback edition), pp. 3, 115, or A. Wenzl, *Philosophie der Freiheit*, (Muenchen, 1949), p. 7, where the third question is also mentioned. These two examples (to which one could add others) have been chosen in order to show that the tradition is still alive today, and that even philosophers belonging to entirely different schools agree in this respect. G. E. Moore also gives some other formulations which are helpful, such as (1) 'What kind of actions ought we to perform?' and (2) 'What kind of things ought to exist for their own sake?' *Ibid.*, p. viii.

which we discover. The third question concerns the freedom of will which must be the basis of any such obligation, for commands would be senseless if we were unable to obey.

The significance of these questions may be more fully appreciated if some further details are added.

1. The first question asks whether—beyond the necessary practical considerations of life—there are principles which ought to determine our behaviour, such as 'Thou shalt love thy neighbour as thyself', and whether these principles (if they exist and can be discovered and stated) are of general validity. Whether they are valid, that is, under any circumstances, overriding all practical considerations. They might turn out to be a mere guidance for those who want to come near to a cherished ideal. The validity of the sense of unconditional obligation which seems to accompany them must therefore be established and tested.

2. As the word 'good' is used in many different contexts, its special moral meaning has to be isolated. This gives rise to the question whether there is something which, in the moral sense, can always be called good, and this demands an inquiry into the nature of value-judgments, of relative and absolute values, which will throw further light on the problem of obligation. To call something good is to make a value-judgment; all moral commandments imply the word 'ought'. But if the good were ultimately derived from merely arbitrary or conventional requirements or from social or psychological influences, value-judgments would remain dependent on these factors and an unconditional obligation to accept this 'ought' would not arise.

3. Morality must be based on freedom of choice, decision and action, for unless one is free to choose and to act upon one's choice one cannot be held responsible for one's actions. A sense of responsibility, however, is probably the most clearly recognized expression of morality, so it cannot be dismissed easily. Yet to believe in freedom has become particularly difficult because of the findings of different sciences, particularly psychology. The prevailing tendency is to assume that all our actions are effects of causes upon which we had no influence. Freedom of will is thus denied,

6

though the implicit denial of responsibility is not so openly professed and is sometimes not even seen. In fact the survival of the concept and feeling of responsibility appears to be a strong support for the belief in freedom. Science provides theories which could help to shake off responsibility, and responsibility, after all, is more often than not an irksome burden; yet it is still felt, demanded and accepted. The age-old problem of freedom must obviously be reconsidered in the light of present-day thought.

All three questions require an investigation of what it is possible and what it is impossible to know. Without a decision on this, the relevance of scientific theories for ethical knowledge, the problem of human freedom and the status of absolute values could not be judged, nor a valid decision about their conflicting claims be made.

Even this short introductory exposition of what ethics means may be sufficient to show that this is the part of philosophy which is most essential for dealing with actual experience. Here philosophy is concerned directly with practical questions of immediate importance which we can hardly avoid answering—consciously if we want our choices to rest on a proper foundation, unconsciously if we neglect or suppress this inner need, for the questions are answered by our decisions and behaviour, whether or not we make the answer clear to ourselves. Thus ethics is of basic importance, because it will make a difference to our attitudes and actions, which answers to these questions we accept or take for granted, whether we believe in good and evil in an absolute sense, in an ultimate right and wrong, or whether we believe that morality is only of social importance, more or less conventional, determined by needs or custom, by inheritance and psychological make-up.

It is true that many do not take the trouble to come to a conscious decision; even those who accept responsibility often divide their lives into two separate compartments—a private one where morality applies, and a public one where it does not, either because of practical needs or theoretical convictions or because the end seems to justify the means. Family life and friendships are frequently protected in this way from the otherwise accepted immorality of, say, the struggle for material or political success. This split may also take another form: influenced by what is commonly believed, some people agree that all morality is merely socially determined, yet they behave in a way which only makes sense as the response to a belief in something like an absolute. They may try to explain this as a subjective survival of old prejudices, but even this does not make sense in the light of what they actually experience and do. They overtly deny, and at the same time tacitly presuppose, absolute standards. Inevitably such inconsistencies must sooner or later harm one's integrity; these problems should at least be faced. We may not always be fully aware of moral problems when we act, we may even refuse very often to be worried by principles or moral demands, but these will force themselves upon us when we are confronted with difficult situations or decisions of consequence when it will be essential to know whether morality is simply a prejudice, now unmasked by modern science and thus to be subordinated to utilitarian considerations, or whether it is something reliable to direct us, something ultimate to rely upon. If ultimate, the good may require sacrifices, even the sacrifice of life, and such sacrifices have been made. Is it simply foolish to contemplate such a course of action at all; should we not just seek our own advantage? In short, it will be rather difficult to disregard all such questions all the time; they will have to be answered in times of stress, and it is therefore better to face them beforehand. Seen in this light, it is one of the main tasks of the philosopher to help us to do so—that is, to develop ethics. Neither the questions nor the answers may be as simple as this first tentative approach suggests, which makes the need to deal with them systematically even more urgent.

When we look at the development of ethics however we discover an unexpected and surprising fact. Despite its obvious and widely accepted importance and even though most philosophers —at least until very recently—agreed that a philosophy without ethics would be highly unsatisfactory, the place of ethics within the general framework of philosophy has remained uncertain throughout the ages.

The difficulty arose because philosophers were mainly striving to create a metaphysical system which was intended to provide a full explanation of the universe and man. This system had to be unitary and all-inclusive; therefore the philosopher had to find a common basis for external reality and for the moral law and had to deal with metaphysics and ethics in the same terms. In other words the universe and goodness were explored simultaneously and it was taken for granted that one and the same method could yield results relevant to the knowledge of both. It proved impossible however to include them in the same system without a falsification of either metaphysics or ethics. One of two things always happened and was obviously bound to happen—either goodness came first and prejudiced the explanation of the universe, or attention was concentrated on the external world and this, instead of explaining goodness, reduced it to something much less than itself.

Typical examples of these two kinds of shortcomings are the systems of Plato and Aristotle—typical because they exercised such a profound influence on the development of European philosophy that they remained the models of its two main types right up to the end of the last century.

Plato's system of ideas—his claim that our world is founded upon the spiritual realm of eternal and unchangeable 'perfect forms' and that these are the prototypes and origin of all the changeable things we know—fits the conception of goodness well. When we want to do something good, we are influenced by the idea of perfect goodness; we try to deduce from it what we really ought to do. This conception itself has hardly changed at all, however much its possible applications have. In fact, some of Plato's own purely moral statements prove it, for they are as valid as they ever were. His assertion, for instance, that it is better to suffer wrong than to do wrong, continues to make its impact; it has become neither obsolete nor conventional, but has remained a challenge. T. Haecker, for instance, made the following entry, dated 30.1.1945, in the secret diary which he wrote in Nazi Germany:

The glory of Europe, its high point, and the sign of its election, is that a sentence in Plato, which says that it is better to suffer injustice than to commit it, should touch from afar the divine revelation of Christ. If there is injustice in the world, then the greater worth belongs to him who suffers the injustice, not to him who commits it. That is astounding, and belongs to another world. Injustice! Not power, be it noted, for the good and the wicked can use power, but not injustice.*

It seems justifiable, therefore, for Plato to accept the good as valuable in itself, as being in no need of any further support—that is as an absolute value. But Plato also makes it the highest of all ideas and thus the basis of his whole system. 'The Idea of good' is 'the universal author of all things beautiful and right, parent of light and of the lord of light in the visible world, and the immediate and supreme source of reason and truth in the intellectual.'† However, this leads to increasing difficulties. While it is one of Plato's great achievements to have established the connection between the three absolute values—truth, goodness and beauty—it is less convincing to make goodness the source of reason. The connection between the good and the visible, external world—that it creates the 'lord of light', namely the sun, —remains, at least as a philosophical thought, entirely unconvincing. The attempt to find a unitary and all-inclusive explanation and to base it on ethics prejudices metaphysics.

Aristotle tries to avoid this failure by relying on sense-experience and its logical elaboration. There are, in his later philosophy, no perfect forms. He refers first of all to sense-data and insists that we must judge what we cannot see by the evidence of what we do see. With him, we come down to earth and his system fits external reality well, even though difficulties arise concerning the transcendental aspect of reality which he does not want to dismiss. It is no accident that this kind of philosophy later led to materialism. While Plato's system can inspire goodness and

---

* *Journal at Night* (London, 1949), p. 221. (I have used in the text the word 'wrong' which is the literal translation of the word 'Unrecht' used by Haecker; but 'injustice' is frequently used as well in translations of Plato.)

† The Republic, bk 7. Quoted according to *The Dialogues of Plato*, transl. by Jowett (Oxford, 1953), vol. I, p. 379.

kindle love, Aristotle is the master of sober investigation; his greatness lies in the development of logic, of a systematic and critical accumulation of knowledge, in leading man a long way towards scientific thinking. Consequently, however, his ethics is mainly matter of fact, a collection of practical and political rules; the good is not considered as such. For him, 'virtue is concerned with pains and pleasures', and the cardinal point is that 'excess and deficiency' are equally fatal; he always tries to find the mean, the reasonable middle way. If 'good craftsmen work to the standard of the mean, then, since goodness like nature is more exact and of a higher character than any art, it follows that goodness is the quality that hits the mean. By "goodness" I mean goodness of moral character, since it is moral goodness that deals with feelings and actions, and it is in them that we find excess, deficiency and a mean . . . the first two being wrong, the mean right and praised as such.'* He compares the effects of excess and deficiency of meat and drink with those of courage, temperance and other virtues; he wants neither complete avoidance nor licentious enjoyment of all pleasures; neither an excess nor a deficiency of truthfulness. The mean thus becomes a useful practical criterion, but it cannot help us to decide what the good itself is. Artistotle does not deal with that good which could be and ought to be done for its own sake. Emphasis on metaphysics does not allow for a full development of ethics.

That this is inevitable is shown even by those later followers of Plato who concentrate more exclusively on metaphysics. Hegel's idealistic system, for instance, leaves as little room for ethics as Marx's materialism. Both agree that 'such an empty thing as good for the sake of the good has no place whatsoever in living reality'.† Other philosophers tried to counteract this trend by writing on ethics alone and making a special discipline of it, independent of all other philosophy. But this too is unsatisfactory, the validity of ethics is obviously doubtful if it is not rooted in our knowledge

---

* *The Nichomachean Ethics*, transl. by J. A. K. Thomson (London 1953), pp. 47, 51.
† Hegel's formulation.

of reality, just as this knowledge remains insufficient if it is irrelevant to our moral experience.

The difficulty of combining metaphysics and ethics in a unitary system arises mainly because morality (meaning 'fundamental morality') must remain autonomous. In the moral sense, the good is only good if it is pursued as an end in itself. When it is done not solely for its own sake, but for some other reason, such as to acquire a good reputation or riches, then the resulting action, though it may still be useful, is no longer morally good. The implication of this need for autonomy is that any complete explanation of the whole of the universe endangers the purity of ethics; even a metaphysical system which is dominated by the good makes doing the good a means to a different end, to finding one's right place in a presupposed world-order, which is a kind of reward. The decision to do the good must spring from the striving for the good alone. And yet ethics should be an integral part of philosophy.

Is there a way out of this impasse? This book will attempt to show that there is, by trying to establish the right kind of interconnection between philosophy in general and ethics in particular. In fact, the success of the investigation will depend on how far such a connection can finally be shown to be indispensable.

A help in discovering this way out can be found in certain parts of Kant's philosophy and in certain aspects of Existentialism, but they have to be seen in a context which is rather different from that in which they occur. This will be discussed more fully later; it may be useful, however, to indicate briefly which of these elements are important and how they influence the relationship between metaphysics and ethics. At this stage the statement of the position will of course appear in a simplified form and often in the shape of dogmatic assertions. These will be explored in later chapters.*

---

* It is due to our concern with this problem that, from among the great philosophers of the past, we shall single out Kant and Kierkegaard; only to them—or rather to relevant aspects of their teachings—will separate chapters be devoted. (See chs VII, VIII, XII.)

The base of our investigation is an elaboration—both extension and modification—of Kant's theory of knowledge, of his insistence that our knowledge is strictly limited. According to Kant, we have no immediate, ultimate and therefore absolute knowledge of reality because our knowledge is dependent on the working of our minds, which imposes its own requirements upon our thinking. Our minds do not allow us, as many thinkers have assumed, to know reality as it is in itself, without any falsification due to our apprehension of it; the mind is not, as Locke for instance assumed, simply a 'white paper void of all characters, without any ideas'* upon which reality imprints itself directly and reliably. Kant recognized that the mind is a kind of mechanism, working according to its own laws, and it is only by the application of these laws (by applying, for instance, such concepts as *cause and effect* or *the one and the many*) that we grasp reality. We therefore have only a relative knowledge of reality. We know it as it appears to us and not as it is in itself. We are unable to penetrate to the ultimate nature of the universe because we remain dependent on thinking and cannot know what the universe would be like if it were grasped directly without the intervention of our thought; nor can we grasp anything ultimate so long as we rely on thinking alone. (This has important implications for the problem of faith which will be explored later.) Kant was the supreme realist; he never denied the existence of the reality which we experience (as Berkeley, for instance, did) nor that thinking follows its own laws (which many still do deny); he saw that our knowledge is based upon both the impression reality makes on us and the laws of thinking.

Knowledge consists of two parts: first of the concept through which an object is thought of at all (the category), and secondly of the perception by which it is given. Without the power of sense no object would be given to us, without intellect no object would be thought. Thoughts without content are empty, perceptions without concepts are blind.†

* *An essay concerning Human Understanding*, bk II, ch. 1, par. 2.
† *Critique of Pure Reason*, pp. 146 and 75 of the original edition (my own translation).

Thus all metaphysical systems are inadequate because there is no possibility of finding a complete explanation of the whole of reality which could claim to be objectively true.

As far as this conclusion is concerned, Kant has exercised the greatest possible influence. His assertion that he made it impossible to construct such a system, though pushed aside in the nineteenth century, has since been vindicated. With very few exceptions, system-building has been abandoned. But Kant's views concerning knowledge are still attacked or even dismissed; in particular it is often overlooked that his teaching does not mean that metaphysical problems should be excluded altogether. It is only the all-inclusive systems which have been invalidated; Kant dealt fully with single metaphysical problems, such as space and time, necessity and freedom, and they can now be dealt with better than before because there is no need to force them into the strait jacket of a system. One can approach them in terms which they themselves dictate.

Kant himself shows how this can be done with regard to ethics. His statements about the knowledge of reality which have been discussed so far concern knowledge of external reality, of the universe—the aim of all metaphysical systems. But he also realized that the abandoning of these systems requires the abandoning as well of the attempt to think in a unitary way, which is the way of thinking demanded by them. Kant discovered (though he did not take it far enough) that there are two ways of thinking—pure reason, objective, impersonal, by which we know external reality, and practical reason, which is personal and takes into account inner experience. External knowledge, being dependent on the laws of thinking, cannot grasp anything ultimate and absolute. But we ourselves are embodiments of ultimate reality, and this has important consequences; we hear within ourselves the voice of the absolute; conscience tells us what we ought to do. In other words: we do not know why there is a universe, why there is an earth and man living on it, nor even why there is man; but Kant believed—in agreement with Socrates—that we are able to know absolutely what we ought to do if we want to do the good, if we want to be good. Thus the limitations of knowledge disclosed by Kant are not simply negative; they also allow us to approach reality in an entirely positive manner; they make room for ethics and enable us to deal with it in the particular way which makes it accessible. We may come to different conclusions, but they will be arrived at in a legitimate way.

These two ways of thinking are so different that they do not allow us to build a system, because they cannot be applied simultaneously nor can their results be simply summed up to form a single unity. We must think either in one way or in the other. In external thinking we are concerned with facts; the personal influence of the observer which might falsify results is excluded as far as possible by weighing, measuring, by taking photographs or using (in nuclear physics) photographic plates, and by making experiments. In ethics we are not concerned with establishing what is real but with what we ought to do; not with impersonal objectivity but with personal experience, with our own striving to make the good real. We cannot disregard our value-judgments and individual reactions, but on the contrary must make use of them. Natural science, therefore, cannot lead to a knowledge of the good, which is based on value-judgments, and knowledge of the good cannot fill gaps left over by science because it is arrived at by a method which science cannot accept. Nevertheless, each way of thinking is perfectly adequate for its own purpose: the successes of natural science prove how efficiently it can deal with external reality; at the same time, we can approach ethics directly, without being hindered by metaphysical considerations.

Yet Kant's teaching still leaves an important gap. To make these two ways of thinking acceptable, he emphasizes their difference and shows, first of all, that they can be applied and developed side by side without contradicting each other and thus without any intellectual sacrifice. To a large extent, this is so; it has just been seen that the one way concerns that which is and the other that which we ought to do. This makes it logically correct to say, in the usual phrase, that statements containing 'is' and statements containing 'ought' are so different that they have no influence upon each other and can be developed independently, the more so as statements of fact are mainly based on knowledge of the past and demands for action refer to the future. But is this conclusion true in the last resort? 'Ought' carries a feeling of obligation which cannot arise in the void; demands felt to be obligatory must be rooted in something real, must ultimately be based on facts, for otherwise they could not have the force to oblige us to do something. The two ways of thinking must certainly be distinguished as clearly as possible; but the independence of one from the other must not be assumed and cannot be final.*

The nature of Kant's moral teaching itself confirms the impression that there is some such insufficiency, for it is almost entirely formal; it tells us in general ways how we should act, but not what we should actually do. The basic version of his 'categorical imperative' says merely: 'Act only according to such a maxim that you can will at the same time that it becomes a general law.'† The absence of specific statements leads to an impoverishment of ethics; in the end, even Kant himself is induced to return, to some extent, to all-inclusive metaphysics. All this will be discussed later. What has been said already, however, leads us to see that Existentialism can make an essential contribution to ethics. Two aspects are particularly relevant here.

First, a general principle which is accepted by all Existentialists —that inner experience must be admitted as evidence of reality. This will not be generally accepted in an age which is so profoundly influenced by the methods of natural science. In general, evidence is only accepted as valid if it can be tested by observations or experiments which afford material proof, and this proof is only accepted if the experiments can be repeated. Even in those sciences which, like psychology, present special problems because they deal with the human mind, these requirements are fulfilled as nearly as possible. But there are no such tests and proofs, not even

---

* This problem will be fully discussed later. See pp. 164, 214–15, 239–40, 292.
† *Fundamental Principles of the Metaphysics of Ethics*, Transl. by T. K. Abbott, 3rd ed. (London, 1907), p. 55.

in the widest sense, when one deals with such values as goodness or beauty, or with morality, love and trust. Obviously, this whole region can only be understood if we scrutinize and evaluate inner experiences which may well remain unrepeatable. If we admit this different kind of evidence, however, there is the prospect that the gap between 'is' and 'ought' may be closed, for we thus discover conscience, a sense of values, particular kinds of feelings, such as the feeling of responsibility, all of which must be described as facts, even though they are facts of a different kind.

Second, Kierkegaard's insistence on what he calls man's 'ethical self'. This is not common to all Existentialists; even some who, like Sartre, are concerned with moral behaviour deny that man's nature has a moral aspect. But Kierkegaard and his disciples claim that man is not only determined by his biological inheritance, by social influences, by traditions and conventions; they assert that there is an ethical, a moral quality belonging to man's innermost being and that he is forced by his very existence to make use of his freedom. Naturally, this claim must be treated with the utmost caution and must not be accepted on inadequate evidence. But, whether finally acceptable or not, it directs our attention in the right direction; any ethical teaching is confronted by this question and, if it is to be valid, must answer it. It will be seen, moreover, that this claim also contributes to the definition of the boundaries of knowledge, by separating ethics clearly from religion.

So these are the starting points of the following investigation: Kant's teaching in so far as it concerns the limitations of knowledge and the two ways of thinking; the Existentialists' admission of inner experience as evidence; and Kierkegaard's claim that there is an ethical self. All these points will be elaborated, and they will be tested as thoroughly as possible. This will also help to bring us nearer to a solution of the problem with which we started—that of determining the right place for ethics within the general framework of philosophy. The following are, approximately, the lines upon which we shall proceed.

One of the reasons why the unitary treatment of metaphysics and ethics is bound to fail lies, as has been seen, in the fact that morality must remain autonomous. This autonomy, however, can now be established, for if two ways of thinking are needed, and if the application of each is strictly limited, external reality and ethics can be separated. As there is one sphere to which scientific thinking applies, and another where inner experience must be taken into account, the building of an all-inclusive metaphysical system becomes both impossible and unnecessary. The other difficulty arises because of the need to justify, through a foundation in facts, the sense of obligation conveyed by morality. This reason for having recourse to metaphysics has also disappeared, for the other way of thinking discloses facts, too—of a different kind, it is true, but facts nevertheless. We shall see that these facts, for instance the existence of freedom, will even prove a help in dealing with such metaphysical problems as the existence or non-existence of a transcendental reality. But even if this reality were to be accepted (as it will be in this book) a unitary metaphysical system would remain impossible, because each way of thinking when pursued independently leads to a limited, incomplete knowledge, so that both need to be constantly used and developed side by side.

These indications must suffice for the moment; other problems will have to be discussed before these introductory remarks can be seen as less dogmatic and more convincing than they may appear now. One of these problems has probably become obvious already—can it really be satisfactory to accept two kinds of knowledge, both of which are inconclusive? In fact, it might seem that this approach only creates a more dangerous split in our lives than the habit of 'living in two compartments' which we have rejected. Far from simplifying problems (as the preceding statements might suggest), this investigation will have to face such dilemmas. The separation of ethics from metaphysics will be successful only if this consequence of the existential approach can be accepted as satisfactory.

However, this is as it should be. The philosopher, to fulfil his task properly, should resist the temptation to simplify. Simplification is the legitimate method of science where the ideal form of knowledge is the mathematical equation; philosophy ought to face life as we experience it, with all its complexity, richness, fulness and inherent dangers. At the same time the task of philosophy is to lead to greater clarity of understanding, and such clarification of the issues involved in ethics does seem to be attainable if we adopt the attitude which has been outlined in this chapter.

Before embarking upon the discussion of ethics itself, a preliminary question has to be answered. Science, in particular psychology, discloses factors which seem to offer a complete explanation of morality. These factors are undoubtedly of great importance; powerful forces work upon man and within man, which exercise a great influence on his moral behaviour although they are not moral in themselves. Thus we must first decide whether or not they leave any room for ethics at all, for it is widely believed today that in this respect science has superseded philosophy and that morality and conscience can be better understood by consulting science alone.

CHAPTER II

ETHICS COMPARED WITH HISTORY AND PSYCHO-ANALYSIS

1

A prominent characteristic of the intellectual scene of today is the special kind of investigation which attempts to discover the relationship between events in the world and those in man's mind. Though this endeavour is influenced by natural science, its main concern is with man or society. It emphasizes the dependence of any particular happening in that sphere on other happenings, in contrast to any final knowledge—metaphysical, ethical or religious—such as was previously sought.

Of the disciplines concerned with this sort of investigation, our discussion will be confined to history, psychology and sociology (leaving out others, such as anthropology and economics, though our general conclusions also apply to these).* Some of these disciplines are of fairly recent origin, some are developments of earlier ones, but this does not matter because the earlier ones have been transformed to bring them into line with more recent trends.

History is the oldest of these disciplines, but during the last two centuries it has been more and more preoccupied with establishing that 'historical sense' on which we pride ourselves; in other words, most historians are no longer content with reconstructing external events nor even with their obvious causes and effects; they want to know how these events fit into the general trend of human development over a long period, and how single causes and effects

---

* I have so far called psychology a science because it also shows the effects of using the method of natural science. But I shall from now onwards use the word 'discipline' because, even though all these investigations are, to a greater or lesser extent, scientific, they cannot be equated with natural science in one important respect. This will be discussed on pp. 53–5.

are produced by more fundamental conditions and can thus be related to each other. All events are to be seen in an all-inclusive historical perspective. A more recent discipline is psychology which, with its experimental methods and close relationship to physiology, aspires to become a pure natural science; but some of its schools, especially those of Freud and Jung, try to explore a deeper level, that of the subconscious and the unconscious, so as to be able to discern more interconnections between the processes within man's mind, in the hope of including all of them, even phenomena which may seem unique. Another younger and still developing discipline is sociology. The movement in this direction has also left its mark on philosophy; linguistic analysis is mainly concerned with the relationships established by language, with the investigation of how these determine man's thought, and with the 'contextual' meaning of words.*

These attempts are of particular interest for our investigation, because they seem to replace ethics in its traditional sense. Their common denominator is the emphasis on man's subjection to conditions—the endeavour to recognize everything which man does or believes as caused by other factors upon which he has no influence, and the desire to discover how these causes in their turn are produced by historical, psychological, social or other conditions. All activities of the mind, including moral impulses, are seen as dependent on something else, and thus as relative. It is this web, created by innumerable cases of dependence, which is explored. The search for an all-pervading and inescapable relativity has, to a large extent, replaced the search for an independent, ultimate, absolute truth. Previous ages would have considered this attitude as the kind of scepticism which implied a resigned acceptance of man's inability to acquire any reliable knowledge at all; scepticism then demanded a stoic turn of mind difficult to

---

* The emphasis on such relationships may also bring to mind Martin Buber's *I and Thou*. But he is concerned with final knowledge, with man addressing God and being addressed by God. It is, however, in line with what has been said so far that the first part of his book, dealing with human relationships, has made a much greater impact than the third part which deals with the access to the absolute.

sustain, a painful renunciation never far from despair. Today the restriction of knowledge to the relative is accepted as desirable, as the only way of grasping reality or of acquiring a knowledge worth having. One even professes scepticism, but it has become a means to an end—to the avoidance of error. No room seems to be left for a fundamental moral law which is not determined by anything else.

In fact, our age could be seen as dominated by a tacit agreement to exclude the absolute, to present as unreasonable any striving for the possession of an ultimate truth, for anything which is true in itself and independent of further conditions. Theories may contradict each other, but they are only taken seriously if they do not admit any thought of absoluteness. Can we really rest content with this web of relativity?

At one time Einstein's theory of relativity was used to support the belief that everything is and must be relative. The basis of this theory is the assumption that there is an ultimate fact, namely that the speed of light is constant, unchangeable, and the greatest which can exist. This basis is as absolute as anything that can be thought of within the realm of natural science. This example may serve to remind us that the two concepts 'relative' and 'absolute' actually belong together, that something can be seen as relative only in contrast to an idea of absoluteness; there must be, at least, the ability of the mind to decide whether something is relative or absolute. The belief that everything has to be entirely relative (rarely explicitly stated, but basic to the endeavours mentioned) is evidently dogmatic, because such a belief, to be meaningful, has to be accepted as absolute truth, in disregard of the limitations of knowledge which make man unable to establish any all-inclusive claim. Despite the emphasis on relativity the belief implies the trust that the power of man's mind is unlimited. This absoluteness of the mind provides the contrast which makes it possible to grasp relativity.* This goes even beyond the original scepticism which saw the boundaries of knowledge and deplored them; by seeing

---

* Neither psychologists nor sociologists pay attention to the theory of knowledge. A few historians do, but they are exceptional.

the mind as all-powerful and yet unable to achieve any final knowledge, it can lead, and frequently has led, to nihilism.

The Existentialists are aware of this danger. They pay attention
to the fact that originally European civilization was essentially
based on belief in God, on the Christian revelation which was
equated with absolute truth. If this core of European civilization
disappears, so they say, a void must be left at its very centre; we
are faced instead with nothing, with mere emptiness—with
nothingness, as it is usually called—and nihilism is bound to
follow.

What this means is probably best explained by Nietzsche. He
asks the question 'What is nihilism?' and answers: 'The fact that
the highest values lose all value. There is no aim, no answer to the
question "Why?". Radical nihilism is the conviction that the
highest values which one wants to accept are really untenable, and
added to this is the insight that there is no justification whatever
for assuming that there is another world or a true nature of things
or anything divine or a given morality.' And he mentions as 'the
clearest symptom of nihilism: Man has lost all his dignity in his
own eyes.'* In other words: it is the undermining of all unconditional standards. It is true that some Existentialists are so fascinated
by this insight that they do not go further, and instead embrace
nothingness with enthusiasm. Others see it as a challenge; they want
to lead an 'authentic life', a life which could face this challenge
and still be of value. They try desperately to reach beyond the
relative, even though many disregard ethics and thus try in vain.

The diagnosis itself however is undoubtedly a merit of Existentialism. To the vast majority today this reliance on the relative
seems very satisfying, for the search for relationships can be of
absorbing interest and can go on indefinitely; they are never
exhausted. Moreover, man's critical faculties can be exercised
without any inhibition. One tends, therefore, to overlook the
possible consequences of this uprooting of modern man through
the dismissal of the absolute which would have to be accepted

---

* *Der Wille zur Macht*, §§ 23, 24, 36. For a fuller treatment see P. Roubiczek,
   Existentialism—For and Against (Cambridge, 1964), ch. 3.

unquestioningly. Yet the dangers seen by the Existentialists have visibly grown since they uttered their first warnings.

The purpose of this book is to try out the opposite way: to attempt to break through this web of the relative; to raise, most emphatically, the question of whether there is an unconditional, absolute truth. Instead of being satisfied with critical analysis, from which, of course, one must start in any case, we shall go further and inquire whether there is in the phenomena seen as relative any aspect which is valuable in itself, or true as such, and which could thus be accepted as final and ultimate. As critical faculties are valued so highly today, any kind of acceptance which would put an end to further criticisms seems difficult and may be denounced as dubious, but this is no reason to refuse it. On the contrary: even if the Existentialists' diagnosis were only partially correct, the path of least resistance would have to be avoided. Certainly, the philosopher cannot hope to discover absolute truth itself; he must pay attention to the limitations of knowledge; all-inclusive, unitary truth, as we shall see, is accessible only through faith. Yet I hope to show that he can go some way towards this truth, towards making statements which indicate what could remain valid at all times and under all conditions; he can explore approaches to fundamental truth. Naturally, to be aware of the dangers inherent in its dismissal is insufficient reason for accepting the absolute; any acceptance must be based on conclusive arguments; yet since the dismissal appears to be dangerous, the attempt to find such arguments is obviously worth making.

There is one point which the Existentialists usually do not consider and which is particularly relevant to our purpose. All the disciplines mentioned, as well as the natural sciences, yield results which are undoubtedly of great importance, but their value is endangered when they are seen as the only results which matter. If the emphasis on conditions—that is, on relativity—includes all reality, the limitations both of the special discipline and of knowledge in general are disregarded, with the consequence that these results are then applied where they are not appropriate. Thus even the most useful results can produce harmful effects.

How this happens, and why the effects are harmful, can be recognized, for instance, in the following statement of W. Ritchie Russell. When discussing 'Ideas on the Brain', he says that 'ancient philosophies are of great interest, but their influence on present-day thought is undermined by the fact that the great thinkers of the past had no conception of what we now know about the brain. Man's ideas about himself have naturally changed since it was discovered, only a little over half a century ago, that the brain consists of a universe of separate and highly complex units' and that 'there are about 10,000,000,000 of these units.'*

Nobody will denigrate the great achievements of the physiological investigation of the brain, nor deny that man's ideas about himself have changed, even though knowledge of the brain has hardly played a conspicuous part in bringing about this change. But this statement is harmful because it tries to invalidate ancient (and by implication all previous) philosophy by mixing up two spheres which must be treated in different ways. Plato's assertion, for example, that it is better to suffer wrong than to do wrong is neither confirmed nor refuted by anything biologists can discover; it is either valid or not valid at all. Results achieved in one sphere cannot—and therefore must not—be applied in the other. If any confirmation is needed, the emphasis put on a number provides it, for it shows clearly how misleading such a statement is. No knowledge of a number can tell us whether we are counting cells or apples or days, and inner experiences cannot be dealt with in a quantitative way. Of two people whose brains are bound to be of the same kind, consisting of about the same number of cells, one may accept Plato's philosophy and the other reject it, or one be an atheist and the other believe in God. Even if we ever knew how many cells correspond to each belief, we would have to know the belief first to make the number relevant. This example may appear too blatantly wrong to be a valid illustration, and certainly such plain statements are fairly rare; yet they give expression to an attitude which is characteristic. Fred Hoyle asserts,

* *The Listener*, vol. 62, p. 735.

Ethical values in the age of science

I think it can hardly be denied that the cosmology of the ancient Hebrews is only the merest daub compared with the sweeping grandeur of the picture revealed by modern science. This leads me to ask the question: 'Is it in any way reasonable to suppose that it was given to the Hebrews to understand mysteries far deeper than anything I can comprehend, when it is quite clear that they were completely ignorant of many matters that seem commonplace to me?'*

Others are less conscious of this attitude, or give it a more equivocal expression, or do not care; on the other hand, of course, there are many scientists who know that such statements are nonsensical. But I think we should be grateful for such professions which bring into the open this dangerous way of arguing; for though common enough, it is not always obvious.

If one of the aims of this book is to oppose such distortions, this is in no sense anti-scientific. On the contrary, it is an endeavour to safeguard the value of scientific research by defining its scope. Our concern is only, as has just been said, to prevent an application of scientific method where it does not apply. This also means that there is no intention of allowing philosophy to interfere with science; the philosopher should be conversant with science and use its support whenever it can be used. In fact, natural science has relieved philosophy of a great burden; philosophers need no longer struggle with apparently metaphysical problems which are outside the sphere of philosophy and are better dealt with by science. This process, however, has often gone a great deal too far. It has led to encroachments on philosophical territory by science and by the other disciplines mentioned above, encroachments which we shall try to prevent or undo. The following criticism of some aspects of scientific thinking should therefore enable us to go beyond science and to concentrate on ethics as such, undisturbed by considerations which are not ethical. The achievements of scientific thinking, especially those of the disciplines mentioned, will be kept in mind, however, for they can help us to exclude from the realm of morality those rules and actions which appear to belong to it, but are actually produced by different causes. The criticism of the misapplication, therefore, does not imply a criticism of these disciplines or of science as such. Nor is a value-

* Fred Hoyle, *The Nature of the Universe* (Oxford, 1950), p. 115.

26

judgment implied about the books from which examples will be taken; the objections refer to, and are strictly confined to, the specific points which are mentioned.

2

As a complete survey of the trespasses of science beyond its proper sphere is obviously impossible, I shall first briefly discuss two examples; one a particular aspect of history, and the other taken from psycho-analysis. They are meant to indicate the correct approach to all such problems. Afterwards, I shall go on to discuss sociology and some aspects of the methods of natural science.

History, as we have said, has been transformed. As a basis for a discussion of this transformation I have chosen *The Idea of History* by R. G. Collingwood, because some parts of it deal directly with the problems of this new approach. In these parts of the book (we are not concerned with all its arguments) the attitude which brought about the transformation is more clearly defined than by most other historians who are less preoccupied with the conditions of their research.

Collingwood characterizes the general direction in which history has developed when he says that the historian 'is investigating not mere events (where by a mere event I mean one which has only an outside and no inside) but actions . . . His work may begin by discovering the outside of an event, but it can never end there; he must always remember that the event was an action; and that his main task is to think himself into this action, to discern the thought of its agent' (p. 213).* This approach has undoubtedly led to great achievements. We no longer apply the standards of our own age when we want to understand historical events; we do not judge them from a point of view which is completely foreign to them. While the Age of Reason, for instance, considered itself as the crown of all human development and judged the past

---

* Page numbers in parentheses on this and the following pages refer to *The Idea of History* (Oxford, 1946). The Roman numbers refer to the Preface, and the two quotations from p. xvii are statements by its author T. M. Knox.

entirely by its own standards, thus failing to do justice especially to the Middle Ages, we seem far more able to appreciate all civilizations, both the primitive and the highly developed, both those similar to our own and those very different from it. Collingwood is probably also justified when he claims that history has thus 'taken a place in human life from which its influence has permeated and to some extent transformed every department of thought and action' (p. 232). We certainly find ourselves compelled to pay attention to history when considering many aspects of life which previously were not seen in the light of history at all; we are interested, not only in human history, but also in the history of the universe, of matter and of life. Thus we also tend to emphasize historical development in morality. Naturally, historians disagree, but more often than not their disagreements bring the period under discussion more fully to life. Their differing views do not necessarily cancel each other out, but show different aspects of the period. Only when trying to assess the present and our own situation do we seem to have become very uncertain; belief in progress and belief in an ultimate decline alternate or struggle against each other.

This understanding of history, however, the 'historical sense', is bought at a price. It imposes limitations upon the historian's understanding in other respects. He must be content with the discovery of what Collingwood has called the 'basic' or 'unquestioning acceptance' which is at work in each age. This means that he is led to recognize that each age is founded upon a belief which is accepted as self-evident, even though the belief itself has no proper foundation. These beliefs constantly change; since each belief is unfounded, it is dismissed soon afterwards, only to be replaced by a similar belief—again unfounded, yet apparently self-evident—which becomes the basis of the following period. The historian can do no more than discover these ever-changing prejudices; he can never discover basic truth. 'In these circumstances questions of truth and falsity cannot arise' (p. xvii). Christianity, humanism or materialism are seen as cases of such an 'unquestioning acceptance'; they are therefore only seen as historical phenomena among others and never appreciated for their value in themselves.

If the historian did not make any further claims, such a view of his task would probably be acceptable. However, by thus including these beliefs in the chain of historical change, he is implicitly denying that any belief in itself could be of a permanent value; all beliefs are simply treated as historical facts, and the 'questions of truth and falsity', since they do not arise, must not be asked at all, even by the philosopher. In fact, this conclusion is frequently drawn, as can be seen, for instance, in Collingwood's discussion of Kant's theory of knowledge and of morality.

Collingwood does not admit that these theories could be correct, because for him they cannot possibly be more than historical phenomena and must thus belong entirely to a particular historical period. 'The positive function of so-called sciences of the human mind, whether total or partial (I refer to such studies as those of the theory of knowledge, of morals, of politics, of economics and so forth), has always tended to be misconceived. Ideally, they are designed as accounts of one unchanging subject-matter, the mind of man as it always has been and always will be. Little acquaintance with them is demanded in order to see that they are nothing of the sort, but only inventories of the wealth achieved by the human mind at a certain stage in history' (p. 229). Is this really the whole truth about Kant's theory of knowledge and his ethics? Collingwood believes it is. For him, 'even Kant, in his attempt to go beyond the "question of right"' is wrong, because 'when he asks how experience is possible, he means by experience the kind of experience enjoyed by men of his own age and civilization. He was, of course, not aware of this' (p. 224). The attempt to apply Kant's teaching about the boundaries of knowledge to modern science is rejected: 'To demand that such criticism should be anticipated by the theory of knowledge is to demand that such a theory should anticipate the history of thought' (p. 230). In other words, Kant's thought cannot be of any use today.*

* It is certainly surprising that Collingwood brackets Kant's theories together with economics.

Here we can see a special knowledge being treated as complete and allowed to invade spheres which are outside its scope; all beliefs have to be robbed of their validity in order to make the special knowledge appear all-inclusive. Consequently, this approach has become destructive; the exclusive emphasis on historical conditions points the way towards scepticism or even nihilism. 'Any form of historicism is confronted by the difficulty of avoiding complete scepticism' (p. xvii).* It is because of this scepticism that judgments of the contemporary situation have become so uncertain, for one can hardly judge it without evaluating its different constituents. To decide whether, at present, society and civilization are developing in the right direction, one must test Christianity or humanism or materialism and ask whether they are true.

Yet Kant (to come back to our example) can also be discussed in a very different manner; one can try to find out how much truth there is in the theories themselves. This will be done in a later chapter, and it will be seen that his theories can be of use today. Similar attempts, after all, have been made and are being made, and they make sense. But they have to be based on the acceptance of a different presupposition—they require the acknowledgment of the limitations of historical knowledge.

That it is a mistake to make history condition all knowledge is shown by a contradiction at the very basis of the historical method. Collingwood mentions it, but does not resolve it satisfactorily, and no unanimity seems to be reached among historians on this point. On the one hand, Collingwood states that 'genuine history has no room for the merely probable or the merely possible; all it permits the historian to assert is what the evidence before him obliges him to assert' (p. 204). Yet, on the other hand, the historian finds so much material that he cannot possibly include all of it; 'he selects from them [his authorities] what he thinks important, and omits the rest' (p. 235). This selection from the available material

---

* The Existentialists are in a better position, for their diagnosis is based on experience and not on historical reasoning. Thus they can face and some of them even defeat the danger of nihilism, instead of unconsciously contributing to it.

rests on an evaluation; he 'forms his own judgment of its value'; he is forced to go beyond the available evidence. Nevertheless Collingwood claims that history is a science, but even if we accept his definition 'The word "science" means any organized body of knowledge' (p. 249), history is not entirely scientific, for scientific principles of organization are objective, and the historian's selection and evaluation must needs be subjective.

The contradiction arises because the limitations of historical knowledge, though seen, are not fully taken into account. There is no doubt that a large number of facts and even some trends can be ascertained with scientific accuracy. As soon, however, as the historian wishes to deal with more than a small particular problem or a very short period (as soon, that is, as he wishes to write 'history' in the generally accepted sense), he is bound to select his facts and data, and this selection, however cautious and restricted, has several characteristics which all show how different historical and scientific knowledge actually are. The historian must sift the material, leave out a number of data and fill in gaps; his selection is not made on purely historical grounds, for he cannot help being influenced by the interests and the attitudes of the time in which he lives. Collingwood himself says: 'St Augustine looked at Roman history from the point of view of the early Christian; Tillemont, from that of a seventeenth-century Frenchman; Gibbon, from that of an eighteenth-century Englishman; Mommsen, from that of a nineteenth-century German. There is no point in asking which was the right point of view. Each was the only possible for the man who adopted it' (p. xii). Moreover, the survival of documents is already due to a selection, for men do not preserve what they think unimportant, and the accidental survival or disappearance of documents may also play an important part. It is true that the natural scientist may have to select his facts, too, but he can test the results of his selection and verify his predictions by experiments and further observations, while the historian, confined to the past, cannot make any such test and must rely on his own judgment and on his power of persuasion.

Sometimes a line of argument is used, especially tempting in history, of which one must beware. A theory may be developed, say, to explain the fall of Napoleon, and as this fall happened, it is then adduced as a proof of the theory. In fact, however, the theory starts from the event and is only accepted if it leads back to it, so that the use of the event as a proof is fallacious. After all, different theories can be brought forward to explain the same event (the cause of Napoleon's fall could be seen, for instance, either as his betrayal of the ideals of the revolution, the megalomania which made him invade Russia, or the dialectics of the historical process which must lead to a reaction), and if this line of argument were accepted, each of these different theories would seem to be proved by the actual occurrence of the event.

There is an obvious reason why this contradiction between the scientific approach and the need to select is so easily overlooked—both seem to confirm the desired and assumed relativity of all knowledge. Therefore it merely seems satisfactory that, in history, the range of relativity is even extended beyond its usual scope. In general, values remain outside science and are often accepted as ultimate, even by those who in theory deny any kind of absoluteness. In this case, however, even the values seem to be dependent on ever-changing conditions, because the selection is determined by an evaluation based on the 'unquestioning acceptance' at work in a particular period and thus ever changing. History appears to bar the way to any escape from relativism; our 'historical sense' strongly supports the tacit agreement to exclude the absolute. Yet it hardly needs repeating that a selection of this kind, made more or less arbitrarily by the individual historian, cannot but lead to a one-sided account of certain aspects of reality, so that no general conclusions should be drawn from it. As the historian only chooses what can be part of an historical process, constant values are not his concern.

History, therefore, because it cannot disclose absolute values, should not be used to deny the possible existence of such values. Christianity, humanism, Kant's theories are historical phenomena, but they also have a meaning in themselves, and the latter cannot be discovered by an analysis of the conditions of their occurrence in the past or of their historical significance. It may be partly true, as Collingwood says, that 'it is only in the historical process, the process of thoughts, that thought exists at all' (p. 227); we may agree that thought does indeed exist within this process, but we must object to his 'only'; thought also has a content, a meaning of its own, which can be valid outside the passage of time and therefore cannot be understood as part of the historical process. Within history everything is relative; but this does not justify the conclusion that events are entirely relative nor that everything is relative. Ideas, beliefs, convictions, though they are historical events, also exist outside the realm of history and can only be discussed meaningfully if the 'questions of truth and falsity' are admitted. It is thus that history confirms our dictum that special knowledge must not be applied outside its legitimate sphere.

We have to remember that many a one-sided view can appear convincing because, to an astonishing degree, reality seems to be pliant; it seems to fall in with entirely different explanations. The triumphs of classical physics led to a mechanistic philosophy which, from the eighteenth century onwards, was widely accepted as entirely plausible; in the later part of the nineteenth century the theory of evolution seemed even better adapted to give an all-inclusive explanation of existence, and to many this still appears true today. Marxism can be made very convincing indeed, and so can belief in progress and humanism. Ultimate values, if accepted, disclose a world of values which can give a real foundation to our lives, and there are several religions which, even though they lead to interpretations of reality which contradict each other, can give believers the feeling of absolute certainty. All these explanations work—up to a point. In fact, no scientific explanation solves personal problems and no religion solves scientific ones. Yet since these explanations function so well, man is tempted to go beyond the point where their validity ends, and then everything is falsified. By their unjustified extension, even the valid results of such creeds become dangerous, because too great claims are made for them. That an explanation works or appears plausible does not prove much, therefore. We must not forget John Oman's warning; he says that reality is so far from 'feeling obliged' to reveal itself to us 'that it only dimly unveils itself to our most sympathetic and far-reaching insight. This may be highly unphilosophical on the part of our environment, yet the fact remains, and even philosophy can only accept it.'*

This does not entitle us to take shelter behind some kind of unjustified 'basic-acceptance'. On the contrary, since reality is pliant, the choice of the right approach to it is an important part of our responsibility; since it does not fully reveal itself to us, or force an explanation unambiguously upon us, we are responsible for our understanding of it. We must constantly make sure that we have exercised all our ability to reach the 'most sympathetic and far-reaching insight'.

3

Some of the weightiest objections to the acceptance of an unconditional morality are made by psychologists. The examples I have chosen this time are mainly taken from Freud's *Introductory Lectures on Psycho-analysis*. I refer to this book because psychoanalysis deals most directly with the fundamental ethical problems with which we are concerned, and because in these lectures Freud succeeded best in making his teaching accessible, for they were meant to explain his teaching to an audience not yet acquainted with it. Some of his later books will be mentioned as well but most of the points taken up from the earlier work are still basic for psycho-analysis; in fact some of Freud's earlier teaching has outlived his later theories, especially his explanation of conscience which has almost become a commonplace.

The great merit of Freud is that he made the unconscious the basis of psychology; according to him, 'psycho-analysis aims at and achieves nothing more than the discovery of the unconscious in mental life' (p. 325).† Certainly the influence of the unconscious

---

* *The Natural and the Supernatural* (Cambridge, 1931), p. 52.
† Page numbers in parentheses on this and the following pages refer to *Introductory Lectures on Psycho-analysis* (London, 1922).

was known before to great writers, to Shakespeare or Dostoevsky; there were also predecessors of Freud and works which he could use. But in the main, psychology before Freud was concerned with conscious processes, and the objective formulation and scientific exploration of the working of the unconscious were of an importance which can hardly be overrated. They have transformed practically all thinking, not alone in psychology. No longer can we think of man as an entirely conscious being; both the sub-conscious (of which man is dimly aware, but which he may be unable to recall or unwilling to face) and the unconscious (of which man is completely unaware, but whose existence and contents can be brought to light) must be taken into account. How far-reaching this transformation of thought has been is thrown into relief when Freud says: 'Whereas, for most people, the word "mental" means "conscious", we found ourselves obliged to widen the application of the term "mental" to include a part of the mind that is not conscious' (p. 270). This was a necessary statement in 1917; but now its first part is no longer true, and its second part, still surprising then, has become self-evident.

To make psycho-analysis reliable, Freud introduces some of the main elements of the scientific method. He tries to find general laws which determine even the most individual phenomena, so as to be able to make generalizations; he reduces, as far as possible, quality to quantity; he develops a completely deterministic view, so as to be able to deny the freedom of the will.* The application of the scientific method has contributed to the successes of psycho-analysis, but it has also led to conclusions which are relevant to ethics and it is with these that we are concerned.

The attempt to generalize can be clearly seen when Freud claims 'that perhaps the sense of guilt of mankind as a whole, which is the ultimate source of religion and morality, was acquired in the

---

* Determinism is no longer completely accepted in nuclear physics, but this does not change that aspect of science which we are discussing here, for the indeter-minacy of the behaviour of particles, the absence of a detectable necessity, must not be equated with the human freedom of the will, the positive ability to act according to one's decisions. For a fuller discussion of this point see P. Roubiczek, *Thinking towards Religion* (London, 1957), pp. 20–1.

beginnings of history through the Oedipus complex' (p. 279). The one-sidedness of this statement has, to some extent, since been rectified, but the method has remained the same. It consists in finding a common denominator for very diverse phenomena, and in making this basic influence independent of consciousness— that is, of any free decision—so that the phenomenon in question can be understood as determined by causes upon which man had no influence. Conscience is nothing but such a product of the unconscious and thus without moral significance. This is also implied in the following explanation of conscience: 'It arose out of the influence of parents and those who trained the child, together with his social surroundings, by a process of identification with certain of these persons who were taken as a model.' Thus conscience arises merely because we make external demands appear internal and thereby our own.

To complete his argument Freud even introduces another common denominator: these influences lead to the formation of an ideal in the unconscious which, because it is unconscious, is forced upon man—the 'Ego Ideal' towards which man is bound to aspire. The enforcement of the ideal takes the form of a censorship; to allow man to believe that he conforms to it, reactions which contradict it (such as the hatred created by the Oedipus complex against the father) are suppressed and replaced by demands which conform to it (you should love your father), and these demands then appear as those of conscience. Thus the reason why these demands arise differs from man's conscious motives; 'he created this ideal for the purpose of recovering thereby the self-satisfaction bound up with the primary infantile narcissism, which since those days has suffered so many shocks and mortifications' (p. 480). Man's striving for goodness is finally shown to be only apparent. While we usually tend to believe that conscience confirms our freedom, because it makes us feel responsible for our choices and actions, Freud's view makes it, like the Oedipus complex, the product of childhood experiences which we are unable to choose.

The more psycho-analysis is developed, the more the role of the individual ego is reduced for the sake of further generalizations. In Freud's earlier theories it is the 'Ego', meaning consciousness and the will, which suppresses and censors anything which threatens to damage the ego ideal. The latter is then replaced by the 'Super-ego', a concept which might indicate some higher, even transcendental power in man. It is nothing of the sort, on the contrary it makes the ego act even more automatically. 'The super-ego retains the character of the father, while the more powerful the Oedipus complex was and the more rapidly it succumbed to repression (under the influence of authority, religious teaching, schooling and reading), the stricter will be the domination of the super-ego over the ego later on—in the form of conscience or perhaps of an unconscious sense of guilt.'* The super-ego is thus created by repressions and is therefore unconscious, it is only a result of processes in man's mind. The conscious ego is more and more hemmed in by the super-ego and the 'Id', namely the unconscious itself. 'Helpless in both directions, the ego defends itself vainly, alike against the instigations of the murderous "Id" and against the reproaches of the punishing conscience.' Conscience is produced solely by this unconscious struggle: 'the more a man controls his aggressiveness, the more intense becomes his ideal's inclination to aggressiveness against his ego.'† According to Freud our inner urges are much less moral than we should like, and being ashamed of this we try to make ourselves much more moral than we actually are; we punish ourselves by excessive demands. But all this has nothing to do with morality in the accepted sense; we are not making free moral decisions.

Freud believes, in fact, 'that our entire psychical activity is bent upon procuring pleasure and avoiding pain, that it is automatically regulated by the pleasure-principle' (p. 298). Later he prefers to speak of instincts in general, which makes this basis of his teaching even clearer and more obviously all-inclusive. 'The theory of the instincts is so to say our mythology. Instincts are mythical entities, magnificent in their indefiniteness. In our work we cannot

---

* *Complete Works* (London, 1961), vol. XIX, p. 34.
† *Ibid.* pp. 53–4.

for a moment disregard them, yet we are never sure that we are seeing them clearly.'* As is commonly the case in science, there is a basic concept which cannot be further explained, and everything is explained or supposed to be explicable as its necessary and inevitable effect.

This attempt to make man more and more dependent on the unconscious and thus to abolish his freedom is supported by the emphasis on quantity, which makes all men amenable to the same kind of diagnosis. The causes of mental illnesses are seen as purely quantitative, for 'it is even possible to conceive disposition as qualitatively the same in all men and only differentiated by this quantitative factor. No less important is this quantitative factor for the capacity to withstand neurotic illnesses (p. 313) ... Whether or not illness will ensue is indeed always a matter of the quantitative factor' (p. 336). What matters is the amount of energy: 'The difference between nervous health and nervous illness (neurosis) ... can probably be traced back to the proportion of the energy which has remained free relative to that of the energy which has been bound by repression, i.e. it is a quantitative and not a qualitative difference' (p. 382). This is certainly correct and a help in judging human behaviour and in the diagnosis of illnesses, but it says nothing about the energy itself which could well be moral strength. If quality is disregarded, the individual differences between a healthy person and a sick one lose their importance; 'you can very well say that we are all ill, i.e. neurotic; for the conditions required for symptom-formation are demonstrable also in normal persons' (p. 300). Almost surreptitiously, a part of human nature has been excluded but all-inclusive generalizations have become possible.

Thus, however, complete determinism can reign supreme and Freud feels bound to attack the man who speaks of accidents: 'Does he mean to maintain that there are any occurrences so small that they fail to come within the causal sequence of things, that they might as well be other than they are? Anyone thus breaking away from the determination of natural phenomena, at any single

* *Complete Works*, vol. xxii (London, 1964), p. 95.

point, has thrown over the whole scientific outlook on the world'
(p. 21). Freedom within the realm of psychology is an illusion and
must be discarded: 'The truth is that you have an illusion of a
psychic freedom within you which you do not want to give up.
I regret to say that on this point I find myself in sharpest opposition to you' (p. 38). Later he remarks almost playfully: 'I have
already taken the liberty of pointing out to you that there is within
you a deeply-rooted belief in psychic freedom and choice, that
this belief is quite unscientific, and that it must give ground
before the claims of a determinism which governs even mental
life' (p. 87). Psycho-analysis appears to have been vindicated as
scientific because even the innermost processes in man's mind can
be recognized as determined in such a way that no loophole is left
for any freedom of the will.

The belief that conscience, the sense of responsibility, in fact all
moral impulses, are preconditioned finds expression in many
different forms, inside and outside psychology. I have quoted
Freud at some length, not only because he is the creator of psycho-
analysis, but also because these passages demonstrate that such a
belief can be held with the firmest conviction and can appear—
at least to those who hold it—as entirely convincing. Nor must
we forget that psychoanalysts can point to numerous cures of
patients who seemed to be inaccessible to any other treatment. To
many people today, perhaps even to a majority, the claim that
morality is absolute seems absurd. Yet Freud's teaching, too, is
based on an essential contradiction which is characteristic, for
similar contradictions occur whenever determinism is asserted.

The purpose of psycho-analysis is to heal patients who suffer
from mental disturbances. Its method is to make them conscious
of previous experiences which were not faced, but repressed, and
which nevertheless survive in the unconscious. By their survival
these experiences create symptoms of mental or apparently
physical disease. When the cause of these symptoms is made
known to the patient by being brought into full consciousness, he
is enabled to behave in a normal way again, uninhibited by the
symptoms which, if the treatment is successful, either disappear or

can be kept under control. The layman would be inclined to say that the patient's freedom of action has been restored. This, of course, contradicts Freud's belief in determinism—but is it not nevertheless justified?

It is true that Freud himself at a different stage of his development would have agreed to such objections; he always believed in the power of reason and sometimes admitted that this implied freedom. But he never clearly saw nor ever solved the contradiction between his belief in determinism and his implied acceptance of freedom. This contradiction is dominant in the book under discussion; and as it is characteristic of many of the attempts to deny the existence of anything absolute, we shall concentrate on this aspect of psycho-analysis here. In chapter VI an example of psycho-analysis openly admitting freedom will be given.

Freud's playful remark—that he takes the liberty of denying freedom—is much more revealing than he would care to admit.*
Thought, to acquire any validity at all presupposes at least a minimum of freedom. If thinking were completely determined by man's physiological and psychological make-up, discussion would cease to be meaningful; arguments would not be accepted because they were convincing, but only because they happened to agree with the constitution of the man with whom one argued. Freud could not hope to convince his audience—which he was obviously trying to do—if men were not free to change their views, he could only rely on treatment. But even the treatment requires some freedom. Freud describes it as 'the substitution of something conscious for something unconscious, the transformation of the unconscious thoughts into conscious thoughts . . . We do nothing for our patients but to enable this one mental change to take place in them' (p. 363). This somewhat strange formulation seems to imply that the necessary processes in the patient's mind are only re-directed by the introduction of a factor which produces a change, so that determinism is not invalidated. But how is the

---

* The remark is even more revealing in the original, for there he says 'Ich habe mir die Freiheit genommen' and thus uses the word 'freedom' twice; he takes the freedom to deny freedom.

factor introduced? The treatment is based on conscious choices made by the doctor: 'Anything which has been inferred wrongly by the physician will disappear in the course of the analysis; it must be withdrawn and replaced by something more correct' (p. 378). The mental change to which it leads must also be consciously brought about by the patient himself; otherwise it will not be effective. Can he do that without freedom of choice? It would be more than difficult to accept all these conscious choices, including Freud's decision to give lectures, as a part of 'the determination of natural phenomena', of the 'causal sequence of things.'* Freud's own teaching would collapse if it were no more than the necessary outcome of his individual childhood experiences. As such it could acquire no general validity.

Actually no attempt to establish determinism can entirely avoid an appeal to the freedom of man's will. Marx, for instance, claims that communism is not an ideal for which man ought to strive, but the result of the actual trend of events. Yet he wants us to recognize that this necessary evolution can be hastened by revolutions and therefore to make revolutions—that is, he tries to persuade as many as possible to make a free decision.

However, as this contradiction is overlooked or disregarded, psycho-analysis, too, is applied where it is inappropriate. Freud states its scope correctly: 'As a science psycho-analysis is characterized by the methods with which it works, not by the subject-matter with which it deals' (p. 325). Nevertheless he makes assumptions about subject-matter as well, for he claims that the unconscious consists of nothing but those impulses, such as the sexual one, which make free decisions impossible; that the unconscious could also be the basis of the 'ethical self' is never taken into consideration.† Psycho-analysis thus includes a factual statement to which, as a method, it is not entitled; man's nature, a given fact, is defined as amoral so that it can support determinism.

* Again, the original is more telling than the translation, for in this passage, quoted in full on pp. 38–9, Freud uses the words 'die Verkettung des Weltgeschehens', i.e. the being chained together of all that happens in the world.
† To this aspect of the unconscious too little attention has been paid.

We are prevented from asking further questions by a circular argument: first the facts are defined in a one-sided manner, in order to make the method applicable, and then the method is used to prove that the facts are as they have been defined. It is true that the method can help us to expose misunderstandings and abuses by showing that conscience and freedom are frequently referred to when actions are due to other causes; but this does not say anything about whether or not conscience and freedom exist. A person may want to appear conscientious in order to acquire a good reputation and may succeed in misleading us; but the fact that conscience is not at work in this individual case, even though it appears to be, does not prove its non-existence, perhaps even in that particular person who may know that he ought to act differently. His behaviour may conceal his true nature. Of course, the psychoanalysts claim that they are able to discover whatever has been concealed, but their method often tempts them to adapt the facts to their theories too readily. As the method has been designed to investigate, not the facts themselves, but the way in which the mind deals with facts, they should logically refrain from defining the human mind itself. For this task a different approach is needed.*

The interference with facts becomes even clearer when Freud extends his theories to take in religion. He is probably still consistent when he goes on: 'These methods can be applied without violating their essential nature to the history of civilization, to the science of religion and to mythology as well as to the study of neuroses' (p. 325). But he then does not proceed to the history or science of religion—that is, to a systematic investigation of its different forms—but dismisses religion altogether as a special kind of neurosis. Belief in the existence of God is simply equated with superstition, as is shown by the very title of his later work on religion, *The Future of an Illusion*. It may be true that many adults, having outgrown the authority of an earthly father, feel lost without his severe guidance or his loving protection and there-

---

* Conscience and the correct approach to it will be fully discussed in ch. VI, section 3.

fore invent a father in heaven; their belief may be founded upon what the psychoanalysts call a 'father-complex'. But God may nevertheless exist, even though some forms of belief are wrong. The reasons for an individual's attitude towards some doctrine cannot say anything about the doctrine itself; one may fail to attain a doctrine which is true by a wrong approach or even discover it by mistake. Once more the application of special knowledge outside its legitimate sphere can be recognized as unjustified and destructive.

All psychology, once it is considered to be all-inclusive, must have this undermining effect because it cannot establish obligations.* As it is concerned with processes in man's mind, it can do nothing more than explain these processes or make the mind work more smoothly if its functioning had been disturbed. As soon as this kind of understanding has been achieved, however, or man's mental health restored, he must deal with his actual tasks and he will deal with them properly only when he knows what he ought to do. Yet in this respect the generalizations of psychology are no help; he must evaluate what he is doing and be guided by a feeling of responsibility; he must be enabled to make valid decisions with regard to his obligations. If he relies on psychology alone, he will have to fall back on some kind of 'pleasure-principle' which, in isolation, will hardly do more for him than allow him to drift, and this lack of any sense of purpose will soon prove to be inhuman and thus highly unsatisfactory.

The distinction between ethics and psychology is probably best understood by comparing mathematics and psychology. The mathematician is not concerned with discovering why certain persons have the gift of becoming good mathematicians and others not, nor why some mathematicians are able to perform one kind of operation well and find another kind difficult, nor why certain persons tend to make mistakes. These are questions for the psychologist. The mathematician wants to discover mathematical laws which are correct and therefore generally valid. Similarly,

---

* This applies also to C. G. Jung's analytical psychology however different it may otherwise be from Freud's psycho-analysis.

ethics is not concerned with discovering why some persons are conscientious and others not, nor even how a particular decision was influenced by the particular characteristics of a certain person; these are psychological problems. In ethics the philosopher tries to discern those facts and laws which form the basis of a morality valid for all persons. Psychology is concerned with processes, with the question of how individual actions are motivated and performed. Ethics tries to evaluate the motives and actions themselves, to apply values which are independent of the individual, and to discover the principles on which these values rest. It is concerned with the moral law. We may succeed in establishing such an independent, unconditional basis for value-judgments, or we may fail, but we cannot dismiss its existence on purely psychological grounds. The content of our thought, our motives and actions must be considered as such.

Certainly all these disciplines—history and psychology as well as sociology—can become important and fruitful for ethics, but only if ethics is made the starting point. These disciplines have contributed to a better self-understanding of man and to a better appreciation of his entanglement with the world and society; they can thus enable us to define more accurately the way in which ethics functions and enable ethics to operate more effectively in practice. This can only come about, however, if ethics is accepted first. If one does not start from ethics, all these disciplines fail because they deny the existence of a fundamental morality and therefore cannot even bring into view the main problem of ethics —the problem of unconditional obligations. They merely ascertain as much as can be discovered from outside; whether or not morality—and what kind of morality—is held. But it is impossible to decide moral problems merely by looking at the historical or social situation or at the intricacies of man's psychological make-up. To make ethical decisions, morality has to be approached from within, for we must be involved; we must decide for ourselves what we ought to do. And this may well mean that we have to dismiss and overcome many commonly accepted convictions.

CHAPTER III

ETHICS AND SOCIOLOGY

1

Sociology was included in the discussion in the preceding chapter because the general remarks made there apply to it. We now turn to discuss it at some length, and to clarify and sum up our earlier conclusions, for sociology is a discipline that can more easily appear all-inclusive than the others, and its very merit—its large scope—tends to lead to more striking misapplications.

Among the new insights which sociology has given us there is one of particular importance for ethics: namely the shift of emphasis from the individual to society and, at the same time, the division of any apparently amorphous mass of people into well-defined groups, so as to make visible the structure of society. Since ethics deals with human relationships it can profit from this, and if our main concern is ethics, we can be shown which task is most urgent and how it can best be tackled. Great harm is done, however, if sociology is mistakenly regarded as a substitute for ethics and used to make ethics appear superfluous. The sociologist deals with what he can ascertain in a given society; he can say what kind of morality is prevalent and how far it is effective, but it is not his task to discuss morality itself; therefore he should neither plead for the acceptance of what, in particular circumstances, he finds generally accepted, nor denigrate attempts to change it. As a sociologist, he is solely concerned with relative relationships, which give him no possibility of discovering anything absolute; nor, therefore, is he entitled to deny its existence. Yet all these things are frequently done.

This endangering of ethics has become so obvious that a number of sociologists try to prevent it and make some of the reservations which will be made here. But this has had no great effect because so long as one moves within sociology and does not step outside it these mistakes are difficult to combat; they arise from the sociological method and cannot be seen as long as the method is applied on its own or sociology is accepted uncritically. It seems justifiable, therefore, to reiterate these warnings.

This time, however, one particular book cannot be used as an example. The discipline has only recently become accepted and is still developing at great speed, so it is impossible to select a representative work for discussion. But it is possible to discern tendencies which infringe upon ethics, and since these—and not special sociological investigations—are relevant to our purpose, we shall concentrate on them. There are five main tendencies of this kind which throw further light on the relationship of sociology (and by implication of all these disciplines) to ethics: (1) to see everything as relative; (2) to discredit, or 'unmask', moral or ideal motives; (3) to 'internalize', as psychology does, external demands; (4) to personify abstract concepts; (5) to claim that the discipline is a pure science.

(1) The preceding discussion has shown that any investigation which restricts itself to seeing everything as relative cannot be accepted as an exploration of ethics. This conclusion applies to sociology, too, but apart from the methodological disregard of anything which could possibly be unconditioned or absolute, the restriction also takes the form which we have already met in the case of history, and here it is particularly revealing.

The claim that sociology is a pure science—that is, as objective as natural science—will be discussed later; but in one respect the claim has been substantiated: Max Weber's demand that sociology should be 'value-free' has been generally accepted. This demand had to be made because values—utility as well as moral—belong to the subject-matter of sociology; it has to pay attention to the values which are accepted or dismissed in order to understand any existing society. 'Value-free' does not mean, therefore, that values are excluded, but that they are dealt with in an objective way; sociology must treat them as facts and must not embark on evaluation. When a sociologist ascertains, for instance, that in a particular society absolute moral values have been replaced by a relative and ever changing morality, or Christianity by utilitarianism, he has to register such facts and their effects upon society, but he should not conclude that the existence of absolute values has been disproved, nor that one of the two beliefs is better than the other. The sociologist himself as a person will, of course, accept certain values and hold certain beliefs, but scientific integrity demands that, within this discipline, he must not allow his convictions to have any influence whatever. Whether he be Christian or agnostic, as a sociologist he is only concerned with the social aspect of values and beliefs, with their existence as constituent elements of society and their social consequences. The discipline, therefore, should not include a demand for reforms nor an establishment of aims. When its findings are used to support demands it is serving an activity which is not sociological.

These few remarks show how difficult it is for a sociologist to refrain from mistaking his findings for ethical conclusions. All values have a social aspect because their acceptance plays an important part within society; in this respect even the highest values—such as truth and the good—appear relative in a social context. Yet these values are traditionally believed to be permanent because of their intrinsic value and are accepted as ends in themselves—that is, as absolute. This may or may not be correct; but the matter can only be decided by investigating these values as such and not their role in society. Nevertheless the sociologist, since he is forced by his method to deal exclusively with their relative aspect, is easily misled into believing that they are nothing but relative. We have seen something similar happen in the case of history and psychology. With sociology the conclusions appear even more inescapable because the pressure of society is most directly felt.

This mistaking of sociological findings for ethical conclusions is due to the failure to distinguish between the role which values play in society—which can be observed from outside—and their part in personal relationships, which means an experience of the values themselves. The sociologist can ascertain, for instance, how the commandment to love one's neighbour operates in a particular society, but only individual experience of an actual confrontation with other individuals can reveal whether or not the commandment is absolute.

The following example is typical. A sociologist who emphasizes that the scope of sociology is limited—very much as we have done —nevertheless feels entitled to assert: 'It is impossible to exist with full awareness in the modern world without realizing that moral, political and philosophical commitments are relative' because 'one's own culture, including its basic values, is relative.'* Despite his acceptance of Weber's demand, he does not succeed in keeping sociology value-free; he obviously assumes that values are fully understood when seen as social factors, and by thus making relativity final and denying the very possibility of absoluteness, he in fact evaluates the commitments he mentions. He wants to leave room for other approaches, but actually deprecates any non-sociological investigation of values and precludes any ethical, existential or religious approach which judges values on the basis of their intrinsic merits—approaches which may well show some values to be at least so far absolute that they necessitate a rejection of beliefs held by society.

Max Weber himself tries, according to R. Dahrendorf, to unite 'the rigour of a value-free science and the passion of a moral position', but in this respect he too fails; Dahrendorf considers it to be his fault that 'whereas sociology, after some decades of rapid development has come considerably closer to a rational understanding of the fact of society, the autonomous human being and his freedom have been lost sight of in the process.'† The fault, however, is not the attempt to make sociology value-free, but disregard for the vigorous demands of science. The tendencies working against morality which we have enumerated are based on scientific investigations, but since it appears legitimate to pursue any scientific endeavour wherever it may lead, many sociologists are encouraged to indulge these tendencies for their

---

* P. L. Berger, *Invitation to Sociology* (Pelican Books, 1966), pp. 64, 63.
† *Essays in the Theory of Society* (London, 1968), pp. 85, 77.

own sake and to use them for unscientific purposes; they want to see everything as relative and to discredit all absolute values. The situation which Dahrendorf deplores arises because a scientific apparatus is often used to support arguments against the belief in an absolute morality, and thus sociology encroaches—illegitimately and unjustifiably—upon the sphere of ethics. The whole man is lost sight of because sociology itself is used to determine a moral position; the fact that values have also a social (or historical or psychological) aspect makes it appear superfluous even to consider that the validity of morality might reside in morality itself.

(2) This wrong intrusion of sociology into the field of ethics is strongly supported (much more strongly than in history and perhaps also more strongly than in psychology) by an 'unmasking imperative', a 'debunking motif';* any social system, any moral or idealistic striving and any belief is shown to be based, not on the motives which are professed or believed in, but on social exigencies. Sociology concentrates on the disclosure of social influences which reveal that even motives which appear purely moral or idealistic are merely results of an unthinking acceptance of the dictates of society; it shows that people believe they are acting conscientiously when they are only obeying the laws which are in force. They support, for instance, severe punishment for petty theft or unconventional sexual behaviour, capital punishment and war and think that they are forced to do so by their conscience; but in fact they simply follow convention and have never allowed their own conscience to interfere.† Religion, when included in sociology, is usually treated in much the same way.

These and similar statements contain considerable truth about human behaviour and historical processes, and there are undoubtedly pernicious social influences, conventions and superstitions which should be unmasked in this way. But only on the basis of ethics are we able to decide which beliefs should be dismissed, which freed from abuses and which judged on other grounds or

* P. L. Berger, *op. cit.* p. 51.
† That the existence of such an 'authoritarian conscience' does not contradict the existence of an independent conscience will be shown in chapter VI.

upheld against society. If the unmasking by sociology is considered to be the whole truth and to disclose the true nature of all convictions, the belief in an all-inclusive social relativity becomes an absolute creed, and this can produce a 'disastrous result—the destruction of the validity of all values and beliefs.

This devaluing becomes all-pervasive because sociology includes even knowledge within its sphere; it shows how much of our thought is determined by social conventions, and this easily leads to the claim that nobody can escape the logic imposed by society. Knowledge is no longer tested on the basis of the assumption that it could be valid in itself; it is solely valid within the framework of a particular society at a particular time. As an example we can recall Collingwood's attitude to Kant's theory of knowledge.* The arguments of historians and sociologists are practically identical in this respect; sociologists, too, believe only in the basic assumptions of historical societies and not in a permanent truth. Since natural science with its material proofs cannot be attacked in this manner, the unmasking means in practice a total discrediting of any belief in the permanent validity of morals and ideals. A one-sided approach is allowed to destroy the foundations of morality although ethics is not even considered.

(3) The processes of making all judgments relative and consequently devalued are made apparently unassailable by 'internalization'. Within society, every person has to play a number of different 'roles', for instance that of man, husband, father, scientist, citizen, member of a class and of a nation. In each of these roles everyone knows what is expected of him and once he accepts a role, he wants to play his part well so as to live up to these expectations. Therefore he makes these demands his own and believes that he is exercising his free will and obeying his conscience while in fact he is merely submitting to external demands. In this way any demand can be seen as social, even if it is experienced as an inner urge; no behaviour can ever escape this kind of explanation. 'Sociological theories equate the playing of social roles with the whole of human behaviour.'† In cases of

* See pp. 29–30.   † R. Dahrendorf, *Essays in the Theory of Society*, p. 91.

doubt refuge can be taken in the past; the pattern of some roles, such as those of father or priest, was developed long ago, and we are also determined by tradition. As an example we can here remember Freud's explanation of the super ego and conscience;* in this respect, many sociologists agree with the psychoanalyst, though some of them are not aware of it.

Again, there is a great deal of truth in many of these explanations. But if they are mistaken for the whole truth, human behaviour can only be seen as apparently and never truly genuine; even if a person has no shadow of doubt that he is acting according to his own convictions, he is still performing a role. This makes it impossible to distinguish morality from mere convention; the ethical self is bound to disappear. Dahrendorf emphasizes: 'What sociological theory does not tell us about man is his moral quality.'† But since social roles seem to determine so much of human behaviour, even those sociologists who try find it extremely difficult to limit sociology to its legitimate field, for they can hardly admit that morality could have a different source.

(4) Human behaviour, however, is so individual that the absence of the personal element is still felt—even if I am only performing roles, I still experience that it is I myself who accept and perform them. But this personal element cannot properly be accommodated in sociology, and therefore society is personified instead. Society assigns roles, performs actions and has knowledge of its requirements. 'Society sees farther and better than individuals.'‡

I have not yet mentioned this tendency to personify abstract concepts, but it is common to the disciplines just discussed and is also found outside them. It occurs, for instance, when biology is made the basis of a philosophical explanation of existence. Biologists attempt to eliminate teleology—that is, determination by purposes—from their science, because only a biology based on

* See pp. 36–7. † *Ibid.* p. 101.
‡ E. Durkheim, *The Elementary Forms of Religious Life* (London, 1915), p. 444. Durkheim's mistake has been recognized, but we shall see later that it is still characteristic.

causality or probability can become a reliable science. Purposes characterize human actions and would thus introduce a non-scientific element into biology. Yet so far as evolution is concerned, scientists have not entirely succeeded in introducing causality, and the latent human element comes to the fore whenever biology is interpreted philosophically. Evolution then becomes an active agent, in the same ways as persons do, in addition to nature which also demands and acts; both seem to have aims and to do themselves what is needed to reach them. In Bergson's *Creative Evolution*, for instance, nature really becomes a kind of goddess who, with the help of evolution, aims at producing greater and greater variety and finally at transforming men into gods.* But this personification is hardly ever noticed, either here or when history or the unconscious play similar parts. Once more it is sociology which shows most clearly what is at stake.

The personification of society is not simply a manner of speaking. When one says that science or philosophy do this or that, nobody will assume that this can be done without scientists or philosophers. Society, of course, is also composed of individuals and only they can act, but if it is personified it becomes a kind of superior being with all the qualities of a person. Not its individual members, but society itself imposes conventions, laws and creeds; it exercises coercion and supports it by sanctions. This remains true, even if the extreme views of Durkheim (who was influenced by Bergson) have by now been rejected, because the concept of society has only been refined and made more convincing by the elaboration of the tendencies which we have described. Dahrendorf, after using the concept in this personified way, asks who it is that defines and enforces social roles and states unambiguously: 'Although many recent writers would answer "society", just as we have so far, the term is hard to justify. Society is patently not a person, and any personification of it obscures its nature and weakens what is said about it.' But it is difficult to avoid this

* The example of Teilhard de Chardin shows that this approach is by no means obsolete.

personification because 'in some sense society is not only more than the sum of its individual members, but something significantly different in kind'.*

Nevertheless, society should be seen for what it is—a particular form or combination of human relationships. Though obviously extremely important, it cannot possibly reveal the core of man's existence, because society as an entity has no conscience and no feeling of responsibility. These are entirely personal experiences which cannot be formulated as general rules, not even by the individual concerned, and therefore they can never be divorced from actual experience. It is the individual who is responsible for society, not society for the individual; persons in influential positions may try to govern in a responsible way and draw up laws accordingly, but each individual still has to decide himself, for his own sake and for the sake of society, which laws he can obey in good conscience. If, however, society is seen as a self-centred entity, conscience and responsibility are ascribed to it; man is seen as a part of a superior being which prescribes his beliefs and takes decisions on his behalf, so that one need go no further to explore his deeper motives and true nature; and since society is the highest authority, it also replaces the transcendental. Whether one likes it or not, it acquires some divine characteristics.

(5) Sociology has accepted the scientific method by attempting to be value-free, but it cannot become an exact science comparable with the natural sciences because it influences and thereby transforms the subject it investigates. Many of its findings are no longer correct once they become known because the findings exert an influence.

Natural science leaves its object intact. It is true that the influence of the observer has become a problem in nuclear physics, but this apparent similarity only clarifies the difference. The uncertainty in physics occurs in a boundary region of the science; it influences the object under observation but does not transform it, and the uncertainty can be expressed by an equation—the uncertainty principle—which exactly defines its very narrow scope. In

* *Essays in the Theory of Society*, p. 44.

sociology the uncertainty is created actually by the main body of the discipline; the object under observation can be completely transformed; and the degree of influence cannot be foreseen. Therefore the test which is successfully employed in science—the prediction of events—is no help here; the very forecast may change the situation.

This applies to all the disciplines discussed here. The interpretation of history influences man's actions and thus his future; psychological knowledge influences man's behaviour. But sociology also shows how the claim that these disciplines are purely scientific may interfere with ethics.

There can be no doubt that the belief in nothing but relative relationships and particularly the 'unmasking motif' have deeply influenced contemporary society, and if sociology is accepted as a pure science, nobody seems responsible for this influence because scientific endeavours are pursued regardless of the consequences. (That this raises a problem even in natural science will be discussed later.*) Nevertheless this attitude is wrong, not only because of the actual effects of sociology, but also because these effects are often deliberately aimed at; for despite the fact that sociology should not include demands for actions or reforms, it is not only frequently used for this purpose, but also seen as having this purpose. Sociologists do try to determine future behaviour, which can be seen when they apply their knowledge as advisers of publicity campaigns; many of them fashion their investigations in such a way that they support either existing governments or revolutionary movements and such activities are not separated from sociology proper, but advanced as arguments in favour of it. Since sociologists deal with society, it is naturally difficult for them to prevent even their political bias from directing their research. If they nevertheless claim that their investigations are purely scientific, they disclaim responsibility for what they are doing, for pure science does not include the concept of personal responsibility. Without noticing it, they allow them-

---

* See ch. x, section 1. There we shall discuss this aspect of sociology more fully.

selves—and are allowed because of the general acceptance of their claim—to act irresponsibly, even though they really shoulder a grave responsibility.

An example of this discrepancy is the sociological technique of taking opinion polls. To produce statistics on the basis of what people tell interrogators seems to be a purely objective activity. There are difficulties of which most sociologists are aware: the questions may be biased and suggest the desired answer, or people may not tell the truth, so that the statistics may not become entirely objective. But even if they were, they could not remain objective; when they are published, they influence the opinions of those concerned; polls made before an election, for instance, undoubtedly influence its result and nobody accepts responsibility for this effect. The claim that they are purely scientific bars the feeling of responsibility from a sphere where it should be particularly strong—the sphere of social activity. Ethics is replaced by an apparently impersonal process which nevertheless interferes with personal decisions.*

All the tendencies at work in sociology therefore confirm that, to make it a beneficial influence, one would have to start from ethics; for only then could sociology be kept within its actual limits and be entirely profitable.

2

There is also a further problem which is peculiar and fundamental to sociology as well as to ethics—the relationship between social and individual morality.

In order to make a society possible man's instincts and desires have to be curbed; he has to be persuaded or forced to recognize obligations to his fellow men and to obey certain laws. These obligations are obviously more moral than his selfish urges, so that morality is partly produced by the formation, development and demands of society. No society could ever work without imposing

* See also pp. 254–5.

some moral rules upon its members. This has given rise to the belief that morality is mainly or entirely created to serve the needs of society; individual morality appears merely the result of the working of social morality—the expression of social demands. Yet all the claims for ethics which we have so far made presuppose that individual morality is fundamental, while social morality belongs to the sphere of the application of morality.

In order to be able to decide which point of view is correct, three facts have to be born in mind.

(1) We have distinguished between fundamental morality and its application.* With regard to social morality, the word 'morality' is used in an even more vague sense; any regulating relationship belonging to the structure of society is called 'social morality', even if it has little to do with fundamental morality. In this sense, social morality is never absent; the most primitive tribes accept certain obligations and taboos, and even the worst society has some kind of it, just as criminals have their own moral codes. Our problem concerns fundamental morality and its ethical foundation; therefore we are only concerned with that social morality which is an attempt to approach or embody fundamental morality.

(2) It is true that, since any society must enable men to live together, it starts with at least a minimum of a valuable social morality which thus seems to precede individual morality. But social morality can never remain static; each of its stages is an initial stage for further developments, it must either improve or deteriorate. The next stage may be better or worse than the preceding one; it may allow fundamental morality greater scope and protect the exercise of man's freedom, or it may sacrifice a great part of true morality in order to fortify the power of state or church. Since we want to find out whether social or individual morality leads to the fulfilment of ethical demands, we have to ask how the improvement of an initial stage of social morality is brought about.

(3) To see this process in perspective, we must once more

* See pp. 4–5.

beware of any personification of 'society', for any organizing is done by individuals, and the creation of social morality at any stage, including the original one, is no exception. Important developments within society are sometimes due to single individuals, to lawgivers such as Moses and Solon, or to despots and dictators. Usually it is a comparatively small number of individuals who are active—those who feel a greater responsibility than others and want to protect them, men who want or have power and therefore subjugate others, and those whose motives are a mixture of these two extremes. The influence of individuals only recedes into the background when tradition is unthinkingly upheld, but before long individuals will again struggle for change. To recognize the relationship between social and individual morality, we have therefore to consider the actions of those individuals who introduce improvements.

Men who are concerned with society cannot establish values merely because these are valuable in themselves, nor can they simply follow their moral impulses and do what is right because it is right. They must constantly check how far their moral values and demands are useful for the particular society in which they live. Pure morality can easily become a danger to society. When we look back today on the trial of Socrates, we recognize that, from the social point of view, his persecutors were right when they feared that his wider, universally valid concept of the good would become a danger to the narrow city state. Nor has any society yet been able to accept Christ's demands to offer the other cheek and to love one's enemy, though few would deny that these demands represent a very high morality. For society, not only man's selfish instincts but his moral urges, too, have to be curbed.

I shall show later (in chapter VI) why goodness has to be accepted as valuable in itself—that is as an absolute value—and why, to be safely and fully realized, it must be aimed at for its own sake. But we can already see here, in the social context we are discussing, that to subordinate the good to another purpose, such as usefulness for society, falsifies its nature and thus falsifies morality. If our motive is to achieve not the good itself, but something useful which can be achieved with its help, such as a well-functioning social order, considerations of usefulness are allowed to override moral considerations; once this happens, it will be well-nigh impossible to safeguard morality. Even if the good were the original inspiration, social purposes will always have priority. Moral demands themselves may thus lead us to sacrifice the good —when, for instance, the rule of law, which was meant to support morality, is enforced for the sake of society regardless of whether or not the existing laws can be morally justified. Such an attitude has been mentioned before—when support is given to severe punishment for petty theft and unconventional sexual behaviour, to capital punishment, and when members of society are forced to kill in war.

Obviously, such laws will only be changed if individuals oppose them; social morality itself cannot lead to an improvement in what it defines as moral. Since fundamental morality is always concerned with relationships between men ('Thou shalt love thy neighbour as thyself'), social needs may make men aware of truly moral demands; but to remain moral, social morality needs the constantly renewed impact of individual morality.

This need for individual morality becomes obvious when we ask in what way different kinds of laws are relevant to morality. The laws which are enforced range from those which are morally completely neutral to those which have a definite moral content. An example of the former is the rule that one has to drive on the left or right side of the road; an example of the latter the laws concerning marriage.

The laws of the road acquire an almost absolute moral significance because to disobey them would endanger one's own and others' lives. But the decision for left or right is completely arbitrary and has nothing to do with morality; the rule itself is a mere convention and could be changed without any moral consideration. Its significance derives from the moral law that one should not kill, although the moral law is not embodied in it.

Thus it is not only society but also morality which requires that the law of the road should be obeyed.

The laws concerning marriage, on the other hand, regulate a human relationship and thus have a moral content, therefore they should be based on the moral law and constantly revised in its light. But it has been shown above that the forms of marriage are frequently mistaken as belonging to fundamental morality;* formal rules tend to reduce the moral content and to overshadow the human relationship with which they deal. Then the real task of morality is abandoned; instead of being concerned with the actual relationship between husband, wife and family, it is only asked whether the conventional form has been preserved. Yet marriage should not be just a convention. In this respect, social morality can become a hindrance to the full development of a moral life and disobedience can be desirable or even necessary.

Thus social morality can either support or hinder the exercise of individual morality. In a well-ordered, humane society laws will make it easier to lead a moral life, so that social morality appears to form the basis of individual morality. This leads to the belief—which is frequently held—that individual morality is dependent on social morality and cannot fully develop without it. But this belief is false. It is true that living in a moral society may help the growth of individual morality, but it is not true that the easier situation guarantees a better moral life; individual morality can also develop fully in an immoral society. In a totalitarian state the moral person who wants to remain moral will have to break the law and the need to take great risks can make individual morality exceptionally strong and forceful. In fact, this latter situation is more significant than the former, because all laws tend to become rigid and inhuman, and when they do, obedience to them is enforced for the sake of the rule of law and regardless of their moral content. It is true that in bad societies more people behave badly than in good ones, but even good laws have to be confronted again and again with their original moral meaning,

* See p. 4.

59

otherwise their form and wording becomes more important than their moral purpose.

In other words, all laws tend to develop in the direction of such morally neutral laws as those of the road. The mere existence of such laws strongly supports this process. Since they must be rigid and yet acquire moral significance, the strictness of all laws seems morally justified. It appears that any law, simply by being a law, is beneficial to moral life and obedience in any case better than disobedience. Moreover, since fundamental morality is concerned with the 'neighbour' and thereby also implies an order of human relationships, any order may appear more moral than disorder. Therefore the distinction must be made between laws with and those without moral content, for otherwise the acquired absoluteness of the neutral law will support belief in the absoluteness of laws which are detrimental to morality—of laws which, through their content, are really connected with the absolute moral law but distort it.

This distinction is often difficult to make because many laws are neither as obviously neutral nor as obviously connected with the problems of morality as our examples. For instance, the demand that we should pay taxes is to a certain extent morally neutral but not entirely so. Money itself acquires moral aspects only by the way in which it is gained and by the use which is made of it; but we have the duty to support society when it needs money, so that we should neither gain money by cheating it nor withhold our support from it. Yet to strengthen a totalitarian regime is immoral and in any society it may be immoral to contribute to armaments. At the same time, it seems highly improbable that refusal to pay taxes will achieve anything beyond causing harm to the individual who refuses—a thought which can hardly be avoided, even though, as we shall see, moral decisions should not be based on guessing whether success or failure is more probable. Contradictory arguments will have to be evaluated.

Evidently, any such distinction can only be based on individual morality, for so long as society is the criterion the preservation of order will always be of paramount importance. Only an individual involved in a particular situation will be able to decide whether a law should be obeyed, opposed or broken even at great risk; and only if the decision is based on individual morality and succeeds in influencing society will social morality remain really moral. This does not mean, of course, that social morality is unimportant; since fundamental morality is concerned with human relationships its exercise must aim at establishing and improving social morality, and any success in such an endeavour will be a great moral triumph. But it does mean that social morality has to be subordinated to individual morality.

The fundamental role of individual morality can be illustrated by the Ten Commandments. I am concerned here with the commandments which express purely moral demands* and the surprising fact is that these have survived so many centuries. They always have to be experienced anew, if they are not to become a dead letter, and therefore we have to take into account the background of our own lives. But their essential meaning has not altered; in their essence they are still valid while everything else has changed. In particular the societies in which they have remained valid have been constantly transformed and, for a long time, have been completely different from the society in which they were originally issued. This permanence indicates their individual nature already, for social morality has to be adapted to the changing forms of society. This indication is confirmed by two particular characteristics of the commandments: they are not formulated as rules to be applied in certain situations, as morality usually was before (if this happens, this or that must be done), but they appeal to the individual and command 'thou shalt' or 'thou shalt not'; and they do this unconditionally, without any reference to the needs of society or the individual. It is in this way that they break through to fundamental morality which does not change.†

* All references to the Ten Commandments in this book should be understood as excluding those of purely religious significance.
† Cf. R. N. Anshen (ed.), *Moral Principles of Action* (New York, 1952). Her own contribution to this anthology, 'Thou shalt not . . .' explains admirably why the Ten Commandments are still as valid as ever.

It could be—and has been—said that the commandments survive because they simply insist on the minimum demands without which a society (once it has outgrown the most primitive stage) could not exist. But this is not convincing with respect to several of the commandments: the prohibition on killing has never yet been accepted without qualifications; the prohibition on coveting cannot be made law; adultery has remained a problem for the lawgiver. That the commandments actually have a different significance can be seen even when we consider the law which most obviously appears as merely social—the prohibition on stealing. Some interpreters claim that this is not an unconditional law, but only a protection of society, for it is found in very primitive tribes, at least with regard to stealing within the tribe, and it is valid only in a society which protects private property. Although it is difficult to imagine a society without any private property, this interpretation could be correct if the formulation were 'stealing is forbidden'. The usefulness for society would then remain in the foreground, for many things are forbidden which—like driving on the wrong side of the road—have no moral significance in themselves. Yet the personal appeal forces us to become aware of more than social demands; since we are directly addressed, our conscience and feeling of responsibility are awakened, and we realize that we are forbidden—in this commandment as well as in the others—an activity which must damage our integrity. Stealing is obviously dishonest and usually disavowed, and it interferes with the life of another person without his consent; therefore it must fail to respect the ethical self in the doer and man's moral freedom in the victim.* The prohibition is—and has to be—unconditional because it is no longer related to the very different, social question—discussed by sociologists, Marxists and others—of whether private property, what kind and how much of it should be protected. The Ten Commandments articulate the nature of the good as experienced by the individual.

That it is individual morality which is at work in the command-

* This aspect of the commandments will be discussed on p. 204.

ments can also be seen from a different point of view: they help to transcend the initial stage of morality offered by society because they do not allow the individual to rest content with the existing social morality. When issued, they were immediately interpreted, in order to make them acceptable at all, in a way which narrowed down their scope considerably; hatred of the stranger and killing were not generally forbidden, but allowed if faith or war demanded them. Yet in spite of their adaptation to cruel conditions the exacting appeal to the individual has survived, and thereby the application of the commandments has gradually become less restricted. It is true that, in this respect too, the situation has not changed fundamentally; political groups and governments still try to restrict the scope of some commandments; but such restrictions still do not put man's mind at rest. We know that the stranger, even if he be of another race, ought to be accepted as equal; and it is to a large extent due to the constant pressure of the commandment 'thou shalt not kill' that less and less killing is condoned by society. Capital punishment and killing in war have now emerged as moral problems which enforce individual decisions, whatever society may ordain. Capital punishment has been abolished in some states, and war became a moral problem even before the advent of the atomic bomb, which shows that the pressure had made itself felt, but also that it is still needed. It is by this constant pressure of the commandments upon individual conscience that any stage of social morality becomes merely an initial stage which should be—and sometimes is—transcended. Without individual morality, society would never be influenced by fundamental morality. Instead there would be a perpetuation of that state of affairs—whether moral or not—which best suited its preservation. The Ten Commandments would have been replaced by social rules and lost their challenging power long ago.

An acceptance of this primary importance of individual morality could ensure a fruitful approach for sociology and remove the dangers which even those sociologists who see them find difficult to combat. If it were accepted that individual morality is the basis of social morality, sociology could be more easily seen for what it is—as a discipline which, instead of establishing the rule of the relative, is itself of relative importance (which would not reduce, but safeguard its value). It would become obvious that one has to start from ethics.*

All that has been said so far leads unambiguously to this conclusion. Only the individual is able to decide whether he ought to accept or reject social morality and its values, obey even an unjust law, because it is important that laws should be obeyed, fight for its improvement, or break a law because it is utterly wrong; and moral insight will always force him to struggle against mere conventions which pretend to be moral. Sociology cannot solve the problems which thus arise; these have to be decided according to the verdicts of the individual's conscience and his feeling of responsibility. The sociologist can ascertain the existing situation. On the basis of presupposed standards he may discover how far it should be changed to come nearer to these standards, and he may support some demands of the good as socially beneficial. But, as a sociologist, he is neither entitled nor able to set the standards himself; nor can he decide which standards ought to be adopted. Such questions as whether it is the power of the state or the scope of individual liberty which should be increased have to be decided beforehand—that is, outside sociology—before he starts giving sociological advice. Nor can sociology ever grasp the good itself.

It is false to believe that society creates morality; the process is exactly the reverse: every new development in individual morality (its successes and its failures) deeply influences society. If, however, morality depends in the last resort on individual morality, its basis is not society but ethics, for it is ethics which is concerned with exploring the foundations of human relationships in the personal sphere and is thus valid for every individual man.†
We could also introduce here, as is often done, the concept of mankind. For in the ethical context (and perhaps in any context)

* A good example of this use of sociology is G. C. Zahn, *In Solitary Witness. The Life and Death of Franz Jaegerstaetter* (New York, 1965).
† See the definition of the scope of ethics on pp. 5–7.

mankind does not mean the sum total of all individuals or societies, but the embodiment of the basic qualities of man. In this sense mankind is not a society, but an idea which is the source of the transformation of society. It was the struggle of individuals in the name of mankind which led to the abolition of slavery. Some sociologists say that slavery was only abolished because it was no longer profitable, indeed this kind of 'debunking' can be pursued indefinitely until no moral motive whatever is left intact—but is it really convincing? Slavery still pays and exists in some parts of the world, especially in Africa, and it is still fought in the name of mankind.

It was said at the end of chapter 1 that we should begin by considering the question whether or not science has superseded philosophy, for many people believe that there is no room left for ethics, that morality and conscience can be better understood by consulting science alone. This claim is mainly based on the disciplines which we have discussed. All of them, however, confirm that, if something of real moral consequence is to be done, an exclusive concern with conditions and their interdependence must be transcended. Otherwise we remain caught within the web of relativity and no escape is possible so long as we move inside it. Therefore I persist with my attempt to embark on the quest for an ultimate, absolute truth, in spite of all the besetting doubts, for only in this way can the present situation be judged properly from outside.

This conclusion will be supported, in the next chapter, by considering in general the methods used in natural science; this will show that ethics has to be approached in a different way, and will thus lead on to a discussion of ethics itself. But a further preliminary question has still to be raised: is this quest for an ultimate truth at all possible, is it not utopian? Because the preoccupation with the relative is so prevalent today, even the word 'absolute' has nearly lost its meaning, so that a quest for it may seem unreal. Moreover, since the disciplines which have been considered so far cannot deal with the absolute, it remains to be shown how it could be ascertained. Our next step, therefore, must be to discuss its meaning and the possible ways of approaching it.

CHAPTER IV

THE ABSOLUTE AND ITS RELATION TO THINKING

1

The examples just discussed show that some theories when applied to ethics leave gaps and give rise to contradictions. This may be characteristic of all scientific or nearly scientific theories; there is no doubt that many more such gaps and contradictions could be discovered. But does it really matter? The general tendency of both our historical knowledge and our daily experience is to make the existence of any kind of unconditioned and unconditional morality seem so questionable that it may well appear that even tentative attempts to replace it by something more realistic ought to be welcomed. The evidence of man's behaviour throughout the ages can be used to provide very powerful support to all those who claim, in one way or another, that morality is relative. If one looks at history, past and present, a belief in the moral law can easily appear no more than a traditional prejudice, one of those 'basic acceptances' which ought to be questioned. This view can be based on such a large number of almost self-evident facts that there is hardly need for much elaboration; a few indications will suffice to show how the argument goes.

We admire ancient Greece, the fortunate birthplace of European civilization; yet when the Greeks conquered a town, they slew all the men and sold the women and children as slaves. Rome succeeded in establishing the 'pax romana', and those who have lived through two world wars can appreciate this achievement, but there were still wars on the frontiers of the empire, while inside it, in the towns, the climax of circus performances had to be the killing of men in a spectacular manner; the spectacle of suffering and death was the most popular form of entertainment. Christianity, the religion of love, led to ruthless religious wars and the burning of heretics, Jews and witches; cruelty and death were again a popular feast. The Age of Reason seemed to promise enlightenment, but it was not long before the French Revolution, despite all its humanitarian aims and achievements, turned to terrorism and war; it mobilized a whole nation and thus introduced a new kind of warfare which involved more people and was more destructive than any before. The twentieth century seems to demonstrate once more that man does not improve; despite its great achievements, it has brought, instead of the millennium which many had expected, more destructive wars than ever, culminating in the dropping of the atomic bomb. There have been ruthless dictatorships, concentration camps, gas chambers, purges—terrifying new forms of legalized mass murder. Today it seems as if the atomic bomb—in itself evil— may actually prevent war on a large scale, but there still is war, racial hatred, terrorism, murder, increasing delinquency. It may be true that the will to power, though by no means absent, is at the moment not as important a motive of human action as it used to be; but the expectation that moral ideas could one day determine political action or international relationships remains as utopian as ever. At the same time the majority today are influenced more and more by desire for material gain and less and less by any feeling of responsibility. There are exceptions, as there always were, but do they count? The moral nature of man, if indeed it exists, does not seem to be fundamental or absolute.

It would be possible, of course, to reject any conclusions based on this pessimistic view by showing that there is also an aspect of history which could support a more optimistic outlook. The inheritance of Greece and Rome has contributed to the rise of a new civilization built on, and mainly indebted to Christianity, and Christianity, after all, has been the source of other achievements— and these among the very greatest. There have been great geniuses, poets, artists, composers, philosophers; there have been wise rulers, great scholars and saints, and much of what they created or exemplified has enriched our lives. Democracy, despite its faults, has developed far beyond its Greek model. Science has practically abolished epidemic diseases, prolonged human life, and enabled man to reach a higher standard of living than ever before. For the first time—at least in the West—a reasonably comfortable life is enjoyed by the majority and no longer by minorities only; the average man can live better today than the privileged classes lived in the past. It could even be argued that this general material improvement has made man, in some respects, morally more sensitive than he used to be. It may be true that responsibility has been weakened by recent developments in our society, but not with regard to the world at large; we are so shocked by misery, cruelty and injustice wherever they may occur, that we respond by giving aid in all parts of the world on a scale which is without precedent. An enumeration of the achievements of man could be made to match the account of his failures.

Yet it would be utterly wrong to try to prove the existence of anything absolute in this way; absoluteness remains outside the scope of any such argument. Some of the reasons why this is so have already been mentioned. Since the historian has to select his facts, he can make many beliefs or points of view seem convincing: belief in progress as well as belief in decline. The opposing views, just outlined, obviously depend not on conclusive arguments but on our inclination, on whether we accept a pessimistic or an optimistic interpretation of history, on whether we are more deeply impressed by the shattering experiences of recent years or by their astounding scientific developments. From a moral point of view the failures and crimes of man are so stultifying that optimism may appear nothing but a shallow consolation, a superficial escapism; but this is an emotional reaction and not a valid argument either for or against progress. Moreover, to show the importance and influence of morality in a historical context would require some kind of belief in steady progress. But any such belief—even if we could wholeheartedly accept it, or even if progress could be proved—would have to be interpreted as showing that the latest achievements of man are due, not to

68

morality or faith, but to other factors, to the pursuit of scientific knowledge and material betterment. This is inevitable; for all historical considerations, since they are concerned with conditions and interconnections, must lead away from absoluteness and deal with those phenomena which are relative. Ideas, as we have said, seen only as historical phenomena, are no longer appreciated as ideas. We look for support to history because we have a wrong notion of what the absolute is; we believe that it should exercise a greater influence than anything relative and that this influence should be indubitable. We expect it to manifest itself as an evident and irresistible compulsion. But historical knowledge—including the diagnosis of the present, so long as it is based on an external survey and not on existential experience—keeps us confined within the realm of influences which condition each other. Any possible experience of the absolute, however, is entirely different and knowledge of it must be gained in a totally different manner.

Therefore, there are two possible lines of thought which will not be pursued in this book. Support for ethics will not be sought in any kind of historical investigation; only occasionally will historical evidence be used to test conclusions, as was done in the discussion of the Ten Commandments above. Nor shall we concern ourselves with the wickedness of man as revealed by the frightening aspects of history as well as by the knowledge of man —that is, the problem of evil will not be fully discussed, though it will be referred to. This does not mean that we deny the enormous power of evil or would attempt to cover it up by an undue optimism; its existence, though not always mentioned, is always presupposed. The task of this book is to build up an ethical teaching and to make it consistent; therefore it is necessary to concentrate, first of all, on man's ethical self. Once ethics has been established, the reader will have to decide for himself whether or not it is a help in fighting evil and can withstand the doubts which the existence of evil is constantly bound to create. In the end, these doubts will also be used as a test.

The next aim of the investigation is to make sure that there is a place for that necessary different kind of knowledge which can do justice to the absolute. The purpose of the preceding two chapters was neither to discover the absolute itself nor to deny the value of the historical, psychological and sociological approaches, but, as has been emphasized, to guard against the application of these approaches where they are not justified and to discover those gaps and contradictions which may leave room for the absolute. The task of the following chapters will be to show that the acceptance of the absolute is justified.

The direction in which to look for this knowledge of the absolute is indicated by the very meaning of the word 'absolute'. In philosophical terms something is said to be absolute when it is recognized as ultimate and underived; when it confronts us in such a way that, if we want to understand our experience, we must accept it unconditionally, even though—because it is underived—we remain unable to explain it further or fully. Originally, the word is an adjective; it does not tell us anything about a content, about what it is that is absolute; it is purely formal.* It is true that we are often also forced to use the noun 'the absolute', and this goes one step further; it implies the assumption that the different contents which we call absolute have not only a common quality, but also a common factual basis. Yet even the noun remains purely formal; within philosophy it can neither be defined nor grasped more directly, nor replaced by more definite concepts. The word itself is empty. The situation is entirely different in religion; for the believer 'the absolute' is not empty; it is God (or a spiritual reality of some kind) and thus totally real and of inexhaustible meaning. For the believer, therefore, God is the starting point; for the philosopher, the absolute is the farthest point he can reach; he can become aware of its existence, but is unable to include it as such in his system; it shows the boundaries of his knowledge and thus of philosophy. It indicates that there is a farther realm beyond thinking which thinking itself cannot reach. Nevertheless, the philosopher should not avoid facing

* For a fuller explanation of the concepts 'form' and 'content', see P. Roubiczek, *Thinking in Opposites* (London, 1952), pp. 27–8.

absoluteness or the absolute. On the contrary whenever he is forced to use these terms he should acknowledge and make clear if and when he finds anything absolute in his discussion. (He should not include the claim that there is a god, for faith remains outside the scope of philosophy. This we shall discuss later.) He will thus acknowledge the boundaries of philosophy, and this is of the utmost importance; for a philosophy which confronts something that transcends it will obviously be different from one which presupposes the possibility of unlimited knowledge. The philosopher who disregards the absolute will always be tempted to find a unitary interpretation of all reality and to falsify his necessarily limited knowledge by claiming that it is all-inclusive. Or, even if he is aware of the impossibility of metaphysics, he may still make his philosophy all-inclusive by relying entirely on one particular method—scientific, logical or linguistic—and denying that anything can be known if it cannot be dealt with by this method. It is the acceptance of correct boundaries which ensures that meaningful questions are being asked: that is, those which can be answered and not those which, because there is no answer to them, must needs produce misleading conclusions. The acceptance of limitations is therefore just as important in philosophy as in history, psychology and science.

If the absolute is understood in this way, philosophy can find out how we can advance towards it, and can develop that totally different kind of knowledge which is needed to approach the absolute in the right way. In fact, the meaning of the word itself, though purely formal, indicates several conditions which govern the way in which this different kind of knowledge is to be developed and thus helps to define the direction in which philosophical thought should move.

(1) As the word 'absolute' has no content, the philosopher must not go beyond the purely formal meaning which has just been stated; he must not include the absolute as such. The absolute itself, whatever it may be, remains outside the realm of philosophy.

(2) At the same time he must be aware of it, and this need,

combined with the lack of a content, forces him to consult his own experience as well as that of others. The absolute cannot be defined by abstract concepts of general validity, even though such concepts can be valuable as guides, nor can it be grasped with the help of historical or other external evidence. Absoluteness is part of our experience and is revealed by experience alone; it cannot be established, confirmed or tested by anything else.

(3) An awareness of the absolute arises when a particular content of experience has made a strong, final impact upon us. As the word means ultimate, such an impact can legitimately be called absolute only if it cannot be superseded by anything stronger; a weak impact could be made relative by being overshadowed or replaced by a stronger impression. This means that the content experienced as absolute has to be of fundamental importance, of real significance to us; unimportant or trivial experiences could not impress us sufficiently; we could not accept them as truly and ultimately essential. We must be able to take the experience 'absolutely' seriously.

(4) As we have to become aware of the importance and significance of the content, anything which we are to call absolute must appeal to our understanding. If we are to trust such an experience, we obviously have to know what it is that we experience; even though the word 'absolute' can be applied to different contents and does not specify them, we shall be entitled to use this weighty attribute only when we are sure that we understand to what content it refers. This does not imply that we should be able to explain it in theory, but that we understand what the content means in the context of our lives, what it actually means to us. Thus, however, the meaning required here is different from that discussed hitherto. If we speak of 'absolute goodness' or 'the absolute moral law', understanding is not confined to the meaning of the words (which is presupposed), but refers to that meaning which must be grasped from within, to the personal, inner experience of a meaningfulness which is related to our existence. It must be capable of being lived, must force us to live accordingly and to make it part of our life.

The absolute and thinking

We shall frequently have to refer to this kind of meaning and shall call it 'existential meaning'.

(5) Absolute does not mean universal. We can never know the whole absolute nor can we ever achieve an extensive knowledge of it; since absoluteness always resides in the individual experience and its compelling nature, we only catch those single glimpses of it which are based on actual experience. We remain unable to generalize. We cannot even exclude contradictions, as will be seen when dealing with moral principles.

(6) Nevertheless, a reality which is justifiably called absolute must be fundamental; therefore all reality must partake in it even if we merely grasp its conditioned, relative aspect. Everything we know is bound to be an appearance of absolute reality. Moreover, although we are unable to recognize the absolute as universal, it must be *one*, for otherwise it would still be dependent on something else and not absolute. Since we can never grasp reality as a unity (as the failure of all metaphysical systems proves), this means that the absolute has to be equated with—and forces us to take into account—the existence of another, a transcendental sphere. Thus we are entitled to claim that any glimpse of the absolute, though pointing beyond philosophy, reveals something of general importance and should exercise an influence upon all our knowledge.

All this shows the philosopher's task with regard to the absolute. He cannot hope to include the absolute itself, but should try to develop a way of thinking which, in contrast to the methods used by the disciplines discussed in the previous chapters, enables him to include experience as evidence of reality as well as that understanding from within which is demanded by the concept 'absolute'. He should develop a method which enables him to recognize when he is entitled to admit that an element of absoluteness can no longer be excluded. Only with the help of such a way of thinking can he discover, on the one hand, how the absolute can be approached, and on the other how its impact can be recognized and distinguished from convictions which are mistakenly accepted as absolute. If, by such a method, he succeeds in this, he will be able to avoid two paralysing mistakes: he will neither accept the absolute too soon, which would strangle necessary further investigations, nor will he be blind to its existence when it has to be acknowledged, a blindness which would invalidate his investigations.

2

In order to be able to do justice to the absolute we have to differentiate between what I shall call 'two ways of thinking'—that is, between two ways of using reason to arrive at valid conclusions, by which two different kinds of knowledge are established. The distinction required for this purpose is probably best understood if we discuss the two methods of thinking known as 'objective' and 'subjective'. The preceding points concerning the absolute apply to the subjective method alone, and so they can help us to recognize, on the one hand, why there are two methods, and on the other, why the subjective method is a way of thinking which can open approaches to the experience of the absolute. It may be useful to keep these points in mind, particularly during the discussion of the objective method which has to be dealt with first.

The objective method is applied to external reality. It is most highly developed in natural science and is therefore well known. A short consideration of some of the characteristics of different sciences thus suggests itself as the simplest way towards a clarification of the two concepts 'objective method' and 'external reality'.

The most exact of the natural sciences is physics. Here the observer tries to suppress, so far as is humanly possible, all personal elements and any influence exerted by himself; he relies upon measuring, weighing, experiments, photography (or at least, in nuclear physics, on photographic plates)—all of which can be tested without any appeal to individual sensitivity, especially as most of these procedures can be repeated. Scientific instruments extend man's senses in such a way that he cannot make errors as a result of bias. There are regions where the observer cannot be completely excluded, but in those cases physics becomes, to a certain extent, uncertain. In quantum theory, for instance, in the region of the infinitesimally small, any observation exercises an influence upon what is observed, so that the observation is no longer entirely objective; therefore the 'uncertainty principle' has to be introduced. But nevertheless this uncertainty hardly reduces the reliability of the objective method, nor does it change its nature. It must not be compared with the uncertainty of human affairs; the principle is formulated as an equation which confines uncertainty within very narrow and well defined limits and which can be used like any other equation. The physicist's ideal remains the completely impersonal mathematical formula.

The achievement of physics—and now also of chemistry—is to translate quality into quantity and thus to allow the application of mathematics. The reality grasped in this way, be it matter or energy, is obviously external to man, and the method is as objective as man can make it. It is true that the scientist himself cannot be excluded; it is the knower who knows. But the method concentrates so much on what is external to man that, for all practical purposes, this personal element can be disregarded. (We shall discuss why it should not be neglected altogether when we try to assess the validity of the objective method.)

At the same time, the application of mathematics is made possible by abstraction. Abstraction means the leaving out of the particular characteristics of an object or event in order to arrive at a general concept which has a wider scope and can thus include many single objects or events. We disregard all the special characteristics of individual tables, for instance, their size, shape, colour, weight—and in this way we form the abstract concept 'table'. From such simple beginnings we gradually advance towards more and more abstract concepts which include less and less of the objects and events we actually perceive: the table is an object; the wood of which it is made is a material; this material is composed of matter; if we deal with an action which produces an event, we form such concepts as motion and force. This is a natural process at work in all thinking; in physics it is carried farther, to concepts such as fields and energy, or waves and particles. These are so abstract that they can be fully identified only by mathematical formulae.

All this is necessary because science aims at generalizations which can be applied to every object or event of the same class. Abstraction therefore serves to develop another tool of the objective method—the use of theories. A scientific theory is a general set of principles advanced to explain observed phenomena and thus a combination of speculation and ascertained facts. The main element in any theory is an abstract working hypothesis, an assumption which makes sense in the light of knowledge so far gained, but it is nevertheless merely an assumption based on abstractions from ascertained facts. Assumptions are needed because there are gaps in all sciences; each new step fills gaps, but also discloses new ones, as for example the advance from Newton's theory of gravitation to the theory of relativity and to the quantum theory shows. These gaps introduce another, more profound uncertainty into this kind of knowledge; any theory may be wrong. Even this uncertainty, however, does not reduce the efficiency of the objective method. As long as the possibility of being wrong is slight and, in the light of new observations and discoveries, diminishing, the theory is accepted as valid. Yet because of the gaps, new discoveries are sought and acknowledged, and if these contradict the former theory, changes within it are made or a new theory developed. This procedure is reliable, because once again the tests are completely impersonal—observations checked by instruments and experiments which can be repeated.

This sheds further light both on the objective method and on external reality. What is certain and unchanging in this sphere are the ascertained facts from which the theory starts. As soon, however, as we seem to be approaching deeper levels of reality, those which demand understanding, we are confronted with those parts of the theory which are uncertain—with hypotheses and speculation. The objective method cannot disclose that meaning which we have called existential;* its certainty is confined to the impersonal region which we can grasp from outside but cannot understand from within. Moreover it is impossible that this method should ever disclose anything absolute or that external reality could include it, for we must be prepared to admit that theories have to be changed or completely replaced if the discovery of new facts demands it. Science would soon cease advancing if any theory were finally accepted as absolutely true. Theories must remain relative, and in the sphere of understanding —which we would have to enter to find approaches to the absolute—the objective method leaves us dependent on theories.

Theories work the better the more they succeed in showing that we can rely upon a cause necessarily producing an expected effect. Theories are developed in order to find such laws. We try to establish the existence of strict causality as part of a general rule of necessity. Because of the nature of theories, necessity can never be complete, but the attempt to establish it is nevertheless another important part of the objective method and one which contributes a great deal to its effectiveness. Obviously, as every switching on of electric light illustrates, causal laws can be relied upon in vast spheres of external reality. It is true that in nuclear physics, the boundaries of a recognizable necessity have been reached; in some fields causality is not even regarded as a meaningful term. But an endeavour is made instead to establish a probability so great that it approaches necessity, in order to bring probability closer and closer to certainty, and this confirms that necessity remains the aim of this kind of knowledge. In fact, even here causality cannot be completely dismissed, for it would be impossible to 'infer the properties of the observed object from the results of measurements if the law of causality did not guarantee an unambiguous connection between the two'.† In general the ideal achievement of the objective method would be to grasp external reality as entirely subordinated to necessity. This ideal, even if beyond reach, is

* See pp. 72–3.
† W. Heisenberg, *Philosophic Problems of Nuclear Science* (London, 1952), p. 20.

justified because it ensures the development of the method in the right direction.

This criterion is confirmed by the usefulness of predictions which are based on this acceptance of necessity. In practical matters we are all bound to rely on predictable effects of known causes; life would become well-nigh unmanageable if, for instance, I could not be sure that the table on which I write will obey the law of gravity and not suddenly jump into the air. Predictions help the scientist to test a theory and to decide whether or not he is conducting his research on the right lines; their importance in science is well illustrated in the case of the astronomer Le Verrier. His calculations led him to assert that a further planet, unknown at his time, must exist, and thanks to him Neptune was discovered soon afterwards. Later he predicted the discovery of yet another planet which he named in advance Vulcan but this time he was wrong. His failure, however, turned out 'to be of far greater scientific importance than success would have been. For success would only have added a small body to the solar system, whereas failure meant that at long last a flaw in the Newtonian theory of gravitation had been found.' Predictions confirm theories or redirect research; 'about forty years later the resolution of this issue was to form one of the cornerstones of Einstein's general theory of relativity'.* In nuclear physics, too, predictions are possible within limits and are constantly used. On the whole, correct predictions prevail and their extreme frequency in everyday life and in all the sciences shows that necessity, despite all the gaps in it, must not be lightly dismissed.

Necessity of this kind however, still remains within the sphere of the relative; for even correct predictions which seem to amount to proof are based on impermanent theories. It is true that predictions may remain valid even if the theory changes: the theory of electricity, for instance, has changed since the invention of electric light, yet electric light still functions in much the same way as before, which means that the prediction that certain causes will produce the desired effects has not been impaired. But

---

* F. Hoyle, *The Nature of the Universe*, p. 19.

these predictions refer to simple facts which can be ascertained. Once more we do not enter the sphere of understanding where the absolute could make itself felt.

Other sciences can help us to recognize which of the enumerated procedures are always essential, for the sphere of external reality is, of course, wider than that of physics and chemistry, which merely show most clearly the working of the objective method.

A different degree of uncertainty arises as soon as a point is reached where history and the phenomenon of life cannot be disregarded. The influence of history can be seen even in physics—namely in astronomy when trying to explain the origin of the universe and the history of the stars. Several theories exist and none can be proved, because historical processes cannot be translated into experiments which could be exactly repeated. This uncertainty is also inevitable in biology when attempts are made to trace the history of life or the origin of man, and to base generalizations on single instances of evolution. Here again both the past and the emergence of new species defy repetition and consequently experimental proof. Repetition—which has been mentioned before but not yet emphasized—is thus shown as another of the essential elements of the objective method, for only if tests can be repeated can the personal element be excluded and the observation of events made fully independent of the observer, as is required if exactitude is to be achieved. The sciences become less exact the less they can make use of intentionally produced repetitions; even the observation of events which recur cannot quite replace such planned experiments.

Yet the objective method is not invalidated even by this further uncertainty; astronomy and biology (and the sciences bordering on biology, such as physiology) are still dealing with external reality in a largely successful way. Most of the other aids which we enumerated, such as measuring, sometimes weighing and often photography, can be used; theories may be less certain but they show where further fruitful research can be undertaken; there are generalizations and approximations to laws. Despite the absence of predictions some theories in this field, such as the theory of evolution, seem even less open to criticism than some physical theories. Moreover, astronomy and biology use physical and chemical methods wherever possible; radio-astronomy, chemical analysis and molecular biology have achieved very important results and thus narrowed down the sphere of uncertainty outside the purely historical field. In fact, all sciences accept the quantitative method as the best one and apply it as far as possible, which confirms that physics and chemistry are the best examples of how the objective method works. Yet astronomy, biology and other similar sciences still grasp their subject-matter in fundamentally the same way—from outside and as objectively and impersonally as possible. Despite the fact that history and life cannot be completely divorced from human experience, we are still safely embedded in external reality—and thus kept, too, at a safe distance from dealing with those personal experiences which reveal the existence of the absolute.

Psychology, too, even though it attempts to grasp the innermost processes of the human mind, uses the objective method, in an attempt to include the mind, as far as possible, in external reality. Again, some parts of the objective method cannot be used because man is never entirely impersonal; but the method can still be applied to a large extent with success. Here another of its characteristic aids—generalization—comes to the fore. Psychology (as a science, not as an art of healing which does not concern us here*) tries to understand even the most individual experience with the help of laws and theories which are generally valid; individual cases are used, necessarily, in a one-sided way as test-cases of generalizations. All inner experiences are seen as events or processes to be observed from outside, which is possible if we concentrate on what is common to many people and can thus be repeatedly observed or even produced at will. It is true that introspection has to be admitted; no one else will ever know what is going on in my mind or in my dreams; but it is exercised in a detached way as self-observation; inner participation must be

---

* The good doctor, when confronted with a patient, will not rely on his theories only, but attempt to establish a personal relationship.

circumvented so as to allow generalizations. As everyone of us reacts automatically in some parts of his mind—that is, impersonally—psychological theories can attempt to express human experience in terms which are sufficiently general and abstract to remain within the sphere of external reality. This is true even of the different forms of depth psychology, of Freud's Oedipus complex as well as of Jung's archetypes. Much can be understood in this way. But as individual experiences thus become the raw material of generalizations, these psychological statements, which must be generally applicable, cannot help anyone to understand himself as the unique person which he is. This time the application of the objective method, though less obvious, is even more drastic because we are deliberately cut off from all those experiences which enable us to recognize the impact of the absolute. It has been said above that abstractions and generalizations may guide us towards such experiences, but can do no more, because absoluteness can only be confirmed by experience—that is, a particular experience must not be seen as a 'case', but must be participated in by the individual person in all his uniqueness.

These characteristics of science have already shown that the objective method is not the privilege of scientists—that, on the contrary, it is used to a large extent in the performance of even the most common activities. We must constantly deal with that reality which is external to us and to deal with it effectively, we must be as objective as possible.

This will have become self-evident by now. We are bound to use numbers and all kinds of measurements all the time. The example of abstraction was taken from everyday life; in fact, life would become well-nigh impossible if we had to remember different names for every table, chair and house; it is difficult enough to remember the names of different kinds of trees or birds and of different people. Most of our intentional actions are based on a belief in strict causality; we rely on it whether we strike a match or take a train or a car. Any decision, even a moral one, is made easier if it can be based on generalizations, theories or laws which we know to be reliable. If we are forced to go beyond what is familiar to us and to face a new, unknown task or problem, we shall attempt to discover causal sequences which enable us to predict the effect of the new cause. Man himself is frequently made part of external reality and treated as impersonally as possible—as a means to an end, as a mere number, as an exchangeable entity; this has its dangers, but it cannot be avoided in any society. In our complex society, to make the best use of man as a means to an end, even carefully devised tests based on measurements and generalizations are applied, at school and in some professions such as flying. Technology, medicine, psychological methods and even statistics have become part of everyday life to such an extent that we cannot avoid using some of the elements of scientific thinking. We constantly depend on a proper grasp of external reality.

To sum up: the objective method mainly consists in using impersonal measurements and experiments, numbers and abstractions; it aims at generalizations and laws in order to establish necessity and to be able to predict. Some of these elements can be left out if they are not appropriate, but the objective method works as long as its basic attitude can be preserved. By it we grasp that aspect of reality which can be known objectively, as impersonal and external to man (or at least without reference to purely personal experiences)—that is, we grasp external reality. As the objective method has such a wide range, extending from the simplest affairs of everyday life to the most complex mathematics, it could well appear that it is all-inclusive and that external reality is the whole reality. But we have seen that to remain within the objective and external sphere also means that we can never hope to find approaches to the absolute. Of course, the absolute could be dismissed as non-existent, as mere prejudice. Yet even within the external sphere itself we can discover that we are dealing only with a particular aspect of reality; that there is a need for another method and another approach.

There are several consequences of the objective method which show this need, quite apart from the fact that it is self-evidently unsatisfactory to disregard purely personal experiences and to treat men as numbers. All these consequences indicate strongly that there is room left for the subjective method, whether or not we succeed in developing it satisfactorily.

(1) One of these flaws we have mentioned already—the objective method must neglect the knower; but he obviously cannot be neglected altogether. It must be of some consequence that even the most objective knowledge is *our* knowledge. If we were restricted to external knowledge alone, this would support the view that there is nothing but relativity, but we have seen that relativity presupposes some kind of absoluteness to become distinct at all.* Thus the disregarding of the observer has actually drawn our attention to him, for he must provide the contrast which makes it possible to distinguish relativity. The objective method alone, therefore, cannot be sufficient; we must also be able to concentrate on the knower.

(2) The scientist may be passionately interested in his science, and this personal interest may help him to achieve success. He may also rely on, or be helped by, intuitions. Much in science is certainly achieved by sudden insights which carry with them great enthusiasm. Once the sphere of science has been entered, however, both personal participation and intuition must be left behind. Their results will only be acceptable if they stand the test of completely impersonal observations or experiments. Even the most cherished ideas have to be discarded if they cannot be thus proved as correct or used as a working hypothesis. This shows again that the knower is excluded, but also, and even more clearly, that the objective method deals only with a particular aspect of reality and that there is a vast personal realm left over which calls for another method of approach. Interest, enthusiasm and intuition are obviously of great importance and undoubtedly real; it would be a distressing impoverishment of knowledge if they were looked on as its merely private accompaniment and therefore excluded from serious consideration.

In an attempt to bridge the gap between science and personal experience it is often argued that the scientist's work is not really

* See pp. 22–3.

different from that of the artist, for both experience intuition. The scientist, it is said, is not some kind of mechanical worker who merely makes experiment after experiment and collects a large number of observations, but he, too, has illuminations, even of an almost artistic kind. This is certainly true but the place of intuition in science and in the arts is entirely different. In science it does not matter whether a discovery or theory is the result of intuition or of diligent mechanical labour, for it can and must be tested objectively; many great achievements are due to intuition but the acceptance of the result is independent of the way in which it has been reached. The results, moreover, are communicated as such; they need factual understanding, but not any knowledge of their history nor a re-experiencing of the intuition. In artistic creation, however, the unique intuition of the artist (apart from his technical achievement) is essential for the final result; the work of art is not only based on intuitive knowledge, but the individual form of the intuition is also preserved in the work and becomes part of it, frequently appearing as the individual and often surprising way in which a particular artist deals with his subject matter. Moreover the value of the work is mainly determined by the quality of the intuition. At the same time, it must appeal to, and awaken the intuitive knowledge of those who appreciate it; the individuality of the artist and the newness of his achievement must be experienced. In other words a new, individual, original approach in science must, if it is to become valid, lead to an impersonal formula; but if an original artistic method becomes a formula, then the artist using it is in danger of producing works which—if not dead from the start—are of diminishing value. The scientist must make use of repetitions: the artist must not repeat himself. In science intuition is a handmaid to be dismissed after fulfilling its limited function, which is mainly that of solving problems;* in the realm of art, problems may be solved too, but here the more important function of intuition is a different one; far from being

---

* This does not rule out, of course, that endeavouring to recover the intuition which led to a new scientific discovery or theory may be a source of excitement to the scientist or a help in teaching science.

dismissed, it must remain alive in the work and the work itself only lives so long as it can kindle intuition in others. It is this kind of intuitive knowledge which gives access to the absolute. We shall see that, outside the arts, it is developed by the subjective method.

(3) The need to pay due regard to the role of personal participation in our experience is clearly seen if we consider what happens if we rely on the objective method alone. Within its scope everything is relative, which by itself need not exclude the use of another method. But if we think that we cannot possibly know anything beyond it, our involvement in relativity becomes complete, and since any complete involvement is an experience of absoluteness, relativity itself becomes absolute. The dismissal of the very possibility of absoluteness and the consequent belief in the exclusiveness of the objective method are actually dogmatic and are evidently considered in every way as absolute, though absoluteness is not openly acknowledged. For we cannot help participating in something; personal participation, rejected as a method, therefore reappears, but now it exercises a falsifying influence as a dogmatic insistence that everything must needs be relative. All the elements which are merely requirements of the objective method are misinterpreted as giving us the only kind of knowledge which is possible, and thus everything is made relative for us. Even the assumption that, perhaps, there could be something absolute can no longer be admitted, though this assertion of relativity is itself based on an absolute judgment. The tacit agreement which we discussed* is a consequence of accepting the objective method alone. The subjective method is needed to restore the balance.

A good example of this misinterpretation is the belief in determinism. The establishment of necessity is only part of the objective method, and its scope is strictly limited, because it does not enter the sphere of that understanding which can disclose existential meaning;† it is a means to an end, not final knowledge. If the method is accepted as covering the whole of reality, necessity also

* See p. 22.   † See pp. 72–3.

appears as all-inclusive, which leads to the conviction that a full knowledge of reality would establish complete determinism. Because of this conviction complete determinism—that there is only necessity and no freedom—comes to be taken for granted; every event or action is assumed to be entirely determined by a cause which, in its turn, has been necessarily produced by a preceding cause. In fact, however, 'determinism is a faith' which can never be proved, nor based on conclusive knowledge; 'the determinist is in no position to plot out the most part of human conduct, as the simple example of established uniformities, whether before or after the conduct occurs. He is singular merely in holding the hope, the pious hope, that under ideal conditions it could be done.' At the same time, what we feel when a determinist view 'is talked to us, is not that human liberty is being disproved, but that it is being threatened';* unless we are completely dominated by a blind faith in determinism we feel that our existence as persons is threatened, which shows that internal reality is involved. We obviously have to find a way of discussing these questions from a different point of view.

It is true that there is within the objective method a limited certainty which practically amounts to absoluteness, where ascertained facts are concerned. If we refuse to eat we know for certain that we shall die. We are, moreover, absolutely certain that we and the world exist, whatever method of thinking we apply. Those philosophers who tried to undermine even these certainties have failed.† This kind of certainty, however, does not satisfy us, it is a challenge—the challenge to establish absoluteness, too, in the full sense of the word, namely in the sphere of that

* A. Farrer, *The Freedom of the Will* (London, 1958), pp. 298, 249.

† Bishop Berkeley, the most radical of the idealists, claims that things exist only by being perceived; their *esse* is *percipi*; but ultimately he uses this argument to prove the existence of God which also restores the existence of things. David Hume develops a total scepticism which makes him doubt everything which our reason and senses tell us, yet he is forced to admit: 'We may well ask, what causes us to believe in the existence of body? But 'tis vain to ask, whether there be body or not? That is a point which we must take for granted in all our reasonings.' (*Treatise*, bk I, pt IV, sect. ii.)

understanding which the objective method cannot enter. If there is absolute certainty, we ought also to be able to understand it.

All this does not amount to proof that we are able to develop a subjective method which works, but undoubtedly it makes it worthwhile investigating this other approach and seeing how far it can lead.

3

The subjective method enables us to grasp internal reality. This statement, however, is not as unambiguous as the corresponding statement about the objective method and external reality; while the words 'objective' and external' can be used without preliminary explanation, the words 'subjective' and 'internal' can be misleading and require comment before being used.

The meaning of the word 'subjective' has deteriorated. Very often it is used simply as a derogatory term, meaning 'biased', 'falsified by prejudice', or even 'attributable to wishful thinking'. But in the phrase 'subjective method' it ought to mean nothing more or less than that approach to reality which is the opposite of the objective approach, that which is needed when only personal participation can lead to the acquisition of knowledge, as is the case when personal experience, certain values or faith have to be understood. The subjective method, to deserve the name 'method' should be, in its own way, just as reliable as the objective method actually is; and the word 'subjective' should therefore equally have neither laudatory nor derogatory overtones, but describe an attitude which is both the opposite and the equivalent of the objective attitude. It is only in this sense, as implying personal participation, that we shall use the word 'subjective'— that is in the sense in which Kierkegaard used it.*

It is characteristic of our present situation that the word 'objective' should be directly intelligible, while the word 'sub-

---

* Although our usage of the word 'subjective' is derived from Kierkegaard, we need not enter into his thought here because we are going to explain the subjective method. For a discussion of his approach see P. Roubiczek, *Existentialism—For and Against*, pp. 99–107.

jective' has first to be rescued. Since scientific knowledge is most powerful and most highly regarded today, all other knowledge has been pushed into the background, neglected and thereby impoverished; as science must suppress the subjective element, this has become suspect in itself even in a non-scientific context. The description and development of that other kind of knowledge with which we are concerned has become difficult. The same trend can be seen even more clearly in the case of the word 'internal'.

This word has been chosen for lack of a better. It is used in physiology and psychology in a more or less spatial sense, to describe what is inside the body or mind. This is not the meaning intended in the phrase 'internal reality'. If the doubtful venture of inventing new words is to be avoided, some such expression has to be chosen, because all the words referring to a reality of that kind, such as 'soul' or 'spirit', have unfortunately become so vague and overlaid with misleading connotations that they can hardly be used in philosophy. This, too, is characteristic of our situation— we are estranged from our own inner knowledge. But no attempt will be made here to rescue either of these words because internal reality, though in some ways related to them, means something different. It does not refer to any kind of entity, but—like external reality—to an aspect of reality which is grasped, and also isolated, by a particular act of thinking. It is an epistemological term, referring to the nature and scope of human knowledge.* Internal reality is that aspect of reality which becomes accessible through the subjective method.

These explanations are obviously only introductory—provisional safeguards against misunderstanding. Since the subjective method and internal reality will occupy us throughout the rest of the book, it is hoped that the concepts will become more definite in the course of their elaboration. Therefore, the following discussion, too, is still tentative, and for the same reason the term 'value-judgment' is left as yet unexplained. The following example is only one special kind of value-judgment; the nature

---

* It may even be doubtful whether the term 'reality' is justified. This will be discussed in the next chapter.

and range of such judgments will be discussed later.* First, a comparison with the objective method will be made in order to show some of the basic characteristics of the subjective method.

If we judge that something is morally good we can no longer exclude the observer; in fact, we cannot even properly speak of an observer. We must base the judgment on our experience of the good; we must be involved, not detached. An attempt to talk about the good to a person who has never experienced it is like trying to explain colours in visual terms to someone who is colour-blind. We are unable to reduce quality to quantity in the manner required to make a statement about the good completely impersonal; we have already mentioned that numbers cannot operate in this sphere;† quality alone matters, and it becomes accessible through personal experience alone. Thus, however, the subjective method uses tools of thought which are very different from those of the objective method, and certainty is achieved in a completely different way.

The basic tools of the objective method are abstractions and generalizations. Since these can hardly be avoided in speaking about any subject whatever, they play their part in the subjective method too. But here they are no longer basic; on the contrary they can be misleading or even destructive. External reality is made manageable by them; it is to them that success in practical affairs, in scientific and technological achievements is due. In internal reality, such abstract words as 'the good', 'goodness', 'love' are used, and a meaning for them can be derived from actual experience by the usual process of abstraction—that is, by eliminating all particular characteristics from a variety of different actions or feelings which reveal goodness or love. But internal reality is not grasped more satisfactorily in this way; it tends rather to evaporate. If the process is carried to its extreme, we do not arrive at the most helpful mathematical formula, but at conventional phrases. Abstract concepts can provide guidance if they are met and supported by personal knowledge of real experience of the same kind; they can help us to remember such experiences and

---

* See chapters IX–X. † See p. 25.

clarify them; they are even needed because experience alone is not enough; we must be able to recapture it. But if we go on using abstract concepts for too long and rely on them alone, they will destroy our capacity to make them real. In the attempt to communicate moral principles they do more harm than good unless we are talking to the already converted. Therefore, even though they are unavoidable, they must be used with the utmost caution.

Nevertheless we shall use them. It is true that such words as 'goodness', 'love of one's neighbour', 'beauty', have been so much misused that they now seem to have a deadening effect; but to replace them would even further weaken the experiences to which they refer. We therefore believe that they should be revived, and this we shall try to do.

The same caution applies to generalizations. The main tool of the subjective method is the emphasis on the particular event, on individual experience, for only through them can the meaning of inner experience be realized; in fact, internal reality is most fully disclosed by the appropriate unique event, because such an event is bound to break through the surface and to lay bare the fundamentals. The more exceptional the action by which it is revealed the more distinct does goodness become, as it does if we consider saving a child from drowning at great risk, obeying one's conscience even though this means the concentration camp or perhaps only losing conspicuous chances of promotion. The story of Captain Oates has been repeated *ad nauseam* because of its uniqueness. Repetition, however, which is an essential help in making useful external generalizations, can be fatal to internal reality. A ritual or form of worship, originally overwhelmingly significant, can become an empty ceremony; the good intention of helping those in need, when it leads to many repetitive acts (for instance in a committee which has to deal with a large number of similar cases), can kill sensitivity—and thus goodness, too. It is the case which is so personal that the very word 'case' sounds wrong which produces the deepest awareness of internal reality. The generalizations which we are incessantly bound to make are not essential; we have to struggle against them.

The absolute and thinking

It could be argued that such precautions are unnecessary. If there is in everybody what Kierkegaard has called the 'ethical self' and if, therefore, fundamental morality is part of human nature, everyone will be able to give meaning to these abstractions and generalizations on the basis of his own experience. Ethics is founded on this trust; otherwise it could hardly be established at all. Yet even the existence of the ethical self does not affect the need for particular experiences, because it belongs to that class of facts which are, at the same time, potentialities. Conscience, for instance, though a fact, can be developed by the right approach and weakened by its denial; it can even be killed. Moral impulses may exist deeply buried beneath different convictions—such as materalism—which seem incompatible with them. In an age like ours dominated by the objective method many people may be reluctant to acknowledge them or even be ashamed of them; few people can avoid at least the secret thought that it is stupid to disregard one's own advantage. Although different motives are potentially present, they may never develop. Because all the abstract words of this kind have been emasculated by centuries of repetition, they will not make it superfluous to use concrete examples as well. To talk of the desirability of goodness or love will be insufficient to appeal to a hidden potential goodness. (Potentiality is another important characteristic of internal reality; it will be further discussed in a moment.) In mythology, history and fiction there are exemplary saints, martyrs, wise men, and pairs of friends and lovers, whose image is deeply ingrained in our minds, and it is rather by the impact of such particular examples—the admiration and love they inspire and the unforgettable impression they make—and not by abstract words that true goodness, friendship and love are understood.

In fact, even if ethics is accepted, particular experiences are constantly needed because, since abstractions and repetitions are unavoidable, the moral sense, also, is constantly dulled. Mere adherence to rules, even to the best of them, is no substitute. It has become a commonplace to say that to obey rules for their own sake is not enough, because it produces that attitude which was castigated in the Pharisees. The subjective method shows why: rules are based on abstractions and demand repetitions, and as moral awareness can thus be deadened, motives foreign to morality are bound to come to the fore. Everyone needs, again and again, new vivid impressions to keep his sensitivity and moral awareness alive; nothing but a constant renewal of his inner participation can guarantee that they go on having meaning for him.

The particular matters because here we move in the sphere of that understanding which implies a sense of meaning for the individual. Therefore we must not simplify in the hope of arriving at a knowledge of processes which can be used without further consideration or involvement, but, on the contrary, aim at considerations and experiences which disclose existential meaning. The value-judgment that something is good must be based on all the particulars involved, for a misunderstanding of or even indifference to any vital factor may make it invalid; each of the particulars must be fully experienced to be understood. If we enter the sphere of the good, if, for instance, we want to help a friend by an action which fulfils the requirements of goodness, we have to make sure first that our motives are the right ones—that we really want to help and not to gain some material reward or acquire a good reputation. At the same time, we must be fully aware of the friend's situation in order to be sure that our help will be of the right kind and serve a good end; to help him to earn more money may be sufficient if we feel sure that he will make the right use of it, but this may be wrong in a case where money will corrupt him. If our help is to be successful, we have also to use the objective method, to be able to choose means which promise success; but we must use it responsibly, for bad means may spoil even the best end. If we use unscrupulous means, for example, we may, by making them seem legitimate, obscure the good which is our aim. Some special considerations may become necessary, too—we may have to resist our friend's own wishes because we judge that their fulfilment would harm him and thus we may appear cruel; we may, on the other hand, really be cruel if we resist them because they are uncomfortable or too demanding for us. Something similar may happen if we feel forced to make our friend less dependent on us; this may be justified or it may be selfish on our part. None of these details can be left to mere routine; for understanding is only achieved if we know, or try to know, what each of them means to us and to the friend and what it ought to mean to be judged to be good; only if nothing in our act is merely conventional or superficial can our deed be fully experienced as good. If we just give such help as is usually given in such cases without understanding the actual situation, or if we simply think that we must not appear cruel, our action may still have a useful result, but the meaning of the good will not be realized; our own sensitivity will be blurred and the other person will not experience goodness at work. If, however, we fail in spite of all the required considerations, we may still have succeeded in helping in another way, because the sincerity and depth of our friendship can be a great support in themselves. Each particular is bound to influence the result.

By way of illustration one might consider how meaning is embodied in great works of art, say, some portraits by the older Rembrandt. Each single detail contributes to our intuitive understanding. Bright light falling on a place which seems unimportant, on a white turban or a golden helmet, for instance, makes us aware of the all-important expression of the face which is only dimly lit; some parts of the picture, such as the curled hair or the collar, are carefully executed even though they might seem distractions; other parts are merely sketched in, the hands may be simply strokes of colour; and other parts again are nearly omitted, usually the details of the background—one could not change any of these without destroying, or at least fundamentally changing, the impact of the painting. If any detail were arranged or executed even in a slightly different way, the light would illuminate the picture differently and produce different effects, and the direction of our attention would be altered. It is through the treatment of all details and their complex interrelationship that understanding and meaning are conveyed.

It is true that the subjective method does not deal with experience alone; it is also used to develop teachings, especially in ethics, and these cannot help being abstract and theoretical. But even in this case the difference between the two methods is striking. Theories are among the main tools, are perhaps the chief tool of the objective method; in the sphere of the subjective they must remain accessory if the method is to perform its task properly. External theories, moreover, try to approximate laws by combining ascertained facts and abstract hypotheses; in internal reality, laws and facts play a different part because of their different nature; and hypotheses should only be used, if at all, when giving examples or considering the course of possible actions. Actually, the two methods can be clearly distinguished by the different meanings which the words 'law' and 'fact' have in each context.

In external reality, laws are based on causality or probability and aim at the nearest possible approach to necessity. In internal reality, it is probably more natural to speak of principles; an inner principle is a law giving guidance for future actions.* This makes such laws different from external laws in two ways. First, internal laws are more compelling than any scientific laws; the latter may be doubted because of the possibility of new discoveries which would lead to new theories, or because of the growing importance of probability (the law thus becoming more an approximation or a practical simplification); a principle states a law which is beyond doubt. In contrast to the findings of natural science, however, it need not be accepted; it acquires its status as a law only by being acknowledged as such; but, once accepted, it is final and pro-claimed with absolute certainty. A moral principle, for instance, can be tentatively compared with others, doubted or even rejected; it is only valid for us if we want to behave morally and finally come to recognize it as valid; but if we do it becomes an absolute law; it is not a mere hypothesis. We may try to dismiss

---

* The word 'principle' is also used in science, but rather vaguely. Formerly it referred to fundamental laws from which others spring, but now it is sometimes used to avoid the word 'law', or to describe those links within a theory which regulate the combination of facts and hypotheses.

even the commandment 'Thou shalt love thy neighbour as thyself', or ridicule it as conventional or sentimental, but its acceptance means the recognition that it is unconditional and binding. Second, a principle is not concerned with causality or probability, but with ends—such as acting responsibly or being good—and even this should not be overemphasized, for it is not the relationship of means to ends which matters most, but the clarification of the end itself. The commandment to love clarifies what the otherwise vague term 'love' should mean in ethics.*

Yet such demands, despite their absoluteness, are not based on ascertained facts, but on facts which, as has just been said, are potentialities, and this means that, in contrast to external facts, internal facts cannot be fully ascertained. It is a fact that man has, potentially, a conscience, but as a potentiality may or may not develop, its existence as a fact can remain a claim which has to be accepted as being justified, and its acceptance does not depend on factual proof, but on whether or not we find that the claim has a basis in our own experience. No external evidence to the contrary can undermine a principle. 'Even though there might never yet have been a sincere friend', says Kant, and even if it could be historically proved that sincere friendship is impossible, 'yet not a whit less is pure sincerity in friendship required of every man.'† The absolute validity of the principle which demands sincerity in friendship remains unaffected.

All this shows that theoretical statements in themselves are not basic in the subjective method; even laws and facts become compelling only when they are accepted—that is, by a personal decision. This is indeed utterly different from the working of the objective method; subjectivity seems to invade the very foundations. But the reason why this happens can be understood, for each of the two methods gives us a different kind of certainty.

In external reality, as we have seen, certainty is confined to

---

* Cf., for example, Kierkegaard's *Works of Love* in which he deals in great detail with each single word of the commandment and thus shows with its help that the concept of love is indeed clarified.

† *Fundamental Principles of the Metaphysics of Ethics*, pp. 24–5.

ascertained facts. We try hard, often with great difficulty, to achieve more certainty; that this endeavour is extremely important is shown by the significance of practical activity and technology, but its success remains limited. Because the theories upon which this kind of knowledge rests are open to doubt and change, there is no fundamental certainty, and this makes even the limited certainty actually reached precarious. Outside the sphere of simple facts any certainty is provisional and may be called in question; theoretical assumptions may or may not refer to something which really exists.

In internal reality, certainty is immediate and beyond doubt; all inner experiences carry with them an unshakable feeling of certainty. We may not always be certain what we think and feel, and why, but we know that we do think and feel; either experiences are obviously real or they do not arise. We may be frightened by a hallucination or by something completely harmless; nevertheless, our fear is real, however puzzling the content of such an experience may be. This immediate certainty is—almost automatically—extended to the content of experience and thought This may be justified, for example, when we know that we experience joy or pain, or it may be misleading if the imaginary causes of our fear are accepted as just as real as the fear itself. There is, in fact, too much conviction of certainty, not too little. We may embrace, as a personal creed, determinism or the existence of freedom, a psychological explanation of conscience or absolute morality, and in each case feel 'absolutely right'. The problem here, therefore, is not how to achieve certainty, but how to discriminate between true and false feelings of certainty, to discard wrong convictions and to recognize those which should be accepted. Certainty is the starting point and not the aim, it is given and is not in need of being established; but we must constantly sort out the certainties which we experience and make sure which of them are justified. This scrutiny, which will also pay attention to the doubts which assail us, will be one of the main points of our later investigation.

The result is that in external reality, as we have said, we know innumerable facts for certain, but have no certainty concerning theories and the foundations of our knowledge. In internal reality, certainty is basic, for (if we avoid being misled by false convictions, which is possible) we can become certain about the foundations of our knowledge. Here the uncertainties arise when we try to apply the principles to the facts of our actual situation.

Thus, in this sphere, the nature of necessity is changed as well. As we are certain from the start, the derivation of the principle does not require the support of causality; its impact, too, is immediate. Instead, there is necessity within the principle; once accepted, it establishes a law. This kind of necessity, however, does not abolish freedom, it is dependent on the free acceptance of the principle and strictly limited to it. Certain actions are thus made necessary, yet since the principle is purely formal, they are not directly prescribed but still require a further free choice. That we should love our neighbour can become a law for us, but each further step which we discover as necessary is a further appeal to our freedom. Therefore, necessity, too, occupies a secondary place; it remains an elaboration of the principle showing what our certainty and our free decision imply. It cannot lead to determinism because we cannot aim at its extension beyond the scope of the principle.

There is also another kind of necessity. A person may have acquired, by birth or by his development, such a strong inclination to do good that he identifies himself completely with the ethical self and cannot but try to be good, and then all his actions are necessarily good. Naturally such persons are rare; even most of the saints had constantly to struggle. Necessity, therefore, is again limited, this time to the person and again cannot lead to any kind of determinism. But these persons exercise an influence by their example—they show the goal that we ought to reach. Why they are as they are is a mystery or a psychological problem; the subjective method is concerned with the necessity of their actions only in so far as these embody goodness. Necessity in internal reality remains restricted.

The secondary position of necessity is confirmed by the fact that predictions are unimportant. For the objective method, as we have seen, these also are essential.* The more common ones (what will happen, say, when a heavy object is robbed of its support) are frequent and easy but when they come to concern theories—that is, the basis of knowledge—they become difficult because the sphere of certainty is limited. Nevertheless, they must be constantly attempted, for they make it possible to enlarge that sphere. In internal reality, on the contrary, basic predictions would be easy, for we can foresee which principles must always be taken into account, and the principles themselves do not change. But such statements are insights into what goodness means rather than predictions, because they do not cover the details of application which would be all-important for predicting the resulting behaviour. Predictions would only be significant if we could predict the behaviour of a particular person in any particular situation, but this is well-nigh impossible by either method. In external reality, we may succeed if we restrict ourselves to his usual and thus probable reactions, but these may be overruled by free decisions. In internal reality, trust in a person, or an intuition of what he will do, may often be proved correct, but we cannot be certain that they will; we cannot know his free decision beforehand. Our trust is rather a hope and a demand than a prediction of fact. If we believe in freedom, as the subjective method requires, respect for freedom makes predictions irrelevant.† They may even do actual harm by influencing us and distorting our decisions, thus preventing the proper use of our freedom. Since the subjective method depends on the correct interpretation of man's actual inner experience, it is better to exclude predictions completely from its realm. We should remain our true selves; predictions (even our own) can too easily make us do automatically what is expected of us.

All these differences between the two methods are further

* See p. 78.
† Belief in freedom is here presupposed, and it is hoped that it makes sense so far. But it will be discussed more fully on pp. 236–9.

confirmed by what each can achieve. At first sight, external results seem much more reliable; since the time when the objective method was first properly isolated and used—that is, since Galileo—it has made consistent progress and has now, in science and technology, achievements to its credit which would have appeared miraculous to all previous generations. Nevertheless, these achievements are based on theories which are always open to change; there is no constancy once we approach the sphere of basic understanding; all external knowledge, as Heisenberg has put it, is 'suspended over an unfathomable depth.'* The subjective method seems, at first sight, much less reliable; since we are dependent on particular experiences and cannot generalize, we may reach understanding only in particular cases, and this can hardly lead to spectacular results. Absoluteness, we have said, resides in the actual, single experience and can only be renewed by such experiences; moreover, as there is no other test but personal participation, misleading prejudices and wrong certainties may easily be overlooked. However, the subjective method enables us to acknowledge experiences by which we meet the absolute in such an unmistakable way that they can even be formulated, and these formulations have permanent validity. These results are rare, but their constancy transcends anything achieved by the objective method (where only ascertained facts are known as permanent), because they are both basic and lasting. In ethics, as we have seen, the Ten Commandments are still valid,† and this applies also to the moral commandments of the Sermon on the Mount; they have survived everything else which existed when they were formulated—states, nations, legal institutions and scientific theories—and they continue to survive everything in the ever-changing external reality, even today, despite all attempts to abandon them. This is a case not of being suspended over, but of being safely led towards the unfathomable depth.

These achievements, however, also underline the need for a proper understanding and development of the subjective method,

* *Philosophic Problems of Nuclear Science*, p. 93.
† See pp. 61–3.

for the lasting validity of the moral commandments, though beyond dispute, is rarely taken into account. This may be due to the fact that they cannot be taken for granted in the same way as external results; their significance can only be recognized if they are accepted and fully experienced. Any moral commandment becomes a dead letter unless it is understood, acknowledged and felt as binding.

To sum up: in contrast to the objective method, the subjective method touches upon absoluteness—in its dealing with single experiences and principles, both of which are compelling, and by its basic certainty. Because certainty is experienced as immediate, the sorting out of experienced certainties—the distinguishing between justified and false convictions—presents the subjective method with a difficult task, the more so as the absolute itself cannot be included; being made accessible by particular judgments and experiences which it immensely transcends, it cannot be methodically dealt with nor included in internal reality. Philosophy, even here, cannot go beyond the purely formal meaning of the word 'absolute' which we have discussed. But we shall see in the next chapter that the subjective method can help us to recognize justified convictions of certainty in two ways which supplement each other—by disclosing approaches to the absolute and by making us aware of its impact.

To those who expect philosophy to be unitary and all-inclusive the reservations which have had to be made—that we need two ways of thinking and yet must not include the absolute itself—may seem to reduce the importance of philosophy. Nevertheless, its task remains great and of the utmost importance. It is true that, unless we are guided by faith, we can do no more than make sure that both methods are used correctly; but to define, elaborate and separate them clearly would be no mean achievement. We constantly need both methods; the objective method for our dealing with practical life, the subjective method for the understanding of our own existence. Yet in constantly using both, we tend to mix them up, and this leads to a falsification of all our experience. I have emphasized how important it is that the scientific method should not be used where it does not apply; so far as the absolute is concerned, it is essential to keep the approaches to it open and to realize that the question of its existence or non-existence can only be decided by the subjective method. But this method—though neglected and therefore in greater need of being explored—should not be treated as if it could lead to a knowledge of external facts and its results be proved historically or in a material way; it is not concerned with material facts, but with existential understanding. This can even be seen in the survival of the Ten Commandments. In so far as they are an external fact, they survive as a part of history no different from any other part; but if this were all they would only be of historical interest. It is their validity which makes them part of internal reality, and this validity does not simply rest on factual evidence because, to be valid, they must be understood, which is only possible if we realize that they apply to every one of us. Then they will exist even for those who decline to act upon them, for such an understanding shows that they really are commandments and thus ought to be obeyed.

Apart from a further elaboration of the subjective method, in order to be able to apply the objective and subjective methods correctly, we must consider in greater detail the relationship between them and between external and internal reality. If we succeed in both these tasks, the subjective method will make us aware of experiences which are unmistakably due to a meeting with the absolute.

CHAPTER V

THE INCOMPATIBILITY OF OBJECTIVE AND SUBJECTIVE KNOWLEDGE

1

The emphasis put on the distinction between the objective and subjective methods may appear superfluous to some readers, for even though the belief in scientific or similar objective approaches is so predominant today that it usually excludes any other approach, a fairly substantial minority would probably admit that there are two different kinds of thinking—that, for instance, religion cannot be dealt with in the same way as technology. To them, therefore, much of what has been said may appear a matter of course. But this may, in itself, be another mistake. The distinction between the two methods is so much taken for granted that no further thought is given to what this realization implies. Despite the growing influence of Kierkegaard and the contribution of the Existentialists the subjective method is still used only in a vague way, and is thought of as something which occurs naturally and does not need to be developed, and this makes it appear inferior to the objective method.

It is commonly assumed that no art or skill is required in order to be subjective. To be sure, every human being is a bit of a subject, in a sense. But now to strive to become what one already is: who would waste his time on such a task, involving the greatest imaginable degree of resignation? . . . But for this very reason alone it is a very difficult task, the most difficult of all tasks in fact.*

This is the reason why we are still faced with the task of developing the subjective method more fully, which also means that a clear delimitation of the scope of the objective method is still

* Kierkegaard, *Concluding Scientific Postscript* (Princeton, 1944), p. 281.

required. Those who use the subjective method without being conscious of it will be at a loss when confronted, for instance, with some claims of sociology.

There will be differences between the sciences in this respect. At one end of the scale are physical theories such as the quantum theory which will have to be disregarded completely;* at the other end are psychological theories which try to deal with personal problems and thus require attention. But it has been seen in chapter II that even these theories are based on impersonal generalizations which cannot fully take into account individual experience of an individual person.

There is, moreover, one particular point which is rarely even noticed—that the two methods are not complementary. We cannot simply add together the results of each and come to a satisfactory unitary knowledge; the two methods are so different that they remain incompatible. We obviously cannot pursue the impersonal and the personal approach at the same time; we are concerned either with external reality or with inner experience. The scientist must disregard his inner participation once he enters the sphere of experiments, and he cannot rely on his scientific theories alone when he wants to understand his ethical problems. Nor can we reduce quality to quantity and yet simultaneously deal with quality; we need numbers when confronted with practical affairs and must get away from them when trying to evaluate moral scruples. The objective method transforms particular into typical cases, so that they may make generalizations possible; the subjective method refrains from generalizations and concentrates on the individual nature of single cases, in order to make it impossible to consider them as mere 'cases'. A comparison of the two methods shows clearly that they are not only different, but in direct opposition to each other.

This is confirmed by the fact that the application of both

---

* Even this is not always taken into account. But it is entirely wrong, for instance, to use the indeterminacy of the behaviour of particles (a purely negative, mechanical concept) to support the belief in human freedom (which is nothing if not a positive force enabling us to make decisions and to act).

methods can be continued indefinitely, without ever leading to their unification. There is no boundary to scientific exploration and technological advance, nor to the enrichment of inner experience; man is at best only on the way to his ultimate self-fulfilment. But even the greatest extension of external reality will not touch 'the unfathomable depth'; it may cover what a one-sided view regards as the whole of reality, but it will remain one-sided, restricted to the impersonal sphere. On the other hand, knowledge of internal reality will always remain dependent on particular experiences; these are inexhaustible, but they cannot be extended in a generalized abstract way; they may give us a profound insight, but they cannot replace scientific theories. Science can, for instance, deal with the entire universe and increase the knowledge of it immensely, but it will never be able to answer any of the questions concerned with that understanding which gives a sense of meaning in personal existential terms; in the last resort we cannot possibly know why there is a universe and why there are laws according to which it has developed. By contrast, we can, for instance, experience goodness very deeply, and in that way we may catch what we cannot but call a glimpse of the absolute; but we can never say (and it was always wrong, in philosophy, to say) that the universe is good or bad, because we are unable to experience the universe as a whole; it cannot be the content of a particular experience.* Both methods can be developed indefinitely in their own particular directions, but they are nevertheless limited to their own spheres which remain separate.

This incompatibility of the objective and subjective methods has important consequences. We have said that we are bound to use both of them, and it is precisely because of this need that we cannot comfortably rely on either without reservations; we are always confronted with discrepancies. Instead of acquiring a unitary knowledge, we are made aware of different aspects of reality

* I do not want to question the *belief* that the universe is good, as the Christian tends to think, or bad as some other creeds claim, but such statements must be seen as expressions of faith.

which contradict each other. We are not only forced—very sharply—to realize how strictly limited our knowledge is, for since we can never arrive at a sum-total, we must resign ourselves to partial knowledge; the conflict between the two methods necessarily produces a conflict within us, a constant inner tension. Does this argue against the distinction between the two methods —or is it another challenge which has to be met?

Before answering this question, it will be useful to consider a few important objections which could easily be raised against this kind of approach. This will clear the way for a concentration on the essential implications of the need for two methods.

One of these possible objections is that such a division of knowledge would lead to metaphysical dualism, and any ultimately dualistic interpretation of reality is highly disturbing; by splitting up the world into two different parts, it splits up our own selves and thus threatens us with the disintegration of our personality. In fact, the metaphysical systems based on dualism—the explanation of all that exists by two fundamental and usually hostile entities, such as light and darkness or some other embodiment of good and evil—have never proved satisfactory, neither in such older religions as Zoroastrianism, nor in sects like the Manichees, nor in philosophy. The complete separation of mind and body, which goes back to Descartes, is under heavy attack at present, and those who want to prove Kant wrong accuse him—incorrectly, as I shall show—of introducing dualism. The reasons why dualism should be excluded can easily be seen. So long as man is faced with two basic entities, he feels forced to continue seeking that reality from which they spring, and if this search is made impossible, his mind is lacerated because he forces himself to act against its essential requirements.

If the word 'dualism' is interpreted in this purely metaphysical sense the objection can easily be met. We do not aim at any all-inclusive explanation of reality which disregards the limitations of knowledge; on the contrary, it has been emphasized that 'external reality' and 'internal reality' are used as strictly epistemological terms. They refer to those aspects of reality which can be isolated and grasped by a particular way of thinking. This epistemological approach implies, as we have seen, that it is impossible ever to create a metaphysical system. Obviously this approach makes metaphysical dualism impossible, too, because we thus remain unable to explain the fundamental nature of reality, and this is what dualism sets out to do. It could even be argued that this approach is the strongest safeguard against dualism.

But this does not yet take into account all the objections to Kant, nor the possible objection to our approach, because the word 'dualism' is also used, even if incorrectly, in a wider sense than its strictly philosophical meaning, to refer to any duality, whatever its kind. If this more general sense of dualism is meant, the criticism could still be valid, because the two ways of thinking, although they exclude metaphysics, do actually force us, for all practical purposes, to face two different worlds, and thus they could create a dangerous split within ourselves. If we must constantly accept contradictions—if, for instance, science and ethics must be pursued in ways which never meet—the integrity of the mind might well be permanently threatened. Yet there is still another line of thought which has to be taken into consideration.

A short excursion into history suggests that the dichotomy we are concerned with is not artificial or accidental, but has deep roots. It may be that other ages or civilizations—the Greeks, for instance—were able to achieve a complete integration of all the different aspects of existence. In our European civilization, however, a conflict between two different approaches soon made itself felt, perhaps owing to its two distinct—and hardly reconcilable—sources, the Greco–Roman and the Christian. By the early Middle Ages, the claims of Christianity and those of reason were already in conflict. At first, it was fairly easy to assuage the mind. In the eleventh century, for instance, Anselm of Canterbury developed the ontological proof of the existence of God which says that everything we can think of must also exist; therefore, since we can and do think of a final perfection, thought does not contradict the belief in God. But two hundred years later the difficulties had grown to such an extent that Thomas Aquinas, after the elaboration of further proofs of the existence of God, suddenly gave up writing because he could not make theology do justice to his direct vision of God. The conflict came into the open at the beginning of the seventeenth century, with Galileo and the well-known conflict between the church and science. Pascal, writing at the same time, had to support belief in God by proposing a wager, a bet that God exists, which he felt able to win—a rather doubtful way of defending faith and one which shows that reason and Christianity could hardly be reconciled any longer. The Age of Reason seemed to herald a complete victory for reason, but it only intensified the conflict by provoking the reaction of Romanticism with its love for the irrational; Kierkegaard, writing when Romanticism had triumphed, put great emphasis on the absolute paradox; reason could be used in its own sphere, but had to be completely dropped in the other. 'Faith begins precisely where thinking leaves off.'* The split in man's mind due to the two ways of thinking has a long history.

These few indications are not meant to prove that the split is inevitable; there is no proof to be found in history, for historical developments can be superseded by surprising changes. Yet they should help us to see our situation in perspective and to recognize that we are not dealing with a strange aberration, due to some accidental development, nor with an artificial predicament invented by philosophers. Our argument must be based on our present knowledge of thinking, but history encourages our belief that we are concentrating on a fundamental problem.

At present, whether we like to admit it or not, we are bound to use both the objective and the subjective method. Unitary thinking may have been possible before the rise of our civilization and it may still be possible outside it, but it is impossible for us. We have to accept that this has happened and that it obviously could not have been avoided. We can neither reject nor escape the confrontation with the two contradictory aspects of existence—

* *Fear and Trembling* (Princeton, 1941), p. 78.

with external and internal reality. Certainly, an experience of the complete unity of existence can be evoked by a work of art and can occur in mystical experiences. But in the realm of thought which alone concerns us here we cannot transcend contradictions. We shall therefore start from them because, if we are bound to think in this way, an open acknowledgement of the fact should enable us to make the best possible use of our thinking.

We can actually recognize why it was no accident that all the solutions proposed for the conflict between the two ways of thinking failed and why they must still fail, for it is impossible to regard the existence of these contradictions simply as a problem which can and should be solved. All such solutions are merely apparent, because they can only be achieved in one of the following ways. In one, we try to reduce the fundamental opposition of the two realities to mere differences within the same aspect of reality, so that they can be dealt with by the same way of thinking. Either the mind is seen as a product of evolution, as by the Darwinists, or matter is seen as a projection of the mind, or spirit, as by the Hegelians. In another way, we try to reconcile what is irreconcilable. We have seen an example of this attempt in the claim that science and art are of the same kind because both make use of intuitions, and in the using of the indeterminacy of the behaviour of particles as a support of the belief in freedom. But what happens frequently is that we disregard the existing contradictions altogether, by relying on scientific thinking or on inner experience alone and denying that any other knowledge could be significant. Those who rely on science tend to admit feelings, including moral convictions, only as private and unimportant. Existentialism, on the other hand, tries to make one forget that science exists. None of these solutions can remain satisfactory for long, because all of them narrow down the scope of thought and dismiss facts and experiences which will make themselves felt sooner or later.

For all these reasons the contradictions themselves are made the basis of this investigation, in the hope that, by applying the two methods correctly, it will be possible to take into account all the different aspects of man's existence which is, after all, full of contradictions. Thus, the resulting two realities should not create a dualistic split within man, threatening his integrity, but open the way towards a more satisfactory, because more fundamental, reconciliation between thought and existence. In other words: we shall accept the inner conflict due to the two approaches as a challenge and hope to show that it can be met.

Thus, however, another criticism could still be made: if no metaphysical statement is intended, it may seem wrong to use the word 'reality' at all. Yet this further objection only helps to clarify our approach.

The concept 'reality' is one of those which cannot be further defined. Any definition must use concepts which are simpler, more basic and of a more general nature than the concept which is to be defined; but once we are confronted with those concepts which form the very basis of our thinking, we are at the end of definition. As has been seen, a table can be defined because abstraction (which leads to more basic concepts) can be applied. A specific table is defined by its colour, shape, size, weight and its material; the abstract concept 'table' by the nature of its material and its spatial position—a table is a solid horizontal plane held up at some distance from the ground. Even such extreme abstractions of physics as particles can be defined by further abstractions—by mathematical formulae. Reality, however, is a general term which includes everything which exists, so that we are unable to define it with the help of details, and it is so basic that we cannot use more basic terms. Instead we are driven to circular arguments, such as 'reality is all that exists'; but 'reality' and 'existence' are tautological and do not define each other. Not all circular arguments are to be despised (as they usually are), for some of them indicate that we have reached the basic assumptions of our thought and cannot proceed further, and, even if tautological, they can clarify our thought. Thus the meaning of the concept 'reality' is not completely identical with that of 'existence'; I use the former when referring to the impersonal universe, and the latter when man is involved; to use both, therefore, increases awareness. But circular arguments are not definitions.*

Concepts which cannot be given a precise definition, however, can be made clearer by a description of what they represent. Thus, when concerned with reality, we can attempt to show different aspects of it and to elucidate in what forms it may appear to us. This is done by distinguishing between an external and an internal reality. It has been mentioned before that this choice of terms is not entirely satisfactory, even though we have always referred when using them to the objective and subjective method so as to emphasize the underlying act of thinking which makes our terms purely epistemological. We actually mean aspects of reality, but to repeat this each time would be too clumsy. Yet this terminology may also have an advantage; it makes us strongly aware of a distinction which needs to be brought into the open.

Nevertheless, there is still the disadvantage that we seem to be speaking of two realities while the word 'reality' suggests that there is only one, and this I do not wish to deny. In fact, however, the distinction itself takes for granted—and thus prevents us from forgetting—that reality is one, because neither external nor internal reality are separate parts or sectors of reality; each can include the whole of it. The stars, for instance, can be seen as purely external, in terms of physics and astronomy, but they can also give us an impression of beauty or make us aware of the majesty of the universe and of man's insignificance compared with it, or even of the significance of the moral order which alone can help us to face the vastness of the universe.† Thought of in the latter way, even the stars are made, to some extent, a part of internal reality. Conversely, the psychologist, though he deals

---

* Cf., for example, the following attempt which is helpful and yet not a proper definition, because it does not say what reality is: 'We shall use "reality" as meaning that which is needed over and above other propositions in order to make true categorical propositions true, and in this sense it will be synonymous with our use of "existence" or "being".' D. M. Emmett, *The Nature of Metaphysical Thinking* (London, 1945), p. 16.

† Kant's description of this contrast will be discussed in chapter VIII.

with the innermost activities of man's mind which would appear a part only of internal reality, subsumes these in external reality, for he thinks, as we have seen, in terms of processes and generalizations and tries to apply the methods of natural science. He thus succeeds, within limits, in making the mind part of external reality.

It should not be thought surprising that everything can be approached in different ways. Science, religion, the arts do not deal with different worlds or different parts of the world, but with the same world in different ways. This is equally true of the many branches of natural science. Physics is one way of interpreting the whole world and it includes man so far as he is a physical body. Biology is another interpretation of practically the whole world, and includes physical facts, such as size, weight and motion, but from a biological point of view. Psychology, too, can be extended to include almost everything, but this time only so far as these things make an impression on man's mind. The two fundamental aspects of reality can be similarly regarded; not however as different branches of knowledge, but as two different approaches which determine all our thought.

If each method, however, can include the same parts of reality, we are obviously confronted with parts of the same reality. Reality as such is not divided into two, but must be one. This is confirmed, even more clearly, by the fact which we have just mentioned—that both methods can be infinitely pursued because they do not deal with limited sectors of reality. To take into account this oneness and to avoid misunderstandings, I shall also use a third term—'primary reality'. This is to show that there is a fundamental unitary reality which the other concepts presuppose. This primary reality underlies all our thinking about reality, and there we could perhaps find the absolute; but, like the absolute, it is beyond our grasp—beyond the grasp of a conscious effort of thinking. It can only be presupposed and not known. Yet all we have said seems to justify this presupposition.*

* Here it can be seen why we have avoided such words as "spirit" or "soul" as names for internal reality; as external and internal reality represent aspects of the

Thus the advantages of our use of the concept 'reality' are preponderant. It emphasizes an important difference but, since it implies that there is a primary reality which we are unable to know, it also confirms that we cannot be accused either of being led towards a metaphysical dualism or of favouring it; both methods indicate that fundamental reality is one. Our terms indicate two ways of thinking, but not two entities or powers which explain existence. In this we follow Kant, and our exposition, though formulated in a different way, also shows why it is mistaken to believe that he opened the way to dualism. By his distinction between two kinds of reason he intended to prove that metaphysical systems—'for all time' as he thought—are impossible, and he did not make any exception, even for himself.

Another possible objection, of a different kind, must also be mentioned—that this denial of a unitary approach defies reason, that it is purely irrational, and that it cannot therefore be controlled at all. It is true that this reproach is often justified in the case of Existentialism; we have mentioned that, at a certain point, reason is even dismissed by Kierkegaard.* Yet this criticism can be refuted, too. It is relevant in this context that Kant speaks of two kinds of reason because—even though there are differences and contradictions which make it necessary to differentiate—reason plays its proper part in both approaches. In fact, it is precisely with regard to the relationship between reason and the irrational that the two methods are not entirely different, for no possible approach can be completely rational. In external reality, which is usually accepted as the proper domain of reason, one must first accept that which exists; only afterwards can reason begin its work. In the Middle Ages, when metaphysical questions predominated, men wanted to know the first cause and the first motion, and only answers to these questions could have led to complete rationalism—that is, to a full explanation by reason of all

whole of reality and point to primary reality, our distinction is different from that between matter and spirit or body and soul which are different parts of primary reality and yet often seen as having no common ground.
* Kierkegaard's special position will be discussed in chapter XII.

that exists. But the great advance of science began when these questions were dropped and the existing 'brute facts' simply accepted as such—when Francis Bacon proclaimed: 'In physics they [the final causes] are impertinent . . . and hinder the sciences from holding their course of improvement,' * and when Galileo demanded that the search for an all-inclusive explanation, especially for a 'Prime Mover', should cease and scientific investigation be restricted to the observation of existing motion. This acceptance of facts, however, means acceptance of a basic knowledge which cannot be further explained by reason and thus remains beyond it—that is, irrational. Similarly, in internal reality, one first has to know the facts disclosed by experience, without being able to explain them; yet once this has been done, the subjective method can and does summon reason to deal with the given facts; otherwise it could not be a method. But it may well be that the achievements in this sphere are not fully appreciated because here we still expect that every element in an explanation can and ought to be completely rational and forget that even here we must start from what is given.

Of course, as the two methods are so different, there are important differences in the working of reason in each field. Knowledge of external reality can easily appear to result from the work of reason; the knower, as we have said, can be neglected. We can describe and test objects and events with the help of material manipulations and base the resulting proofs on logical thinking; moreover, as the objective method actually aims at abstractions, generalizations and theories, there seems to be, once the facts are accepted, nothing but the work of reason. Knowledge of internal reality is derived from the particulars of experience, abstractions are only of minor importance, and even principles, as we have seen, are much more limited generalizations than external laws; thus it can seem that reason is hardly employed. But value-judgments obviously require reason and logic, though a logic of a special kind, and the need to sort out potentialities and inner certainties also means that they must be judged according to

* *The Dignity and Advancement of Learning*, bk III, ch. 4.

criteria provided by reason. Ethics cannot be proved, but it has to be demonstrated in such a way that it appeals to what man can recognize as his inner need; therefore, ethics must be made understandable and be understood. It cannot be irrational. To be valid and intelligible, it must be accessible to reason and formulated with its help. It is true that reason does not dominate as obviously as it does in abstraction; experience must be consulted at every step; but this in itself means a continuous exercise of reason. We cannot characterize the two methods by saying that the objective method is rational and the subjective—if method at all—irrational, but we can equate them with two different kinds of reason.

In fact, the subjective method is needed to enlarge the sphere of reason and to enable us to make full use of it; if this method is rejected or disregarded, a vast sphere of human experience is left in the sphere of the irrational—to be dominated by prejudice, emotional reactions, blinding passions. Unless we succeed in making the irrational to some extent accessible to the work of reason, it will run riot; the attempt to suppress it will never succeed. It is true that it is more difficult to recognize and specify the task of reason within the subjective method, but this is only another way of saying what we have said before—that it is in need of elaboration.

2

The need for the two methods arises from the fact that we are unable to transcend the opposition between subject and object; all our thought remains determined by it. To be able to grasp the world which surrounds us we must oppose ourselves to it. If we were completely submerged in reality, we could not acquire any conscious knowledge of it. This, however, is bound to lead to the dichotomy already described. If we want to think, we must transform ourselves into a centre of a different kind, a centre from which activities—thinking, feeling, willing,—can be directed towards something outside them which they can grasp, and this centre itself, just because it is different, must then be grasped in a different way. Of course, man remains part of reality, but we cannot consider him as simply one among like parts, for everyone must develop these activities of his own and use them to get at the reality outside himself. The resulting awareness may be dim or clear, it may be achieved voluntarily or under some compulsion, but the fundamental situation will remain the same. It could be expressed by saying: '*Here* am I, and *there* is everything else.'* This is an individual experience, but it is one shared by every man and is therefore a general characteristic of all thought.

Whenever we think, we, as subject, confront everything else and thus make it an object. Since, however, we remain parts of reality, we want to grasp not isolated objects nor ourselves in isolation but in both cases the whole of reality; our individual experience is therefore extended to endeavour to understand all reality either from without or from within, and this gives rise to the two methods which confront us with an external and an internal reality. This happens simultaneously with any development of consciousness and is so much a matter of course that the process itself need not become conscious; what is described here as an activity begins as an automatic reaction, and it is for this reason that the process so often escapes attention. But as it is the basis of all thought, it is essential that it should be made conscious. Otherwise we shall not understand our own thinking.

The opposition between subject and object has the effect that the object is known by the subject and that the subject becomes aware of itself by confronting objects. Therefore the two realities must not only be clearly separated (as emphasized hitherto), but must also both be taken into account. To become understandable and complete, each method must within itself establish the opposition between subject and object. To be able to do so, each method uses certain elements taken from the other, so that external reality can include the subject and internal reality the object. This inclusion of the other reality, however, takes place in each case in an entirely different way and thus explains why the two methods are incompatible—as the following examples will show.

* As formulated by R. Guardini.

External reality presupposes the knower: his contribution consists of those laws of thinking which enable him to develop the knowledge of objects. This knowledge is mainly based on abstraction, but abstraction is not entirely based on the object; it requires laws of thinking which belong to the realm of the subject.

Some of these laws have been stated by Kant, who has shown that the two forms of apprehension—space and time—and several categories, such as cause and effect, are not derived from the impression reality makes upon man, but are, on the contrary, provided by the mind, and that only when they are applied are knowledge and experience possible. If we think of a particular object, say our example the table, we can form by abstraction such concepts as 'table', 'wood', 'material', 'matter', 'particle'; but we cannot form the concept 'space'. This concept is present at all stages of abstraction; the concrete table as well as all concepts derived from it presuppose space; only because they are placed in space can they be thought of at all. If we leave out all particular characteristics so that only empty space remains, we have moved away from objects altogether and are dealing with something entirely different which is obviously not derived from the object.* When we think of an event, say of the falling of a stone, we can arrive at further abstract concepts such as 'motion', 'force', 'energy', but abstraction itself will not lead to the concept 'time' which is again presupposed at all stages and is as such entirely different. Cause and effect, too, are contributed by the mind; we only see sequences, but we try to discover causality because our mind is bent upon discovering those interconnections which help us to grasp the event better; it is because they exist in the mind that we expect to find them. It is true that all the concepts mentioned are abstract—cause and effect as well as matter and force—but the latter are arrived at by abstraction from the object, while the former are contributed by the subject.

* It is no accident that to admit the existence of empty space caused difficulties in physics, for with the complete disappearance of objects external reality vanishes, too. The gap can only be closed if one contribution of the mind, space, is replaced by another one—mathematics.

Objective and subjective knowledge

We shall return in chapter VII to the laws made clear by Kant. But it can be seen immediately that they work because they are taken from internal reality, for we understand their meaning with the help of analogies with inner experiences. For instance, in external reality—where we observe only sequences—we cannot recognize what cause and effect actually mean, but this we know from experience; when I want to do something and then do it— for instance lift a burden—I know how an effect is caused; and I know it, too, when something outside myself prevents me from acting according to my intentions. Thus I base my knowledge of external reality on an analogy with what I know subjectively. Space, by my being a body and moving about, and time, by my living through the hours of a day and the months of a year and by growing older, are similarly very concrete experiences, and as all that happens to me takes place in space and time, it becomes natural to use them as a framework for all that I perceive and know outside myself. But the abstract concepts have been made intelligible through my inner experience. Even those abstract concepts which are derived from external reality, such as that of force, are based on such analogies, because it is from my experience of exercising force—of being strong enough to lift the burden or too weak to do it—that I know what the concept means and can use it in external reality as a purely abstract concept without loss of meaning. In fact, we do not really know what external forces are, even if we give names to them and call them gravitation or electricity, and this shows the importance of our ability to use analogies from inner experience.

It is due to these analogies that abstraction seems to lead to a full understanding without actually doing so. This full understanding which discloses existential meaning* is accessible to the inner experience from which the analogy is drawn. But it is not transmitted by the analogy because, to make these concepts serviceable tools for the grasping of external reality, they must be completely separated from any personal experience. Thus our own force is personal, but it would be wrong to personify external forces, and

* For an explanation of this kind of understanding see pp. 72–3.

we must not try to understand external objects or events by ascribing to them intentions or experiences. Space and time are deprived of any reference to what they mean to us; instead they are made accessible to abstract and entirely external measurements. It was only when the anthropomorphic interpretation of such concepts ceased that the advance of natural science became possible. Therefore the understanding of external reality is never full understanding; it stops short at the point at which abstraction touches upon the concepts contributed by the mind.

These are only a few examples (more could easily be added*), but they will be sufficient to make clear why the subjective contributions, though derived from internal reality, do not reveal it. To make them useful for the objective method, they must be transformed into abstract concepts, and abstraction is not an essential aid in the subjective method. In the sphere of principles it can offer useful guidance; but those experiences from which the analogies are drawn could only disclose the meaning of inner experience if they were treated in exactly the opposite way. Since internal reality cannot be understood with the help of generalizations, but only by concrete single experiences, the emphasis would have to be on their particularity. Inner experience will be revealed to me not by the concept of force, but by actually using force on a special occasion, not by the concept of time, but by actually living through a certain span of time.

For this very reason, however, internal knowledge, to become knowledge, needs external reality; experience, to become concrete, must be embodied in, or connected with, something external to us. This has been mentioned before; the concept 'love', for instance, is not much help; it must be embodied in an actual, if possible a unique deed of love, or in a loving person, or in love for a person. The inner experience of love will remain vague unless I love something or somebody; even in the case of self-love I have to make my own person an object towards which this

---

* For a fuller elaboration of these and the following remarks see P. Roubiczek, *Thinking in Opposites*, pp. 91 ff. and 124 ff., or the extended German version *Denken in Gegensätzen* (Frankfurt am Main, 1961), ch. 3.

feeling can be directed. We experience beauty when we see a human face, a natural scene, or are moved by a work of art; we experience justice when an act of justice or injustice is done. All inner experiences are grounded in, or accompanied by, feelings; but feelings, to be more than a mere vague stirring of emotion or an indulgence in some kind of mood and to be known or to lead to knowledge, must be related to an object. Whether I am interested or disgusted, excited or in despair, the object—something or somebody—is needed to make my feelings clear. The mere statement 'I love' or 'I hate' may describe a psychological state, but it remains well-nigh meaningless so far as the understanding of internal reality is concerned. Every inner experience, to become distinct and meaningful, needs embodiment and thus external reality.

Again, however, this inclusion of external elements in internal reality cannot serve the other, the objective method. All the aids which could help us to grasp reality as external—abstraction, generalizations, theories—must be excluded and manipulations strictly avoided, so that the single objects or events can make their proper impact and be grasped as such. We have to concentrate our attention on a particular object, say an individual table, and to see it as ours, as practical, as aesthetically satisfying, or as the result of human work or action, to make it real for us. It is true that objects must be correctly apprehended, for their falsification would falsify our experience, but a full knowledge of an individual object is developed, not by pursuing abstraction, but by resisting it. If abstract concepts intrude, objects are not realized but dissolved. Only by being apprehended in a concrete way can objects or events serve to clarify that existential understanding which is neither available in nor part of external reality, and through being grasped in this way they can no longer serve the objective method. While in external reality the knower must be subordinated completely to that which he perceives, in order to make it purely objective, in the subjective method a relationship to the person must be imposed on reality, so that external objects and events can become the embodiment of what he wants to express. The aim is not impersonal, but personal knowledge.

Therefore, the contributions which each reality makes to the knowledge of the other do not procure knowledge of that reality from which they originate. The knower contributes abstract laws from which all traces of inner experience have been eliminated; the external embodiment contributes a vessel which is cut out of external reality and isolated in a way which prevents the working of the objective method. It is true that any impression or experience is originally unitary, whether it be looking at the stars or feeling pain. Even such a complex procedure as reading this book will be remembered as a single and unitary event. But this unity cannot be known as such; one of the two methods must be applied in order to achieve knowledge—the star is either an object involved in material processes such as motion or an object of beauty and majesty; the feeling of pain is either the comprehensible result of physiological and psychological causes or an inner experience, and reading a book will either be something to be discussed in terms of eyesight and print or a concern for the understanding of the book's content. In meetings with other people, too, although this is different from all other subject–object relationships, one can make the other person either a kind of object, by concentrating on his external features, his social position and practical activities, or one can experience an intuitive knowledge of oneself and the other person, the I–Thou relationship.* Naturally, knowledge of external reality will be based, first of all, on that of objects, and knowledge of internal reality on that of inner experiences, but as everything can be included in each reality, the two methods can also start from the same unitary impression, from the stars or the pain. But the unity cannot be preserved; we are faced instead with irreconcilable contradictions.

It is this characteristic of the process of thinking—that we actually start from unity, that it seems within our grasp and yet must be abandoned immediately—which makes the impossibility of ever knowing the unity itself particularly agonizing. The incompatibility of the two methods really produces a deep inner division. Man finds himself caught between two realities which he

* This relationship will be explained on p. 125.

cannot fully understand; external reality he knows only from outside; in internal reality single instances of understanding may occur, but these cannot be extended to cover the whole even of this reality. There is the insoluble problem of existence; why is there a universe, why man?—and the insoluble problem of understanding: if knowledge exists, why is it so limited? Thus man is also unable to understand the two main constituents of himself: body and mind. He is born, must grow and die; much of the working of his body is outside his influence; and yet his mind exists with all its wonders. Some limited explanations can be found; the process of birth, the causes of death, the development of body and mind can be traced. But no such explanation makes us understand why the facts are as they are—why men are such creatures that they must be born into this universe and cannot escape death. Neither a concept of the evolution of the mind nor the recent impressive discoveries about the brain are really adequate explanations once we realize how we experience the mind, with all its faculties and achievements, from within, once we confront these theories with what thinking, feeling and willing actually mean for us, with the creations of natural science and of the arts, with justice, goodness and the great religions, and also with man's abysmal failures and crimes. There are innumerable facts and experiences which we do not understand. We seem suspended over an abyss of the unknown and the conflict between the two realities within us seems to be more real than the realities themselves, but even the conflict does not help us to know ourselves completely. It is understandable that the Existentialists should claim that man faces nothingness, outside and inside himself.

Nevertheless there is the absolute certainty that we exist, and we have said that it is a challenge which can be met—that it is possible to achieve a fuller understanding and to do justice to the absolute in the sphere of understanding as well. But it may be said that the conclusions which we have reached so far mutually exclude each other. We began with the assertion that the absolute, if it is to be known at all, cannot be known by any attempt to establish external relationships and interconnections, that some totally different method must be used. Then we showed that the subjective method touches upon absoluteness and that, in internal reality, we are not suspended above, but safely led towards, the 'unfathomable depth'—that we can find approaches to the absolute, even though the absolute itself remains outside our grasp. Yet now the conflict between the two methods has thrown us back again into great uncertainty; if there is no fundamental knowledge, how can we hope to find approaches to the absolute? Instead we seem to hover precariously in the void.

In fact, this is not so. The very precariousness of man's existence shows how the previous expectations can be fulfilled; the confrontation with the two realities makes clear what is meant by the opening of approaches to the absolute. Since the need for two methods makes any final knowledge impossible, the absolute itself still remains outside what we can achieve by thinking. Yet just because we need two contradictory methods, we can recognize that we also possess a different kind of knowledge which is not produced by the conscious effort of thinking, but is given to us by the impact of the absolute. The conflict between the two methods, by making us vulnerable, by revealing a gap, exposes us to impacts of the absolute and throws into relief that there is a third kind of knowledge. We are forced to face an apparent void, but if we remain aware of the two realities we are not engulfed; we may transcend it. Those Existentialists who, like Sartre, embrace nothingness, rely on a unitary way of thinking, but Pascal showed the distinction we are trying to establish when he said:

The infinite distance between body and mind is a symbol of the infinitely more infinite distance between mind and charity; for charity is supernatural. All the glory of greatness has no lustre for people who are in search of understanding. The greatness of clever men is invisible to kings, to the rich, to chiefs, and to all the worldly great.

The greatness of wisdom, which is nothing if not of God, is invisible to the carnal-minded and to the clever. These are three orders differing in kind.*

The existence of this different kind of knowledge can be recognized when we remember the results which each method

* *Pensées*, no. 792 (Everyman edition).

can achieve. The objective method provides us, with regard to ascertained facts, with a certainty which could be called absolute, and yet this method does not touch the absolute itself because it does not provide us with a full understanding of these phenomena; the deeper it penetrates beneath the surface, the more uncertain its results become. The subjective method gives us a full understanding of internal reality and opens approaches to the absolute in many ways, for it enables us to give a sense of meaning to our personal experience, to make value-judgments, to take into account morality and its principles, and to make actual within us all those potentialities which, like conscience, confirm these principles. We also experience the feeling of certainty, and this time it refers to the foundations of internal reality. Nevertheless the subjective method only touches upon the absolute. We remain constantly haunted by the question of whether our convictions are really justified or whether they are influenced by misleading inner experiences, such as personal prejudices and passions; and we also remain aware of the fact that the subjective method leads only to partial understanding, for it does not include external reality. But we have found formulations of inner experiences which have permanent validity—such as the moral commandments—and we could not arrive at them nor assert their absoluteness on the basis of inner experience alone; they are based on the third kind of knowledge just mentioned—a knowledge which is self-evident and at the same time so significant that the problems which beset the two methods are transcended. It is because of this knowledge that we can recognize when the subjective method really touches upon the absolute. Three examples will help to make this clear.

(1) When we consider Plato's assertion (to which I have referred before)* that it is better to suffer wrong than to do wrong, it is at once clear that it cannot be supported by the objective method; from the social or psychological point of view, fighting wrong, if necessary even by another, perhaps lesser wrong, can be defended much more convincingly. The subjective method will help us, in terms of personal experience, to appreciate what Plato means; the

* See pp. 9–10.

demand which this statement implies will immediately appeal to us; but we shall still not be able to subscribe to its claim of absolute certainty; we may, at the same time, feel compelled to resist evil and to do something against it. Even if we take the other translation of this passage and substitute 'injustice' for 'wrong' conscience alone will hardly be able to come to an unambiguous decision. Have we not the duty to abolish injustice, and can that be done if we simply suffer? Yet we are struck by Plato's demand in such a way that we cannot but accept it as absolutely true; we know for certain that we are confronting truth. Plato could not have arrived at this statement by a conscious effort of thinking; he must have been struck by it too; nor can we tamper with it. As with all experiences, we can disregard or circumvent it, but it cannot, in itself, be experienced as other than absolutely certain. It is impossible to make it relative by limiting its application to particular circumstances or by accepting its validity only under particular conditions. We experience an impact of the absolute.

(2) In the commandment 'Thou shalt love thy neighbour as thyself' Kierkegaard sees the breaking into man's existence of the transcendental. Love, if it is to be genuine, must be spontaneous; everyone knows how dubious the result may be if we force ourselves to try to love a person whom we dislike. Yet the commandment is not an appeal to our inclinations; it is concerned with a duty. It commands an emotion which should be spontaneous. Therefore, only a love greater than ours, a love which kindles love within us, can give sense to this commandment: 'In earthly love and friendship partiality is the middle term. In love to the neighbour God is the middle term; if you love God above all else, then you can also love your neighbour and in your neighbour every man.'* This, however, can also be understood in terms of human experience. If we meet a person as a person without inner reservations we know—whether we accept it or not—that our behaviour should be dictated by love, and this knowledge cannot be equated with a spontaneous feeling awakened by the other person. For in

* *Works of Love* (Princeton, 1946), p. 48. For a fuller elaboration see P. Roubiczek, *Existentialism—For and Against*, pp. 67–8.

such a meeting it is possible to love any neighbour; the boundaries of race, creed, social position are transcended. This love may even arise at the very moment when some conflict is brought into the open, when, for instance, the hidden influence of social distinctions is made conscious and could awaken contempt. We experience an impact of the transcendental aspect of humanity and are forced to acknowledge it in every man. We shall understand that *agape* is possible: 'the love and concern which go out to a human person for no other reason than that he is a human person, than that he is "there", not because he is such and such, not because he has agreeable and attractive qualities of one sort or another or is likely to bestow benefits in return.'*

(3) The experience of a meeting with another person probably shows the impact of the absolute most directly—that is, when we meet a person in the way which Buber calls an 'I–Thou' meeting, when lack of understanding really hurts and full understanding is one of the greatest satisfactions man can experience. In any such meeting we know more than internal reality, for we are confronted with our innermost nature from outside, when 'the Thou confronts me', and it is by this confrontation that our most fundamental inner certainty is given to us. Moreover, this revelation is based on grace, and again the meaning of this religious concept can be understood in human terms. We have to be willing to respond to such an experience, to accept it, to live through it; otherwise it will pass unnoticed; we need personal participation. But the will to participate is not in itself sufficient to make the meeting possible. We have to strive, yet none of our endeavours can guarantee the attainment of what we seek; we have to knock at the door, but it has to be opened for us; our striving is necessary, but the successful meaning is not simply its consequence. 'The Thou meets me through grace.'† The absolute has made itself felt.

The subjective method enables us to understand what these experiences mean, but the experiences are not the results of our

* H. H. Farmer, *The Word of Reconciliation* (Digswell Place, 1966), p. 25.
† M. Buber, *I and Thou* (Edinburgh, 1937), pp. 76 and 11. See also P. Roubiczek, *Existentialism—For and Against*, pp. 144–5.

methodical efforts. These insights have an added certainty, a more fundamental one than could be achieved by the subjective method alone—a certainty given to us by the absolute, once we have opened the approaches to it. The results, after they have been experienced, are included in internal reality, and it is true that they may appear so self-evident that they are too easily taken for granted or they may even become matters of convention. But whenever they are fully experienced anew and come to life again, all other problems, solved or unsolved, are outshone by them.

The significance of any such experience can be seen most clearly when we try to dismiss it. If, for instance, we had to reject the statement that it is better to suffer wrong than to do wrong, if we had to admit that love of one's neighbour is a misleading illusion, such a rejection would not mean—as would the abandoning of a scientific theory or of a particular value-judgment—simply the change of a detail within the framework of our convictions; we would have to change our convictions altogether and build anew from different foundations. In external reality, we must be prepared, if necessary, to change or dismiss theories; in internal reality any value-judgment about goodness or beauty may prove false; the knowledge imparted by an impact of the absolute is characterized by a certainty which, though still assailed by doubts, survives confirmed and deepened by them. The mere thought that it could be disproved only throws into relief how much this knowledge, once gained, becomes part of our very being.

This knowledge, therefore, would be distorted if it were simply identified with internal knowledge. It is different in kind; it takes possession of us. We shall call it 'essential knowledge'.

The knowledge is achieved in an existential way, by experience. But I have chosen the name 'essential' partly because some internal knowledge is also existential, and partly because I want to emphasize that essence is to be included as well. Only thus can a proper balance be achieved; extreme Existentialists like Sartre who admit nothing but existence are bound to come to destructive results.*

* For a fuller treatment see P. Roubiczek, *Existentialism—For and Against,* pp. 11, 109–11, 124–5.

By itself this knowledge does not yet solve the problem which we have mentioned—that of distinguishing between justified and false convictions of certainty. Further criteria will have to be introduced to show how this knowledge differs from wrong obsessions; this will be attempted in the next chapter. Yet a fuller description of this essential knowledge will be needed to find these criteria; in the following, therefore, the problem of misleading certainties will be provisionally disregarded.

To appreciate essential knowledge correctly, one has to remain aware of the two methods and their conflicting results, of external and internal reality. This is necessary, not only in order to recognize its nature, but also in order to avoid making wrong claims for it. The knowledge given by an impact of the absolute is bound to be more certain and fundamental than any other, but it is essential and not all-inclusive, which means that it is not without boundaries of its own. It does not abolish the limitations of knowledge; its scope is limited too, and it is this very limitation which shows some of its most important characteristics—mainly in two ways.

On the one hand, essential knowledge neither supersedes nor reconciles the other two kinds; there are still the two realities and with them the two methods and the contradictions to which they lead. We cannot dispense with the objective method, for we must still master practical life; we cannot dispense with the subjective method, because we continue to need value-judgments and must solve personal problems; as always, we often have to make decisions without knowing all the relevant factors and thus to take risks. External reality incessantly reminds us that internal reality is not self-sufficient, and feelings, passions, personal involvement make it impossible to rely on the objective method alone. Nor are the fundamental problems which we have mentioned solved: we still do not know why there is the universe and man, nor why we are born to die, nor why we are endowed with an apparently all-powerful mind and can only achieve limited knowledge. If anything, the contradictions become more bewildering: how can the impact of the absolute be reconciled with the existence of crime and evil, with the atrocious aspects of mankind's history? All this could be more easily accepted if man were completely cut off from the absolute. Essential knowledge may help us to face problems, but it does not serve to solve them; it is an additional knowledge.

On the other hand, any impact of the absolute reveals only one particular facet of it; we do not grasp the whole absolute nor the absolute as such, but have a limited experience which conveys a sense of absoluteness. Essential knowledge does not cover primary reality nor does it make it accessible in the same way as the two methods establish external and internal reality. We do not achieve an all-inclusive, unitary knowledge; primary reality as such cannot be grasped.

Nevertheless, the conflict between the two methods has borne fruit: we are made certain that there is unity and can discern what it implies. The experiences which convey essential knowledge are limited; each gives us only a particular insight, as the examples mentioned have shown; but each of them discloses a facet of the same primary reality; we have just said that all our convictions would have to be changed if one such experience were to be dismissed as invalid. Complete knowledge of the underlying unity remains beyond reach and even the knowledge we have is not unified, but we gain the conviction that primary reality exists, recognize some of its essential features, and thus unity makes itself felt. In each single experience of this kind, therefore, we also experience the oneness of the absolute. The knowledge is essential in the sense that in it we grasp the nature and meaning of oneness.

As an illustration one could think of the basic experience of the Christian. The will of God and the way to salvation are fully revealed to him in Christ, but this does not solve any of the problems mentioned; neither undeserved misfortune and undeserved prosperity, birth, illness and death, nor details of the actual course of history are explained, the revelation gives another kind of knowledge. Not even despair is directly met by faith; Christ himself had to cry on the cross: 'My God, my God, why hast thou forsaken me!' But belief in Christ achieves something different: it helps the believer to break through to another level of existence; leaving all problems behind, he finds in Christ that peace which transcends all other forms of understanding. By grace he receives the certainty of unity in Christ, which is so over-whelming that it outweighs all conflicts.

This religious example, being taken from outside philosophy, is only meant as an illustration. It shows the main characteristics of essential knowledge most distinctly: neither religious nor essential knowledge can be intentionally acquired; they are given to us, but, once given, they break through all barriers: the contradictions, though not solved, are left behind. All the other examples have been chosen from the sphere of ethics, partly because this is our concern in this book and partly because ethics is generally accessible and can therefore be treated philsophically, while religion is not open to everyone. Morality has been correctly called that side of religion which can be discussed, and this implies that it can also be discussed independently of religion. I shall explain later why ethical examples are also the clearest we possess. I hope that those mentioned so far will already have shown that essential knowledge, even if it has to be given to us, is based on a common experience.

Having thus clarified the nature of the different kinds of know-ledge, which was a necessary preliminary task, we can now return to ethics and develop it further.

CHAPTER VI

HUMANISM AND ETHICS

1

To pave the way for a further discussion of the nature and relevance of essential knowledge, we shall first take up another of the conflicts to which it is bound to give rise—a conflict in the sphere of moral decisions—because it will help to define the scope of ethics. We have had to pay attention to the limitations of knowledge in each of its fields, and the scope of ethics is also restricted by boundaries of its own, which must be firmly drawn if we are to avoid being misled by wrong expectations.

An action is truly ethical if it is the result of a personal decision to act in a moral way and if the way chosen can be accepted as truly moral. This apparently self-evident statement has two obvious implications which lead to less apparent consequences. On the one hand, moral demands are not fulfilled if an action, though conforming to moral rules, is done for the wrong reason—if, for instance, we try to help another person because we expect, or want to earn, a reward. On the other hand, even if our intention is to act morally, the demands of morality are not fulfilled when, instead of facing the given situation and making the appropriate personal decision, we rely on what is usually done in similar circumstances—if, for instance, we give money to a person in need, with a friendly gesture, without realizing that both the gift and the gesture hurt because what he was seeking was understanding, sympathy, love. Ethics demands that we come to our own decisions and these cannot be moral unless we are also aware of their ethical basis and framework. We must be completely involved in our actions, so that we act from the right motives, and we must also make sure that the actions which we intend are both good and the right ones in the given circumstances.

In practice, this structure of a moral deed need not become conscious; it may, as has been said, appear self-evident to many people; but it should obviously be brought into the open in a discussion of ethics, the more so as there is always the temptation to avoid painful decisions by relying on conventions.

With regard to the scope of ethics, our description of an ethical action means that the ethical framework must leave room for personal choice and decision. We must not expect ethics to provide us with a closely knit or closed system of rules or laws, with a ready-made decision for every possible situation; it must leave what in future I shall refer to as an 'area of the unprescribed' to allow us to come to our own decisions. Does this contradict our claim that ethics is based on internal and essential knowledge— that is, on the discovery of approaches to the absolute and on the experiencing of its impact? Have we to admit that morality is purely relative?

The limitations of ethics find their expression in the contrast between principles and necessity which has been discussed.* We have seen that there is necessity within the principle, that in them-selves principles are absolute laws, but that they do not force us to accept them; they become absolutely compelling for us only by being accepted. We must choose between various principles and decide which applies in a particular situation, but once we have chosen we become subject to an absolute demand. In other words, principles are abstract formulations of absolute laws, but we have seen that, in internal reality, abstract statements are insufficient; this reality is known by personal participation. Therefore the absoluteness of principles becomes real only when, in a particular situation, we make them absolutely binding for ourselves. We are challenged, so to speak, by a store of absolute laws which often cannot all be applied at the same time, so that we can and must choose between them, and it is this choice which leaves room for both personal decision and absoluteness.

This double aspect of principles originates in their relation to the moral law. The moral law represents the absolute demand to act

* See pp. 94–5.

5-2

morally and it is of universal validity. Yet, since it is a purely general demand, it is in need of specification—namely of principles which articulate different aspects of it, as the Ten Commandments do.* But any such principle, though wholly right in itself, may still prove inapplicable in a particular situation, because no single principle is the complete expression of the moral law. Therefore all principles partake in its absoluteness, but their validity is nevertheless limited and not universal. One must not steal, but a parent may do so to save a starving child and be right. Once, however, we apply a principle and make it valid, it is absolutely binding for us, and we cannot escape absoluteness because the moral law forces us to apply one or the other principle.

This does not mean, in a contradictory way, that principles are relative as well as absolute. A principle, whenever it is valid, is absolutely so. It is never relative; if we do not make it binding for us, we must exclude it altogether. Such a rejection on a particular occasion, however, does not preclude its acceptance in a different situation; we still recognize that it represents an aspect of the absolute moral law, even if it cannot be applied at that moment.

The following example may show how this works. It has been said that the commandment 'Thou shalt love thy neighbour as thyself' belongs to the sphere of essential knowledge, being a result of an impact of the absolute. It is, in fact, so basic that it is often considered as identical with the moral law itself, and it is certainly true that all our moral actions should be guided by this kind of love; it could appear, therefore, that all other principles are merely subsidiary, to be chosen in the light of this commandment and not absolute. This commandment, though basic, is also very general; it says something definitive about our attitude, but not what we ought actually to do in any particular situation, and thus it can come into conflict with other, more specific principles which then acquire equal weight. If we are driven to despair watching an old person whom we love and want to help, hopelessly ill, suffering great pain, a wreck of a human being whose survival seems nothing but an unbearable burden to himself and

* See pp. 61–3.

others, and if we feel that it would be an act of mercy that his suffering should be terminated, we shall still be confronted with the principle 'Thou shalt not kill'. It may be argued that we ought to choose the action which serves love better; but as we are not told what that love requires in that situation, we shall still have to make a genuine choice. We may feel justified in exercising mercy by killing and thus in taking upon ourselves the great responsibility of disregarding that, in general, killing is absolutely wrong; or we may be convinced that we cannot accept this responsibility, either because the situation does not conclusively justify it or because we experience the prohibition of killing as ultimately binding for us, and in this case we may be compelled to suppress our compassion, our desire to help and even the actual feeling of love. We shall have to decide, in the light of our own experience, which of these two principles (each recognized as absolute in itself) we have to make absolute for ourselves by accepting it in this particular situation. Principles do conflict, and no general solution suitable for all occasions can be given beforehand.

It could also be said, of course, that there is no need to introduce absolutes at all, that it is sufficient to consider the relative circumstances, to try to find out, for instance, whether there is any hope for the patient, how far the killing represents a danger to ourselves, whether this risk should be taken, and what are the patient's own wishes. This sounds the more convincing as all these considerations will have to be made in any case when we decide upon which principle we should base our action; paying attention to a situation means taking relative elements into account. But there is, between these two kinds of argument, a fundamental difference which speaks in favour of the acceptance of absolute principles.*

This becomes obvious whether we look at the absolute or at the relative elements involved in such a decision, because of the fact which we have mentioned—that absoluteness and relativity become clear to us in opposition to each other and that neither,

---

* Another objection could also be raised—that the moral part of the Ten Commandments represents social demands and is not an expression of the absolute moral law. This has been discussed on p. 62.

therefore, should be neglected. This also involves another distinction we have made before—that between fundamental morality and its application. The application is determined by relative conditions; but we have also to make sure that it is the fundamental moral law which is being applied.

So far as the absolute is concerned, it is insufficient to rely on accepted principles alone, on a 'natural morality' which has been given once for all. Recent experiences of all the kinds of totalitarianism have shown that this natural morality cannot be relied upon. Although absoluteness means validity once for all (and we shall have to discuss the relevance of the passage of time),* we must still make sure, by our own experience, that principles are in fact absolutely valid, for they must be binding for us. To do that, we must assail them with all the knowledge of the relative conditions we have—for instance, in the case of killing, with the current justification of war, of capital punishment, of the murder of a tyrant, or in the case of a hopelessly sick patient with the defence of euthanasia. We must find out as accurately as possible whether the rejection of the principle would be against the inner evidence we possess and where and when the rejection would really falsify what we in fact experience. We must see where we are really bound to admit absoluteness and when disbelief would be dishonest or even nonsensical in the light of what we cannot help believing.

Nevertheless, even though this assailing of the absolute means an emphasis on relative considerations, the relative itself will be properly judged only if absolute principles remain the basis of such tests; the absolute will make sure that we do not succumb to purely individual emotions, preferences or aberrations. These tests will be helped by willingness to admit that there is absoluteness; if we accept nothing but that which can be proved, we shall be caught within the web of relativity which makes it impossible to judge the weight of the single relative elements given by special circumstances.

Concern with circumstances which are purely relative always

* See pp. 155–6.

leads to attempts to find out how they are interconnected; we are led—as our discussion of Freud has shown—to abstract generalizations. These can be applied to different circumstances; they tend to support straightforward, apparently convincing conclusions which overshadow the particular situation of the particular person. In the case of mercy-killing this probably means one of two things: either emphasis on the duty of doctors to preserve life at all costs, or justification of euthanasia. Life is often artificially prolonged even when this delaying of death is completely senseless and causes unnecessary suffering, but is this a manifestation of love? If euthanasia were to be allowed as many desire, it would be done either to help society, by relieving it of a burden, or because of compassion with the sufferer, but are these reasons sufficient to make killing in such cases a generally accepted solution? Even if it were allowed only on compassionate grounds and the will and desire of the sick person were taken into account, abuses would be bound to occur. As all such cases concern life and death, they demand an extremely responsible decision in each individual situation, and the necessary facing of the problem with all its implications can only be safeguarded if the challenge of absolute principles and their demands forces us to resist the power of generalizations. The necessity of choosing between absolute principles means that these come into conflict with each other, and it is this conflict between absolutes which, in the face of fundamental and profoundly personal problems, ensures that we come to a personal decision in which we are completely involved and that we take into account all possibly relevant considerations. Unless thus challenged, neither our whole personality nor the full weight of the moral law will come into play. We must become genuinely unable to take refuge in impersonal conclusions which all too easily leave loopholes for licence.

This challenge is usually made poignant—and therefore clearer —by another characteristic of morality. Because of the required area of the unprescribed, all positive principles are rather general; they do not, as we have seen, prescribe solutions. But the negative prohibitions can be stated in a much more definitive way; it is possible to know that such actions as killing, stealing, telling lies are wrong in themselves. They obviously cannot, in themselves, be moral. If a conflict arises, the positive commandment usually runs up against a limitation imposed by a negative one—is it wrong to kill a hopeless patient, or to steal to save children from starvation, or to tell a lie to save a person from despair? We are therefore challenged by a conflict between a 'must' and a 'must not' and forced to make a decision. Both the 'must' and the 'must not', however, will only arise if we recognize absolute demands, experience their full weight and thus the true impact of the absolute; and only thus shall we be able to assess the relative factors properly without yielding to secondary considerations or to purely emotional responses. At the same time, this assessing of the relative elements will prevent a dogmatic or impersonal acceptance of the absolute as being independent of any concrete situation.

The moral principles, originating mainly from the Ten Commandments and the moral part of the Sermon of the Mount, are based on an impact of the absolute which was so distinct that it led to a clear formulation, and it can be revived in us by the formulation if we are confronted by a situation which is profoundly relevant to us. The principles show this and also show how all three kinds of knowledge participate. Internal knowledge makes us aware of those facts which exist as potentialities within us. They are transformed into actual facts by the impact of the absolute— that is, by essential knowledge; and external knowledge provides us with the challenge of the relative, contained in a particular situation. The two demands—to love and not to kill—will both appeal to us strongly and force into the open our potential ethical self, while the consideration of circumstances will prevent either of them from overriding the other without allowing us to come to our own decision. None of the three approaches can work satisfactorily in isolation. External knowledge shows us a large number of relevant relative factors; internal knowledge shows some other relative factors and also many potentialities, but both together do not provide us with a final criterion for our choice.

Essential knowledge does, but with the help of contradictory demands; therefore, if relied upon alone, it could mislead us into merely clinging to the principle which we like best and making it a dogma regardless of the situation.

Naturally, as there is no proof in ethics, but instead the need for an area of the unprescribed, errors cannot be avoided. The task of ethics, therefore, is to narrow down the scope of error by sorting out and making clear which of the accepted principles are really absolute and to make them appeal to us, so that we can respond to them and thus make an ethical decision. Ethics cannot and must not dictate or save us from conflicts, but we hope to show that its elaboration can help us to make these conflicts fruitful.*

2

The preceding conclusions can best be seen in perspective, further clarified and thus judged by comparison with what is usually called 'humanist ethics'. In itself, this kind of ethics is very similar to that which we have propounded so far, while the approach to it is entirely different. The comparison can therefore help to evaluate these different approaches, and thereby also clarify the contributions of the three kinds of knowledge.

As a basis for this discussion I have chosen the book *Man for Himself* by Erich Fromm,† for two reasons. First, he is a psychoanalyst who admits the freedom of the will; thus we shall be able to consider another aspect of psycho-analysis and so make our consideration of it more comprehensive. Second—and this is the

---

* These limitations of ethics pose a difficult problem to the legislator who must safeguard obedience to general laws. It is difficult for him to allow for exceptional personal decisions and thus to uphold a balance between what should be law and the avoidance of injustice or cruelty which may arise. This problem goes beyond ethics, but the clarification of principles and values (which we shall discuss later) may help the legislator, too. The demand for a 'value-orientated approach' has actually been raised. Cf. R. W. M. Dias, *The Value of a Value-Study of Law* (The Modern Law Review, July 1965), pp. 397 ff.

† London, 1948. Page numbers in parentheses on the following pages refer to this book.

main reason—the kind of ethics which Fromm wants to establish is based on the acceptance of 'Thou shalt love thy neighbour as thyself' as the fundamental ethical demand; this will enable us to concentrate on what is basically different between the humanist approach and ours. We have said that psychological knowledge could be important and fruitful for ethics if one started from ethics instead of the other way round.* To some extent Fromm chooses this way, and as we can thus agree with him on the actual demands of ethics, his book can well serve as a basis for discussion of the existence of the absolute which we accept and he denies.

Fromm has no objection to, and even adopts Christian ethics, but since he is an atheist, he does so 'not because it is God's will, but in operational terms—loving my enemies, trying to do justice, trying at least to love the stranger'.† His atheism, however, means that there is nothing 'transcending man'; 'Man, indeed, is the "measure of all things". The humanistic position is that there is nothing higher and nothing more dignified than human existence' (p. 13). He denies that there is anything which could be called 'absolute'.

The basic question which the humanist position raises, therefore, is whether the claim that there is nothing transcending man can be accepted. We have ascertained that there is no answer in any fundamental context to the question 'Why?'; that we do not know, and cannot possibly know, why the universe or man exists, nor why man is as he is. Moreover, although we ourselves are part of reality, we do not even fully understand its two elements which constitute us—body and mind. It was the lack of any final knowledge of either side of this dichotomy which has led to our recognition of essential knowledge; the inconclusiveness of external and internal knowledge made us aware of our possession of a more conclusive knowledge and of the impact of the absolute. We can hardly doubt that there is much which transcends our understanding; does it not, therefore, also transcend man? Man surely cannot be the measure of *all* things, and if there exists a sphere which he is unable to explore fully, we cannot confidently

* See p. 44.   † *The Listener*, vol. 76, p. 595.

assert that it is neither higher nor more dignified than man. On the contrary, the mere fact that we must accept ourselves as we are without knowing why seems to indicate that we depend on a reality which transcends us and which, as we depend on it, must be in some sense higher than man. We have found that this is how we experience our existence.

For Fromm, relativity reigns supreme. He feels entitled to dismiss belief in anything transcendental or absolute because of his lofty view of human nature, and thus anything which could indicate a higher reality—such as ethical values—remains relative, being dependent on man who stands highest. But Fromm cannot quite avoid seeing man as dependent too, though not on anything which transcends him; for Fromm, man depends on biological, social and historical conditions. In this way he is able to build his ethics entirely on the consideration of relative interconnections. The content of his ethics is similar to our own, but we have said that it could never be established in that way. Who is right?

Ethics provides us with a very good test for deciding whether or not the existence of a transcendental reality and thus of something absolute should be admitted. When trying to explain essential knowledge we have deliberately used so far only ethical examples; they are, for several reasons, the best starting point. Probably it is religion which comes to mind first whenever the absolute is mentioned; but we have agreed that morality is that side of religion which can be discussed, for the impact of the absolute in this sphere leads to formulations which can appeal to everyone, in contrast to metaphysical or religious statements. (We shall include these and discuss their different nature in chapter XII.) At the same time, ethics refers to action and can thus be tested— again in contrast to other teachings—by action, which makes it more definitive than any other philosophical statement. This probably helps to explain why moral commandments achieve such lasting validity. This testing by action cannot, of course, be included in an abstract investigation, but some of the examples used may have reminded the reader of similar experiences and thus helped him to include his own experience. Moreover, such a test is valid because we have had to admit experience as evidence of the real; therefore, when dealing with ethics, we are in fact well-equipped to judge whether the exclusion of anything transcendental can be accepted.

According to Fromm, ethics serves the well-being of man, 'the sole criterion of ethical value being man's welfare' (p. 13). In his ethics, therefore, '"good" is synonymous with good for man and "bad" with bad for man', and thus, 'in order to know what is good for man we have to know his nature . . . If ethics constitutes the body of norms for achieving excellence in performing the art of living, its most general principles must follow from the nature of life in general and of human existence in particular' (pp. 18, 19). This implies that 'happiness is the criterion of excellence in the art of living, of virtue in the meaning it has in humanistic ethics' (p. 189), and psycho-analysis helps Fromm to discover that 'it is one of the characteristics of human nature that man finds fulfilment and happiness only in relatedness to and solidarity with his fellow men', so that the demand of ethics is 'to love one's neighbour' (p. 14). He believes that this love, too, 'is not a phenomenon transcending man; it is something inherent in and radiating from him' (p. 14); therefore he insists 'on the principle that only man himself can determine the criterion for virtue and sin, and not an authority transcending him' (pp. 12–13).

Fromm's assumptions seem to carry great weight because much of his analysis of human nature and many of his conclusions ring true. But as his intention is to create a different foundation for what is, in essence, traditional ethics, these conclusions in themselves are not yet an answer to our question. We still have to find out whether, by his own method, he could ever have arrived at the results which he accepts as given, and whether his view of human nature is complete enough to form a satisfactory basis for ethics.

Much of what he says agrees with our line of argument. He removes the stumbling block which was found in the early writings of Freud; he never doubts that man is free to choose, decide and act, and he bases his conclusion not on philosophical speculations but on empirical observations. 'There is no situation

which provides for a better opportunity to observe the strength
and tenacity of the forces striving for health than that of psycho-
analytic therapy' (p. 223). He sees, of course, how dependent man
is on external conditions, on his character, on 'destructive and
irrational passions' (p. 234), but asserts nevertheless: 'Man, while
like all other creatures subject to forces which determine him, is
the only creature endowed with reason, the only being who is
capable of understanding the very forces which he is subjected to
and who by his understanding can take an active part in his own
fate and strengthen those elements which strive for the good ...
We are therefore not helpless victims of circumstance; we are,
indeed, able to change and to influence forces inside and outside
ourselves and to control, at least to some extent, the conditions
which play upon us' (p. 233). It is true that we may fail, but this
does not alter man's basic situation: 'One can recognize this
failure and judge it for what it is—his moral failure. Even if one
knows that the odds against the person were overwhelming and
that everyone would have failed too, the judgment about him
remains the same. If one fully understands all the circumstances
which made him as he is, one may have compassion for him; yet
this compassion does not alter the validity of the judgment'
(p. 237). This is a point which is important for any moral approach, a point which we fully accept: a crime or sin may arouse
our compassion and it may be desirable to exercise mercy; nevertheless, the moral judgment should not be watered down by
excusing the deed psychologically or otherwise; the deed should
first be recognized for what it is. Only if the act of forgiveness
does not interfere with the moral judgment will it truly help both
the criminal or sinner and society, for only a clear awareness of
what is basically wrong can lead to inner reform and to the right
kind of social reform.

Moreover, Fromm's elaboration of the concept and nature of
love is in many ways admirable. This concept, difficult to define
and often used in too vague a way, is obviously in need of clarification, and some of the distinctions Fromm introduces are very
helpful. In contrast to the common opinion 'that nothing is easier

than to love, that the difficulty lies only in finding the right object', he sees that 'love is a very specific feeling; and while every human being has a capacity for love, its realization is one of the most difficult achievements'. To distinguish this specific feeling from 'confused and wishful thinking' he calls it 'productive love' which he defines by basic elements which are characteristic of all its different forms, namely by 'care, responsibility, respect, and knowledge' (pp. 97–8), each of which he fully explains. We cannot reproduce these explanations in detail here, but the following example may show how valuable some of his analysis is.

In the commandment 'Thou shalt love thy neighbour as thyself' the last words—'as thyself'—may create doubts and perplexity, because most people, including Freud, hold the view 'that there is a basic contradiction and a state of alternation between love for oneself and love for others' (p. 128), or even that 'to love others ... is a virtue', and 'to love oneself ... is a sin' (p. 119). To explain and justify the commandment, Fromm distinguishes between 'selfishness' and 'self-love'. Selfishness is contrary to self-love; the selfish person 'can see nothing but himself; he judges everyone and everything from its usefulness to him', and because of this concern for usefulness 'he is basically unable to love' (p. 130). The selfish person 'is necessarily unhappy and anxiously concerned to snatch from life the satisfactions which he blocks himself from attaining. He seems to care too much for himself but actually only makes an unsuccessful attempt to cover up and compensate for his failure to care for his real self', because his real self requires 'relatedness to and solidarity with' others. Thus 'it is true that selfish persons are incapable of loving others, but they are not capable of loving themselves either' (p. 131). For 'love, in principle, is indivisible as far as the connection between "objects" and one's self is concerned ... An attitude of love towards themselves will be found in all those who are capable of loving others' (p. 129). Only if man respects the human person in everyone will he be able to include his real self, and only if he thus exercises the right kind of loving care and feels responsible for himself can he truly love others.

Nevertheless, our objections to Fromm's approach are not invalidated. It is not plausible that his results could ever have been arrived at on the basis of pure relativity alone. In fact, they are weakened by this derivation.

Fromm's basing of his ethics on a knowledge of man's nature and the requirements of his welfare brings us back to a problem which has been mentioned before.* There we had to agree that it is logically correct to say that statements containing 'is' and statements containing 'ought' can have no influence upon each other, and we were yet forced to add that they cannot be completely independent of each other either, because the feeling of obligation which 'ought' carries must ultimately be based on facts.

The logical inconsistency warns us of what G. E. Moore has called the 'naturalistic fallacy'. Moore states that 'good' is 'one of those innumerable objects of thought which are themselves incapable of definition, because they are ultimate terms by reference to which whatever is capable of definition must be defined'. The naturalistic fallacy disregards this basic fact; it 'always implies that when we think "This is good", what we are thinking is that the thing in question bears a definite relation to some other thing'. The good is then regarded, not as an intrinsic value, but as a means serving a purpose, such as pleasure, happiness, society, evolution, or other useful or desirable ends. Moore also emphasizes, as we did, that ethics cannot be based on metaphysics. A better starting point for the derivation of ethics he sees in 'the intuitional view' which 'consists in the supposition that certain rules, stating that certain actions are always to be done or to be omitted, may be taken as self-evident premises'. He accepts this fully 'with regard to judgments of what is good in itself' and also accepts as 'correct contention' that 'certain ways of acting were right and others wrong, whatever their results might be'.†

Fromm commits the naturalistic fallacy when he makes ethics serve human welfare. It is true that he believes that such welfare can best be served by love, but love itself thus becomes a means to

* See pp. 15–17.
† *Principia Ethica* (Cambridge, 1962) (paperback ed.), pp. 9–10, 38, 115, 148, 106.

a different end. We have avoided this pitfall by emphasizing the 'ethical self' and the impact of the absolute, which have no such relationship as that between means and ends: our innermost being responds to the good as such, without any interference by a purpose, and the response happens only when we strive for the good for its own sake, again without subordinating it to a purpose. Ethics is rooted in the ethical self, which is a potential fact; the appeal of the good makes it actual; and thus we experience the identity between the demands of the good and the innermost core of our being, without establishing a fallacious connection between the two. What we ought to do is not illogically determined by 'some other thing' outside it; the necessary autonomy of ethics is preserved; yet the sense of obligation arises because the moral commandment corresponds to, and is confirmed by, what we in fact are.

This approach may appear similar to Moore's 'intuitional view', but actually goes far beyond it; the intuitional view hovers in the air and must remain insufficient because, lacking a proper basis, it does not enable us to distinguish reliable from prejudiced judgments. In our case, any final ethical intuition is a response to the impact of the absolute, and Moore, like Fromm, would have rejected both our concept of essential knowledge and the existence of a transcendental reality. Nevertheless, without realizing it, Moore shows that he feels this insufficiency himself. Since he does not give a foundation to his intuitional view, he is led to undermine it and comes very near to committing the naturalistic fallacy himself when he tries to make judgments. When moving on from the 'good in itself' to the discussion of 'rules of action', he says: 'Since what we intuit, what conscience tells us, is that certain actions will always produce the greatest sum of good under the circumstances, it is plain that reasons can be given'—that is, a purpose is introduced.* But I do not intend to discuss Moore's theories further; because Fromm deals more directly with the content of ethics, he is for us the better example.

---

* *Ibid.* pp. 148–9. That this is also a misrepresentation of conscience will become clear in the next section of this chapter.

That Fromm falsifies ethics can be seen in many ways, in his use, for example, of the concepts 'reason' and 'knowledge'. His main line of investigation is external and psycho-analytical; he explicitly rejects 'subjectivistic ethics' and wants 'objectivistic ethics', in order 'to arrive at normative principles which are objectively valid' (p. 14). He never distinguishes between different kinds of knowledge, but claims to rely on the objective method alone. Certainly, ethics should not be based on personal prejudice and predilection, but to arrive at his norms Fromm is actually forced to employ the subjective method and to touch upon essential knowledge. Yet he does not pay attention to them, and the disregard of both undermines the results he wants to support.

Inner experience is obviously consulted when he discusses love; no one can, from outside or purely psychologically, distinguish the love which he wants to make real—'a very specific feeling'— from other kinds of love; the understanding of feelings needs inner participation, personal experience. The psychoanalyst may retort that, by consulting the patient, he is approaching the problem from outside and drawing psychological conclusions, but this will not apply to the patient who must face his innermost motives and feelings, nor even to the doctor who, if he wants to understand his patient fully, must try to share his individual inner experience. To decide whether we are moved by love at all and to distinguish between love of our neighbour and other kinds of love, we must honestly face ourselves, without taking refuge in external or psychological explanations. We have to go beyond a generalized view of the processes operating in our minds and deal with what, as individuals, we actually intend and feel. We must apply the subjective method.

Equally Fromm's discussion of freedom is not solely based on what he admits into his scheme. In the preceding quotation he bases his belief in freedom on the fact that man is 'the only creature endowed with reason', because he can thereby understand the 'forces he is subjected to ... and strengthen those elements which strive for the good'.* But to be able to oppose to

* See p. 141.

such forces the striving for the good, it is certainly necessary to employ two different kinds of reason; the good will be recognized only if internal knowledge has opened a way to it. Otherwise one will be forced, as Fromm is, to find additional reasons for doing good—that is, to commit the naturalistic fallacy—and then the good will not be strong enough to combat the overwhelming forces which, inside and outside man, work against it. The urge to do what is good must be experienced as an inner compulsion exercised by the good; reason, if it deals with external knowledge alone can always find excuses which absolve us from doing the good. Even those who do not believe in an absolute good and reject the two ways of thinking will avoid the naturalistic fallacy only if they employ—whether they acknowledge it or not—the subjective as well as the objective method.

This supporting of external knowledge by unacknowledged inner knowledge is bound to have dubious consequences. We cannot possibly be induced to love our neighbour by objective considerations; this will lead either to our merely pretending that we love those whom we may objectively despise, or to our discovering again and again that not even tolerance can be defended because it seems necessary to fight evil with ruthlessness. Nor can we uphold belief in freedom on this basis, for external knowledge can only make us realize necessity and compulsion; we have to consult inner experience to become aware of our responsibility. Here Fromm's fallacy becomes most obvious. His concern with the well-being of man demands that we obey conscience and accept responsibility, not because we are told to do so, but because our reason shows us that we benefit. But if we feel responsible only to ourselves, as Fromm believes, we can still act completely arbitrarily; only few people will thus feel compelled to accept love of their neighbour. We must surely be responsible to somebody or something that we have to face, be able to confront what we do with the demands of a higher authority,* for otherwise responsibility will not prevent us from doing whatever we

* As we shall provisionally call it; the question of authority will be discussed on pp. 153–5.

like. Those who feel responsible and do not follow their desires and yet deny that there is a higher authority to which they are responsible will find it difficult to account for their feelings. Some Existentialists who have tried to do so (especially Sartre) have been driven to despair by the vain attempt to give a clear meaning to this responsibility of man to himself alone and to nothing else.* Even a denial of responsibility may serve the well-being which Fromm has in mind. Some forms of Islam as well as Marxism, by emphasizing determinism and thereby removing the burden of responsibility, unleash enormous energies in man and are therefore 'productive' in the sense of Fromm's ideas.

Nor is it possible to substitute the demands of society (despite their obvious importance) for those of a higher authority. The insufficiency of responsibility merely to ourselves becomes most conspicuous if we look, as we must, beyond the self-centred view which Fromm elaborates. Planning future actions which have implications for our neighbour will obviously require more than responsibility to ourselves alone. If somebody has to make, say, a political decision, he must look beyond himself. But we cannot say that he is then simply responsible to society, because he may have to make a decision which contradicts the accepted views or even the immediate advantage of the society in which he lives; in Nazi Germany, for instance, the best men felt bound to work for the defeat of their country. We have to accept the challenge of a higher authority, for otherwise either personal or social demands —which may or may not coincide with the good—will remain dominant, and we have seen that even the predominance of justified social demands is detrimental to the good.†

Man must be able to face himself. This is one of the main conditions of ethics, and the question of responsibility only shows most clearly that humanism fails to fulfil it. The necessary detachment cannot be achieved on the basis of the external approach (which Fromm trusts) because it leads away from the personal

---

* For a fuller treatment of the two aspects of responsibility see P. Roubiczek, *Existentialism—For and Against*, pp. 126-9. To Fromm's concept of 'conscience' and 'authority' we shall return in the next section of this chapter.
† See ch. III, section 2.

altogether; nor can internal reality suffice because man is too much involved in it, and seeing nothing but man alone means, as Existentialism shows, seeking refuge in internal reality (even if Fromm does not admit it). To take the measure of himself with all his shortcomings and potentialities, man has to face a spiritual reality outside himself, so that a confrontation becomes possible; he needs, as we have said, essential knowledge and has to accept it as based on the impact of the absolute.

But Fromm is also bound to deny the existence of essential knowledge, and this involves him in a further contradiction. At first he seems again to come near to our approach and the concept of the ethical self when he says 'that our knowledge of human nature does not lead to ethical relativism, but, on the contrary, to the conviction that the sources of norms for ethical conduct are to be found in man's nature itself; that moral norms are based on man's inherent qualities' (p. 7). Then, however, he dismisses the absolute as merely 'rooted in theological thinking in which a divine realm, as the "absolute", is separated from the imperfect realm of man. Except for the theological context the concept of the absolute is meaningless and has as little place in ethics as in scientific thinking in general' (p. 16). Therefore, as an atheist, he is bound to reject the absolute as well as essential knowledge. Instead, he opposes objectivity to relativism; but this is a false opposition, for the objective approach, as we have seen, is always necessarily within the web of relativity.

This remains true even if we make a necessary reservation. It could be argued that our dictum does not apply to Fromm because his usage of the term 'objective' is not identical with ours. He establishes what he calls objective judgment with the unacknowledged help of the subjective method, and it is thus that he often arrives at those valid insights to some of which we have referred. He actually tries to oppose to objectivity (which he sees as having a deadening effect on man) a different living and life-giving objectivity (which is based on inner experience and thus very nearly subjective). Nevertheless, as he does not distinguish between the two methods, the opposition remains wrong, for even his objectivity remains relative. This becomes clear when he goes on to equate ethics with science: 'The history of science is a history of inadequate and incomplete statements, and every new insight makes possible the recognition of inadequacies of previous propositions and offers a springboard for creating a more adequate formulation.' (p. 239). This is certainly true of science, but Fromm is speaking here of ethics as well.

The consequence of the false opposition is thus an implicit denial of the very foundation of his book. As always, relativity is made possible by contrast with absoluteness; the absolute in this case being the assertion that there is nothing which transcends man. This assertion is dogmatic, for it is simply stated before he begins his investigation as a fact which cannot be doubted. Equally dogmatic is his acceptance of the obligation to love one's neighbour; it remains throughout the unshakable basis of his ethics; it is obviously considered as a final truth and not as a hypothesis. At no point does he envisage the possibility that psycho-analysis could ever lead to a different result, nor what would happen if it did. It seems evident that fundamentally his own view of the commandment to love one's neighbour is different from what he says; despite his assertions, he treats it as absolute. But as he insists on relativity, he feels obliged to admit the possibility of change, and thus the book fails to do justice to its main claim. Contrary to his intention, we are almost encouraged not to take 'productive love' as seriously as he does, for actually his approach allows us to look for other sources of productivity and creativeness. This might present no difficulties, in the case, for instance, of a scientist or artist who, in a self-centred way, is entirely devoted to his work.

In fact, Fromm is contradicted by his own psycho-analytical knowledge. He emphasizes the profound restlessness of man, and his ethics is an attempt to quell it. This restlessness, however, is not merely, nor even mainly, due to questions concerning the activity of man, nor to the difficulty of answering the question 'What ought I to do?', though such doubts may contribute to it; in the last resort, it is metaphysical. It is due to the fundamental contradictions which we have pointed out: to the apparent powerlessness of the good, to the insoluble problem of existence, to man's finding himself suspended over an abyss of the unknown.* Ethics can contribute to the healing of this restlessness and prevent it from turning into despair, but only if it touches upon the metaphysical level of experience. It must acquire a power which outweighs all other considerations—that is, it must be based on the impact of the absolute. It must lead to an inner certainty which is only fortified by new insights.

Yet Fromm can also help us to clarify the problem to which therefore we must now return—how to distinguish between justified and false convictions of certainty.

3

The discussion of morality seems to lead to an impasse similar to that of history which is, as we have said, open to contradictory and irreconcilable interpretations; it depends on the bias of each individual whether, for him, the optimistic or the pessimistic view carries more weight.† Similarly, morality, when discussed as such, appears to be a very strong force; one cannot help believing that, by now, it should have become generally accepted as valid; at the same time, we are constantly confronted with selfishness, cruelty, crime and wars, all of which seem to make a firm belief in the power of morality dubious. To come, on these grounds, to a final correct decision remains impossible; we are unable to weigh one kind of evidence against the other; though not directly based on the objective and subjective methods, they are as incompatible as these. It will help us little to remember the great achievements of mankind when confronted with the power of evil, nor will the evidence of evil invalidate our knowledge of the existence of the good. When, for instance, we are frightened by certain aspects of the contemporary world, say by the violence of nationalism or race-hatred, it will most probably help us little to remind our-

* See pp. 120–1.   † See pp. 66–8.

selves how many good or even admirable people we know, nor will our trust in these people be destroyed by the knowledge of, say, the existence of the atomic bomb. Again it will depend on us which facts we consider the more important; the two kinds of evidence do not admit any kind of quantitative measurement and thus cannot be simply compared. They are incommensurable and therefore do not meet.

This ambiguity makes it necessary for us to rely on the inner certainty which we actually experience, the more so as we often cannot predict the consequences of our actions and thus must act on the basis of insufficient evidence in this respect, too. Frequently we have to do what we consider to be right simply because we believe in its rightness, regardless of the historical situation, of the possible, but unpredictable practical consequences, and of our idealistic wishes. Therefore it is of the greatest importance to tackle now the problem the discussion of which we have postponed so far—the problem of how to distinguish between justifiable and false convictions of certainty, especially since the feeling of certainty, as the psychologists correctly emphasize, can also be produced 'from below', by passions, animal urges and the enjoyment of power. (Afterwards we shall also touch upon the problem of evil.) To enable us to make proper judgments, it will be a help to ask the question which is bound to arise in any discussion of morality: what is conscience?

There are many different interpretations of this concept. Once again, Fromm's approach can help us to specify our own ideas and our reasons for holding them.

In agreement with Freud's concept of the super-ego, Fromm first attacks conventional conscience as merely a product of the demands of religion, society or public opinion. That kind of conscience appears to be an 'inner voice', but in fact in its name we merely make external demands our own; this, however, we do so thoroughly that they become part of our mind and subtly enslave us. This 'authoritarian conscience', as Fromm calls it, 'is the voice of an internalized external authority, the parents, the state, or whoever the authorities in a culture happen to be ... Such authorities . . . are either consciously or unconsciously accepted as ethical and moral legislators whose laws and sanctions one adopts, thus internalizing them. The laws and sanctions of external authority become part of oneself, as it were, and instead of feeling responsible to something outside oneself, one feels responsible to something inside, to one's conscience' (pp. 143–4). To this wrong kind of conscience he opposes as the right kind 'humanistic conscience' which 'is not the internalized voice of an authority whom we are eager to please and afraid of displeasing; it is our own voice, present in every human being and independent of external sanctions and rewards'. It is 'knowledge within oneself, knowledge of our respective success or failure in the art of living . . . reaction of our total personality to its proper functioning or dysfunctioning' (p. 158). It is 'the voice of our loving care for ourselves' (p. 159). How far does this distinction prove satisfactory?

There is no doubt that it is important to distinguish conscience in its proper functioning from the distortion which Fromm calls authoritarian; his investigation of this misleading aspect of conscience can clear the way for a better understanding, especially as, unlike Freud, he does not make it a complete explanation of conscience. Yet he fails because his humanistic conscience falls far short of doing justice to the right kind of conscience, and thus he does not enable us to distinguish clearly the authoritarian from the true.

This becomes obvious when he elaborates the 'reaction of our total personality': 'Actions, thoughts and feelings which are conducive to the proper functioning and unfolding of our total personality produce a feeling of inner approval, of "rightness", characteristic of the humanistic "good conscience" . . . Conscience is thus a reaction of ourselves to ourselves. It is the voice of our true selves which summons us back to ourselves, to live productively, to develop fully and harmoniously—that is, to become what we potentially are. It is the guardian of our integrity' (p. 159). Given a proper basis, parts of this could be a good description of conscience, but it is invalidated by insisting that we react only to ourselves.

We have said before that the idea of responsibility is robbed of its significance when we are made responsible only to ourselves.* One of the reasons why this is so becomes obvious here: if we react only to ourselves, we hardly have a chance of distinguishing the internalized voice of external authorities which, after all, we also make our own ('one feels responsible to something inside') from the voice of our true selves. The criteria upon which Fromm mainly relies—happiness and the art of living—are insufficient for such a distinction. Giving in to public opinion may make life easier and more pleasant, so that it need not produce a neurosis. It could even be called the true art of living, and it need not damage a person's integrity; there are conservative public servants who stand for public opinion and whose integrity cannot be doubted. We need more than purely subjective or psychological criteria.

The mistake which Fromm makes is once more due to his rejection of anything transcending man, for thus authority for him means exclusively those external influences which enslave man. But there is also a different kind of authority—that which sets man free. To act freely means to act in full accordance with the fundamental, most essential elements of one's own nature, without being forced either by external or by wrong inner compulsions (such as destructive passions) to act otherwise. If man is characterized by his ethical self—and we have agreed with Kierkegaard that he is—acceptance of the moral law establishes such an authority because its demands bring into the open those potentialities which he cannot but accept as belonging to his innermost being—that is, as fundamental and essential. (As an illustration one could think of the Christian claim that God's unlimited power does not establish another kind of determinism, because belief in Him and the acceptance of His commandments enable man to exercise his freedom fully.) Obviously, to be of consequence, conscience must have authority too, but this authority cannot be derived from man alone, not even from his ethical self as such; it must be derived from something distinct from him, such as the moral law, so that he can face something which confronts him; only such a confrontation can enable him to

* See pp. 146–7.

distinguish between the call of conscience and that of differing wishes and inclinations.

To acknowledge an authority which sets us free is also necessary to avoid a danger which psychoanalysts fear in this context—a morbid conscientiousness and a morbid feeling of guilt. These are often overemphasized and used as an excuse for discarding conscience and the feeling of guilt altogether; yet within limits they are real dangers. It is part of our nature that we are not perfect; nobody is entirely free of guilt, nor can we ever hope to satisfy all the demands of conscience. When we are thrown back entirely on ourselves, we are unable to cope with these facts properly; they either appear to us as the result of irrational injustice, for they persist even if we are not conscious of a particular guilt in a particular case, and then we may be driven to accuse fate and to be weighed down by despair; or we are weighed down by trying to satisfy the excessive demands of perfection. 'A reaction of ourselves to ourselves' is therefore no answer, even though it is true that both wrong reactions are reinforced by the authoritarian conscience. But the other kind of authority has, in this respect too, a liberating influence. Once we acknowledge it, we can face conscience and guilt and yet develop fully, because being set free also points to an appropriate action. We are no longer concerned with ourselves alone, but are brought into contact with our neighbour whom we should love, and thus we can see where our own fault lies and do something to make up for it.

Fromm comes near to admitting such an authority when he says: 'The difference between humanistic and authoritarian conscience is not that the latter is moulded by the cultural tradition, while the former is not. On the contrary, it is similar in this respect to our capacities of speech and thought, which, though intrinsic human potentialities, develop only in a social and cultural context. The human race, in the last five or six thousand years of its cultural development, has formulated ethical norms in its religious and philosophical systems toward which the conscience of every individual must be orientated' (pp. 171–2). In itself, this appeal to tradition is justified, but tradition has constantly to be scrutinized and tested, because there are wrong traditions as well. Again, however, Fromm does not enable us to distinguish between those cultural traditions which should be accepted, and the 'internalized voice' of institutions and public opinion which may be also part of tradition. It is true that, to a large extent, the sorting out of traditions is brought about by the passage of time, but to understand this working of 'the last five or six thousand years' we have to refer to the absolute which Fromm rejects. Otherwise we could hardly understand how it is that, from the moral point of view, we can now assert with confidence that Socrates was right and his persecutors wrong.

When, at any time, a 'new morality' is proclaimed, there is bound to be great uncertainty whether this new morality is correct or as to which parts of it are and which not. This was obviously the case at the time of Socrates, of Buddha, of Jesus, of the Reformation, just as much as it is today. In retrospect, the sorting out can be done, because it has become possible to distinguish between individual or temporal aberrations and a new and valid way of approaching the absolute.* The experience of the absolute, if it occurs at all, is a common experience; if a new access to it has been found, this new way will gradually be understood and will establish itself and survive because the absolute is one and unchanging. Since we never grasp more than facets of it, there is room for new approaches, and these will be recognizable because they give access to the same absolute; they make it possible for a different impact of the absolute to make itself felt. By contrast, the aberrations which merely seemed to touch upon the absolute will be exposed for what they are and not survive.

The Ten Commandments and the Sermon on the Mount, to whose survival we have referred, can illustrate this process. Since mankind develops in the course of its history, it does not seem surprising that morality undergoes the same development. Yet it is surprising that this is true only up to a certain point; once a certain level has been achieved, no further development takes

---

* For the following see also the discussion of the term 'absolute' on pp. 70–3.

place; thus the essence of the moral commandments just mentioned has not changed, but is still valid and alive. Obviously, something real and unchanging has entered into history and has remained independent of it. Therefore, the passage of time is of help; it can reveal what survives and thereby indicate where we should look for the impact of the absolute. The more so as these results can be discerned in different civilizations which developed independently of each other; the fundamental morality of Buddhism, of Taoism and Confucianism differs only in details from that of Judaism and Christianity.*

Yet the passage of time only provides us with indications; the results isolated by it have still to be constantly scrutinized, tested and experienced anew, otherwise they will become a dead letter, or distorted or deteriorated traditions will creep in. Tradition must constantly be confronted with our own conscience; to achieve a reliable sense of morality, we must, again and again, oppose them to each other. The impact of tradition, therefore, has to be assimilated in terms of our own experience, so that we can test our convictions by experiencing for ourselves fully where traditions agree with conscience and can thus stimulate and direct it, and where we are forced to oppose tradition and act against it. This is actually one of the main ways of making sure that we do not succumb to wrong convictions. To be able to make this confrontation trustworthy and fruitful, however, we must admit that the absolute is present both in tradition and in conscience.

At all the points which Fromm touches we are therefore forced to go beyond his concept of a purely humanist conscience, and we have to do this because he does not pay attention to several basic characteristics of conscience. All of them point in the direction of the absolute.†

---

* This constancy can also be seen in the sphere of other values: for a discussion of the relevance of the passage of time to the appreciation of beauty see P. Roubiczek, *Thinking towards Religion*, pp. 158–9.

† For the following I am indebted to the thorough and balanced investigation of conscience by H. G. Stoker in his book: *Das Gewissen, Erscheinungsformen und Theorien* (Schriften zur Philosophie und Soziologie, ed. M. Scheler, vol. 2), (Bonn, 1925).

We have said that he bases his ethics entirely on the commandment to love one's neighbour, but does not admit its absoluteness; at the same time, he defines conscience as 'man's loving care for himself'. He rejects absoluteness because he believes that a psychological investigation can establish this commandment by showing that it is the main condition of man's well-being; thus it should also be possible to derive the commandment from the conscience which watches over his well-being. Yet in fact the demand comes first, imposes itself upon us and is manifested in the promptings of conscience which is directed by it. Conscience is only concerned with the person who experiences it; I do not experience a stirring of conscience with regard to actions of others unless I am involved; it speaks when I myself am involved. It is a reaction to our own deeds. If I actually do feel responsible for others, I must have experienced love of my neighbour first so as to be involved. Therefore the commandment cannot be deduced from conscience: I and my conscience must be struck by it, there must be an impact from something outside which influences conscience—an impact which is never allowed for by Fromm's investigation nor produced by it.

There is a difference which must not be overlooked between conscience and the knowledge of morality and values. All such knowledge can be applied to the character and deeds of others as well as to my own, but conscience only comes into action when this knowledge is directly and unambiguously related to me, when I clearly experience that it does apply to me. Conscience can presuppose this knowledge, but I may still know that my deed was wrong or of no real value without being affected; it is only when I am affected that it is justifiable to speak of conscience. Insensitive persons may well know what morality demands and yet remain indifferent when they disregard it. Knowledge of morality can be developed independently of conscience, and conversely conscience by itself does not lead to supra-personal demands; conscience as such is at work, not in the act of knowing, but in making moral knowledge binding for us. Kant makes this clear when he does not identify his 'categorical imperative' with conscience which is, for him, only concerned with the question of whether or not the imperative has been obeyed.

Once conscience speaks, however, it is impartial to the person experiencing it and only partial for the good and against evil. It may make extremely exacting, very painful demands, in complete disregard of the person one is; it may even demand the sacrifice of life. Obeying conscience may produce a profound satisfaction, even in death, but this transcends any possible interpretation of Fromm's idea of achieving happiness by the art of living and productivity, his main criteria of ethics. Once more we must look beyond man.

For us, therefore, conscience is the appeal to live in accordance with the humanity within us, but this humanity is revealed by the challenge of a higher reality which impinges upon us and wants us to do justice to it. We agree with Fromm that our humanity is essential, but do not believe that it can be fully understood by investigating the conditions of man's well-being. Conscience appears to us as one of the clearest experiences of the transcendental—so clear that it can help us to clarify the vague word 'higher'.

There are several other characteristics of conscience by which this can be shown. One of them is indicated by the rather surprising phenomenon that a truly honest man usually feels reproaches of conscience more frequently and more strongly than the rogue or criminal who ought to be much more exposed to them.

Conscience, we have said, belongs to those facts which are potential. Such facts remain unreal when seen from outside; they can only be known and made real by our own inner experience. Any experience, however, can be disregarded or circumvented; we have therefore relied upon the impact of the absolute to force us to pay due regard to our moral potentialities and to make sure that we are not succumbing to our wishes or to illusions. All this is confirmed by the strange contrast between the moral and the immoral man. The latter may be well aware of the bad nature of his actions and yet be proud of them or ridicule the standards by which they are judged; he has become insensitive because his actions—in which he is truly involved—make him look at conscience from outside, and thus it becomes unreal, a common prejudice, a conventional admonition. Potential facts, if disregarded, may never become actual; they may be deadened instead and even destroyed; therefore wicked behaviour, a way of acting which prevents the development of conscience, will blunt and probably even kill it. Dostoevsky, when coming to the 'House of the Dead' in Siberia, is frightened by finding the criminals, murderers among them, not torn by remorse, but boasting of their crimes, for he discovered thus that conscience can be killed. Later he came to the conclusion that conscience must be awakened by the ideal in which man finds his fulfilment.* But when conscience is admitted and developed by acting in accordance with it, all its potentialities will gradually be made more and more fully actual; the good man will acquire an ever increasing sensitivity and conscientiousness and thus be constantly exposed to reproaches of conscience, the more so as its demands, owing to man's imperfection, can never be completely satisfied. At the same time, the ability to act according to conscience requires a clear knowledge of good and evil, at least in each particular case; we are always confronted with choices, and to be able to make them conscientiously we have to know whether or how far a deed is really good, or better or worse than other possible courses of action. So long as we are in doubt, conscience cannot speak clearly, but it will make itself felt in urgently requiring a clearer knowledge. Thus, whether it speaks or wants to speak, conscience forces us to live in the face of the absolute and is the result of doing so, because the knowledge required is a binding knowledge, and to be truly binding it must impose upon us an unconditional obligation which can only be rooted in the absolute.

That we are entitled to assume an impact of the absolute can be seen when we compare what is usually called 'good conscience' with 'bad conscience'.

---

* For a fuller treatment see P. Roubiczek, *The Misinterpretation of Man* (New York, 1947), p. 262.

Conscience reflects a quality which we have found characteristic of morality—that the negative commandments are more definitive and refer more directly to particular actions than the positive ones; since an area of the unprescribed is needed to allow us to come to our own decision, the positive commandments cannot directly refer to particular situations.* Similarly, the experience of having a bad conscience gives us the conviction that its verdict is absolutely true, however much we should like to alter it; the verdict is independent of our will and overrules it. But the experience of having a good conscience tends to be comparatively vague. We may experience a profound satisfaction, but this is probably rare; usually we hesitate to claim that we have satisfied the demands of the good fully, unless, in some particular case, we know that we have not been guilty of an offence ascribed to us—not that this sense of relief is necessarily a profound experience. This difference is reinforced by further reactions. Having a very bad conscience makes me judge my own character; I feel that I am a bad person, that I am guilty; I shall not even be able to evade this feeling by embarking on metaphysical speculations (to which I may otherwise be prone), namely by accusing fate or God of my failings. I shall accuse myself alone. A good conscience, however, should not—it even must not—lead to conclusions concerning my character; if it is to remain good, I must not make it a proof of my being good; that would give rise to complacency, pride, hubris, and this would immediately destroy my good conscience again and make me guilty. A good conscience can only be preserved by humility and a feeling of gratitude to something outside myself; it cannot simply be accepted as an evidence of my own merit.

This, once more, points to an impact of the absolute. If we are doing good, we move in the direction of the absolute to which we can never do complete justice; however far we go, there is still something transcending us which we cannot hope to emulate; it tells us that we are going in the right direction but it also makes us realize that our achievements can never be final. As the absolute

* See pp. 131, 135–6.

immensely transcends us, it remains, in its completeness, always beyond reach and it cannot therefore give us the feeling that we are perfect. But as it is fundamental to all reality, it also embraces us; its impact is both a challenge and a help, because we are supported by it. This is the reason why an experience of having a good conscience at its best leads to gratitude and why, despite its limitations, it is elevating and not depressing.*

Dependence on the relative, on determining conditions, still applies in many ways, but does not interfere with the experience of absoluteness. Conscience does not merely express moral wishes which may or may not be capable of satisfaction: it tells us that its satisfaction is possible and demanded. It is true, nevertheless, that we may know what we ought to do and want to do it and yet find ourselves in circumstances which make it impossible. But the feeling of unconditional obligation survives and remains essential, for only if we confront the external or inner impossibility with the absolute demand shall we become sure of our decision; only if we honestly—sometimes perhaps even desperately—try to satisfy a demand which we acknowledge as absolute shall we know that if we fail we did not give in too readily. There are, after all, numerous examples of the victory of conscience in apparently hopeless situations.

Conscience may also err; it is not infallible; and yet it provides us, at one point at least, with definite certainty: if I (even erroneously) recognize something as evil and want to do it, my will is evil, and it is good if I (even erroneously) want to do what I believe to be good. This aspect of conscience, however, can be extremely dangerous, because my errors may be grave; so-called 'men of good will' have unleashed wars and given in to hatred and racial prejudice. Thus the relative element, the possibility of error, points once more to the need for a constant reference to the absolute which is needed to make sure that the good will is truly good. As always, meeting something which is beyond doubt

---

* The fact that there is always something transcending us has been elaborated convincingly by K. Jaspers. Cf. *Der philosophische Glaube* (Muenchen, 1948), ch. 1, or *Philosophie*, 3rd edition (Berlin, 1956), esp. vol. 3.

absolute represents a challenge to find the right response to it, and to make it conscious is particularly urgent when the response can be so utterly wrong.

This also shows that I may find out later that I made an error in good faith, but this will hardly relieve my bad conscience; good conscience, once more less definitive, may be shaken by it. I can judge differently at different times; conscience can and has to develop, despite the constancy of basic morality; but the development must take place within the limits of this basic morality. Unless conscience is directed by the impact of the absolute, it will not develop, but deteriorate. It is in some respects relative, but this does not hinder it from relating us to the absolute.

Conscience arises because man is good and evil, and thus it also throws light on the problem of evil. This has proved the most intractable problem throughout the ages, and ethics alone cannot possibly solve it. But, though we do not pretend to offer anything like a solution, conscience can help us to see some aspects of evil in perspective. (The problem of evil must be distinguished from that of the existence of pain. The latter we do not include, because it can be dealt with only in a metaphysical or religious context.)

The cause of a bad conscience is that we have either done or intended wrong, or fear that we may be able to do it. Thus, however, bad conscience is evidence of a victory of the good; we know that we ought to do or intend to do the good, and with this knowledge we reach a moral state which is higher than that before our conscience was bad. To the psychologist a bad conscience may appear pathological and this may be true in some cases, yet from the moral point of view it is, in most cases, a sign of mental health, a first step on the way to conquering evil, because this poignant awareness of it can only have been made possible by an awakening of the good. A bad conscience may still remain ineffective, but it will hardly allow us to be complacent or to feel satisfied with its ineffectiveness. The contrast between a good and a bad conscience, moreover, shows even more clearly that the good transcends evil. A bad conscience, as we have said, pronounces a definitive judgment; thus evil can in particular instances be circumscribed and fully grasped; but the good can never be so restricted; as soon as we think that we have a complete hold on it, we have already distorted it. When we are able to erect definitive limits, we exclude any further development and are in control of the situation and we can do this with regard to single appearances of evil within us, but we are never able to put the good at our disposal in this way. Since we must not believe that we are good because we have a good conscience, the good always transcends all the limitations which we could draw. We experience the duty to be conscientious and thus face ever greater demands.

All this does not amount to an explanation of why there is evil nor why it constantly reappears within us; it does not even lessen the feeling of dread which arises when we are faced with it within ourselves or others, nor the terror caused by our realization of the power of evil in the world and our helplessness when confronted with it. But it shows that the good as such transcends evil and enables us to transcend it, too, the more so as conscience, when it speaks, remains independent of our will and can overrule it. We have said that conscience can be disregarded, circumvented or even killed, but the complete lack of it seems rare and can never be asserted with full confidence, for we do not know what the apparently amoral person really feels. In general, therefore, we may assume that conscience will make itself felt, and once it is allowed to speak, it cannot be silenced by our will again, nor can we force it to tell us what we should like to hear. Conscience, as Farmer has said, raises an 'inescapable claim'; it pays attention to our freedom by establishing, not a compulsion by a definite order which we cannot but obey, but a claim which leaves us free to accept or reject it; nevertheless it is inescapable because we cannot help recognizing its justification; we are unable to reject it without knowing, at the same time, that we ought to accept it.* Conscience, though a still small voice, is powerful, and what it tells us is that which is essential for us as individuals.

* See H. H. Farmer, *The Servant of the Word* (London, 1941), pp. 41–3, or *The World and God* (London, 1935), pp. 70–2. For a fuller elaboration see also P. Roubiczek, *Thinking in Opposites*, pp. 198–200.

6-2

These conclusions are supported by a further characteristic: conscience confirms that we are entitled to claim, as we have done, that the feeling of obligation which accompanies all moral demands must ultimately be based on facts, although it is logically correct to say that statements containing 'is' can have no influence on those containing 'ought'.* Conscience is a fact which connects the good and the corresponding higher values with our own being and thus makes us strive for these higher values, for any such value is desirable and therefore establishes itself as an aim for our striving. The ethical self is both part of our being and a demand.

This also confirms once more what we have said about evil: it is still involved both in our being and in the moral demand which would be unnecessary without it; its existence is the reason why conscience comes into action at all; but the demand points beyond evil, for conscience is not only terrifying, but at the same time, as we have just claimed, 'the final succour'.† This can be seen particularly clearly when we consider another fundamental element of conscience—the feeling of guilt.

The feeling of guilt, too, may seem merely pathological to many, and it may become so if it is taken out of its proper context, but it is a sign of mental health if it is properly experienced. The evidence of evil at large or the weight of an evil deed may be so overpowering that we lose all hope of ever being able to escape evil or to atone for it; yet once we ourselves really feel guilty, once we are really able to say 'I am guilty', we are beginning to find a release from this hopelessness; we know what we ought to have done and that we should atone for it. Despite the external and the internal power of evil we are shown a way either towards an appropriate action, where we can do something instead of remaining a passive victim, or at least towards an attitude which points beyond despair. Despair will not be avoided, perhaps not even lessened, but the very despair itself contains an indication of its possible counterweight. Kierkegaard

---

* See pp. 15–17 and 143–4.
† This is again a term which H. H. Farmer uses. He sees God as making us experience an 'absolute demand' and 'final succour' at the same time.

believes that, if a man is destroyed by despair, he has not experienced it deeply enough; if he had, he would have discovered, in the innermost depth of his being, an indestructible reality and an urge which could have saved him. So long as we do not discard conscience, we constantly remain aware of the fact that the good is more comprehensive than evil.

To appreciate these conclusions correctly, however, we have to remember, as we emphasized before entering into the discussion of conscience, that there are two kinds of evidence which do not meet.* The evidence that conscience is powerful does not invalidate the other kind of evidence which shows that it is terrifyingly powerless. Therefore, as no proofs in this sphere exist, the task of ethics is to strengthen the power of conscience and of everything connected with it, the ethical self, the moral law, the higher values, in the hope of making actual within us those potential facts which support morality. Ethics must appeal to us in such a way that increasing knowledge makes it increasingly difficult to disregard it. In other words, we must do what we have found necessary—confront tradition with our own conscience, in order to single out those parts of tradition which have withstood the passage of time and can be accepted as essential knowledge. Ethical teaching must attempt to communicate the challenges produced by the impact of the absolute.

So far only a limited number of examples of essential knowledge have been used. I shall attempt to add more and also to include the internal approaches to them which can make them accessible.

* See pp. 150–1.

PART II

CHAPTER VII

KANT I—HIS THEORY OF KNOWLEDGE AND OF ETHICS

1

The preceding investigation took Kant's theory of knowledge as one of its starting points.* It is the soundness of this theory which makes the ethics which he founded on it the most appropriate basis for our discussion of ethics. I shall therefore recapitulate those points of his epistemology which are most important for our argument, and then proceed to a comparison of his ethics with our own.

First, however, since in my appreciation of Kant I differ from other and more commonly held views, it may be useful to ask an obvious question: if Kant's theory of knowledge, in its essentials, can be accepted as correct and final—as I claim—why has it not been generally accepted? If some of its main conclusions are really as valid as I believe them to be, they ought to have been made the basis of all philosophy, yet this has not happened. Certainly, we shall have to raise objections as well, but our objections never question the foundations of his theories; yet there are others who reject his philosophy altogether. This seems to contradict our judgment. If it could be shown that it need not, our point of view might become more comprehensible, and this could help to make it acceptable.

A striking contradiction between Kant's own claims and the work of his immediate successors points to the answer I have in mind. Kant himself believed that he had made metaphysics impossible once for all, since he had proved conclusively that any systematic explanation of all existence which pretends to be based

---

* As has been explained on pp. 13–15, on which this chapter is based.

on direct absolute knowledge must be wrong. Yet the nineteenth century witnessed what was probably the greatest flowering of metaphysics of all time. Today all these systems may appear dated; this is especially true of those of Fichte, Schelling, Herbert Spencer and Bergson, and also of the achievements of Hegel and Schopenhauer though these, as systems, are certainly more impressive than any of an earlier date, including even those of the Greeks; moreover, Marxism, though not metaphysics in the narrower sense of the word, represents the culmination of materialism.* Nevertheless it would have been short-sighted to believe that Kant's teaching had therefore been invalidated. By now his claim has been fully vindicated; with very few exceptions, philosophers are no longer preoccupied with 'system-building'. It was merely that, for a long time, the last word had not been spoken.

Even though metaphysical systems have disappeared, however, Kant is still dismissed. Most philosophers now agree that our knowledge is insufficient to explain all reality, but they still reject the two ways of thinking, which, according to Kant, we are bound to employ, and they aim instead at a unitary way of thought. This aim is no fundamental departure from the old systems, for it admits the hope of achieving a full understanding of reality. Kant insists that it is for ever impossible to arrive at knowledge which is both complete and absolute; thinking based on pure reason can include all reality (as science does) but remains relative because it is dependent on the laws of thinking, while practical reason (which we shall discuss in this and the following chapter) reaches absoluteness, but cannot include all reality. If unitary thinking were possible, the shortcomings of our knowledge would not be final, but only due to lack of knowledge, to gaps in the knowledge so far achieved. We could assume that these gaps would be filled in the future, and even though the prospect appeared remote, we

* Metaphysics, in the narrower sense of the word, is a dealing both with this world and with the transcendental, and therefore materialism is usually not called metaphysics. This I consider to be wrong; materialism should be included because denial of the existence of the transcendental is, after all, an important statement about it.

could still trust that we were moving in the direction of a complete ultimate knowledge.

This presupposition is obvious in the attempts to make science a philosophy. We have seen that science is constantly applied where it does not apply; it encroaches upon those aspects of reality which, to be understood, require the subjective method; scientific thinking is used to make them appear explicable. Everything which points towards the transcendental is explained in a way which robs it of its particular quality, so as to enable unitary thinking to include everything, and this implies a confident belief that everything can and will be explained. Even many theologians who, after all, are bound to be concerned with the transcendental give in to this endeavour; they try to reconcile science with religion on the basis of scientific thinking, applying to both the same kind of logic; some even come very near to transforming religion into a complete metaphysical system.* We recognize now that the opposite attempt which was characteristic of the Middle Ages—to achieve unitary thinking by subordinating everything to theology—was wrong, but the successes of science appear to make the new unitary thinking more convincing although it is just as wrong. Nor is it any solution to rely on internal reality alone, as many Existentialists do; for they too openly aim at an all-embracing absolute knowledge, even though they do not try to be systematic.

The reasons which make the acceptance of the need for two ways of thinking difficult are easy to appreciate. There are—apart from the fear of dualism which has been mentioned†—two main obstacles.

On the one hand, it is difficult to think about thinking, which

---

* The number of books in which this 'bridge-building' is attempted is too great to be listed; cf. for example, E. L. Mascall, *Christian Theology and Natural Science* (London, 1956), or A. F. Smethurst, *Modern Science and Christian Beliefs* (London, 1955). Many of these theologians try to avoid metaphysics, though this would be the logical conclusion, for they approach the transcendental from outside and thus make it part of external reality. Others, for instance Teilhard de Chardin, are less cautious.

† See pp. 105–9.

is an activity designed to turn outside to achieve results, and not to turn in upon itself. This difficulty can already be seen in the case of introspection which is needed in psychology and in order to grasp internal reality; it requires discipline if it is to be fruitful; otherwise it lends itself to the production of mere fantasies or to brooding. But even to make one's own inner experiences into the kind of object which thinking demands is easier than to face thinking itself. The latter activity does not appear to provide us with any object whatever; when thinking tries to concentrate upon itself, all its functions seem to be removed, for normally it is brought into action by concentration on something outside itself. For a similar reason many Existentialists fear to confront consciousness directly because, as it is always consciousness of something, the attempt to grasp consciousness as such leads to nothingness. Therefore it is only natural that most people should be reluctant either to embark on an investigation of thinking or to accept its findings.

This reluctance may explain why epistemology has not exercised more influence, which would otherwise seem surprising, since it is that part of philosophy which has, as time is gradually revealing, achieved the most reliable and lasting results. Yet the philosopher must obviously understand the laws of thinking; otherwise he will be led astray, as the fate of all metaphysical systems proves; epistemology must ensure that presuppositions—the conditions of thought—are not mistaken for results. Therefore this difficulty has to be overcome, and Aristotle, Locke, Hume, Kant—among others—show that it can be done and that it is of the utmost importance to do it. We also hope that our investigation has shown by now that the attempt is rewarding.

On the other hand, man wants to know; he wants to acquire a knowledge which is both complete and ultimate. He experiences what has been called the 'metaphysical urge'—the desire to understand all reality absolutely. This urge led to the creation of metaphysical systems during those periods when religion was no longer accepted as a satisfactory explanation: in Greece when belief in the gods vanished; at the end of the Middle Ages; during the Age of Reason; and in the nineteenth century. This urge may have become much weaker now; we rather trust the scientist to find a satisfactory solution of all problems. Such a trust, however, shows itself to be a survival of the metaphysical urge, in that science is thus accepted as a complete philosophy; this in turn leads to the demand for unitary thinking, because otherwise science could not solve all problems. The urge has only changed its form. Therefore, acceptance of the need for two ways of thinking demands a painful renunciation—the acceptance of the limitations of knowledge and of the impossibility of ever achieving knowledge which is both complete and ultimate. We can once more understand why Kant's theory of knowledge does not find ready acceptance.

But does this not contradict what we have said about our age—about there being a tacit agreement to exclude everything which could be accepted as an absolute and to admit only what can be seen as relative? It does not, for we have also shown that relativity itself is then bound to replace the absolute and to become an absolute creed.* In fact, the findings of science are usually accepted at their face value, without doubts or reservations, so that a complete knowledge of all conditions and relations (even if they are, by definition, relative) would also represent a kind of ultimate knowledge. The emphasis on unitary thinking supports the belief that, despite the relativity concerning details and the incompleteness of our knowledge, science is on the way towards this kind of absoluteness. It is thus that the metaphysical urge now seeks satisfaction in unitary thinking.

The renunciation of absolute knowledge points towards the need for faith, which will be discussed in the last chapter. Kant was aware of this, for he said: 'I have therefore found it necessary to deny knowledge (i.e. absolute external knowledge), in order to make room for faith.'† So far as ethics is concerned, we can restrict ourselves to the recognition of essential knowledge. But this makes the painfulness of the necessary renunciation even

* See p. 85.
† *Critique of Pure Reason* (transl. by N. Kemp Smith; London, 1933), p. 29.

clearer perhaps: we have seen that the two ways of thinking, which throw into relief the existence of essential knowledge, are incompatible, and that essential knowledge also does not solve problems; it is an additional knowledge.* We have to remain content with answers which are only partial and which relieve us neither of doubts nor of the feeling of dread when confronted with the terrifying problems of existence. From whichever viewpoint we approach the theory of knowledge, we can understand that it is not easily accepted. By comparison, the uncritical acceptance of unitary thinking appears comfortable and comforting because, since we can safely rely on the constant extension of knowledge, we are not confronted with a final 'unfathomable depth', but only with soluble problems.

All these factors probably explain why Kant has been subjected to so much criticism. There are three main kinds of such criticisms which we must consider.

1. Some critics concentrate so much on criticism of the details of his teaching that they are prevented from appreciating its basic elements.† There is no doubt that such criticism is partly justified, in so far, for instance, as it concerns his predilection for symmetry; he likes his investigation to result in twelve concepts or pairs of concepts and to arrange them in four groups of three, and this occasionally requires some distortions. In such an enormous work as his—and in some respects it is the first of its kind—contradictions and weaknesses are bound to occur; rather is it astonishing how rarely they do. Much of this kind of criticism can actually be refuted. In any case, it is wrong to start from such marginal elements; what matters is Kant's fundamental insight which is disregarded in most of these attacks. Such critics usually rely entirely on logic which, though undoubtedly important, should be a subordinate part of philosophy and not dominate it. These critics, consciously or unconsciously, want to avoid taking any theory of knowledge seriously.

* See pp. 127–8.
† Cf., for example, the chapter on Kant in Bertrand Russell's *History of Western Philosophy*, which is characteristic for this whole school of thought.

2. The most important kind of criticism is based on the assertion that Kant's theory of knowledge applies only to the knowledge achieved at his time, mainly to Newtonian physics, and that the subsequent development of science has proved him wrong. Kant, so the critics claim, insists that we can only think in the way he describes; but ways of thinking have been developed, especially in nuclear physics, which are entirely different, undreamt of at the time of Newton. Therefore Kant's teaching is largely dated or perhaps even entirely invalidated.

So far as this criticism is based on the general aversion to the theory of knowledge, it can easily be disproved. Kant does not restrict thought, but stimulates it. He never doubts that thinking only elucidates a small part of reality and that his theory is bound to leave gaps. He himself tries to fill some of these by adding to his first two critiques—the *Critique of Pure Reason* and the *Critique of Practical Reason*, which seemed to contain his whole theory— the *Critique of Judgment*, in which he extends the scope of pure reason. This third critique should have made the critics more cautious, but they usually disregard it. The criticisms referred to, not being concerned with practical reason (that is, with ethics), are based on the *Critique of Pure Reason* alone; but had the latter been complete, the need would not have arisen to extend the investigation into other fields. For Kant, there are constantly further tasks ahead because, since he is mainly concerned with the limited scope of knowledge and the restricted validity of thinking, he always leaves room for experience.

What this means can be seen, for instance, in his refutation of the old proofs of the existence of God. In these, thinking and logic are made the test of existence; because we can think, say, of perfection, it follows logically that a perfect being must exist, because thinking cannot but reveal existence; or, since our thought makes us assume that there was, at the beginning, a first cause, such a cause must exist and must logically be God, for the first cause is independent of any further causation, while all others are produced by preceding causes. Kant recognizes that it is impossible to prove the existence of anything in this way. On the one hand, we have ideas, even very convincing ones, which need not actually correspond to anything real, such as the religious and the scientific ideas concerning the origin of the universe; on the other hand, we have reality which exists even though we cannot prove that it must exist nor that it must be as it is. In this respect, reality is 'that which need not be but is'.* Existence can only be grasped by experience, and experience is always expanding. Kant is nearer to Existentialism than many Existentialists realize, for he makes allowance for further developments.

At one point, however, any further development seems to have been blocked: in the realm of the laws of thinking. Kant establishes categories—that is, concepts such as *cause and effect* or *the one and the many*—which have to be applied to make clear thinking possible, and he believes that he has disclosed all categories. This the critics deny; but it can be seen that this criticism, too, is unjustified, for these categories have withstood the test of time as the really fundamental ones. At the same time they do not hinder the development of thought; they can be discerned even in modern science, and it is useful to realize their contribution to it. Both the derivation and the application of the categories show that these essentials of Kant's theory should be accepted.

Kant comes to be concerned with the categories because he asks how it is that we can ever say 'must' in the sphere of knowledge. We have to rely on experience, but our experience is limited; the claim that something must be as it is or happen as it does presupposes a complete knowledge which we do not possess. Only if we knew all relevant cases could we say that no exception will ever occur and so speak of necessity, but such a foundation for necessity is impossible. Are we therefore forced to renounce it?

Two different answers are possible. Hume and his followers reject necessity altogether; he says that all statements containing 'must' (such as that a cause must necessarily produce a predictable effect) are merely based on custom and habit, and that therefore the acceptance of a strict causality is only due to laziness of mind. He believes that all knowledge springs from our perception of

* R. Guardini, *Die Lebensalter*, p. 34.

reality, and his argument runs: perception does not disclose necessity; causality is derived from perception; therefore causality
cannot have necessity. Kant, on the other hand, accepts necessity.
He agrees that perception has no necessity, but insists that causality
has; and therefore draws the conclusion that causality is not based
on perception. He believes that 'although all our knowledge
begins with experience, it does not therefore all spring from
experience'.* Knowledge has two sources—perception and the
laws of thinking—and necessity is based on the latter which is the
contribution of our mind. We can say 'must' only because the
laws of thinking apply and only so far as they apply. Thus he feels
entitled to embark on the investigation of what categories exist;
they can be discerned because they alone establish necessity.

This is confirmed by another line of Kant's argument. He calls
the categories 'concepts *a priori*' because they are not derived
from experience, but precede it, which shows that they are
contributed by our minds. Necessity is one of these concepts
and indeed the basic one. We are able to distinguish them just
because they are not arbitrarily produced by our own volition
nor are we able to alter them; they are the given necessary laws
of thinking.

In this derivation of the categories Kant shows himself once
more the supreme realist. We have said before that life would be
unmanageable if, for instance, we could not be sure that our table
would obey the laws of gravity and would not suddenly jump
into the air.† We are bound to rely on strict causality and thus on
necessity in vast areas of our life, and we are obviously able and
entitled to do so. If we want to understand our thinking, necessity
has to be accepted and accounted for. Otherwise we shall not
understand how our thinking actually works.

But has not modern physics left necessity behind? We have
mentioned that in some fields causality is no longer regarded as a
meaningful term. Yet even here the application of Kant's categories—and their essential task—can be recognized. To quote

---

* *Critique of Pure Reason*, p. 41. See also quotations on p. 13.
  † For this and the following see pp. 77–8.

Heisenberg again, this time at greater length: 'The applicability of these forms of perception* and of the law of causality is the premise of any scientific experience even in modern physics. For we can only communicate the course and result of a measurement by describing the necessary manual actions and instrument readings as objective, and as events taking place in the space and time of our perception. Neither could we infer the properties of the observed object from the results of measurements if the law of causality did not guarantee an unambiguous connection between the two.'†

This statement has two implications. On the one hand, as Heisenberg constantly emphasizes, the influence of modern physics (and other sciences) on the working of ordinary thinking should not be overrated. Experience has been enormously enlarged, new facts and possibilities have become known, but the actual working of the mind, outside the extreme abstractions of physics, has not been changed. We hear of a space–time-continuum, but this has not altered the concepts of space and time which we are bound to employ. Modern science has moved into a sphere of greater and greater abstractions, so that now some of its findings can only be expressed by mathematical formulae and can no longer be translated into ordinary speech; they cannot, therefore, influence the basic processes underlying thought. Man's outlook—his *Weltanschauung*—may have been changed, as it was by Copernicus and Galileo, but this does not involve the laws of thinking.

On the other hand, the extreme abstractions are only possible because basically the categories still apply. There is the firm framework to which Heisenberg refers; abstractions, even the most extreme ones, must start from a reality which has been grasped with the help of categories and return to it in the experiments;

---

* Of space and time. These will be discussed later in this chapter; Kant does not call them categories, but forms of perception. Their task however is the same as that of categories: to make thinking and knowledge possible. They can therefore be included in this discussion.

† *Philosophic Problems of Nuclear Science*, p. 20. (The translator has retained the German words 'Anschauungsformen' and 'Anschauung'.)

only because of this framework can abstraction proceed further and further. In the end, indeed, some categories, such as causality and necessity, are omitted, but never all of them because, in the last resort, mathematics is still based on the category of *the one and the many*. It may be that Kant did not foresee the omission of categories, but his theory is not thereby invalidated, for we can never dispense with the categories altogether; the omission of some merely restricts the sphere of knowledge where we can say 'must' and introduces, as Kant makes us expect, an element of uncertainty. In all calculations concerning these extreme abstractions Heisenberg's 'uncertainty principle' has to be taken into account.

This principle shows clearly what actually happens. It states that, in the region of the infinitesimally small, the knowledge of objects or events is no longer complete, because observation exercises an influence on what is observed; the influence of the observer (otherwise excluded in physics) must therefore be allowed for—that is, an unavoidable subjective element produces a gap in objective knowledge. The methods of observation enable us only to know exactly either the place a particle occupies or its speed; the observer has to concentrate on one only of the two to achieve knowledge at all; it is impossible to measure exactly both place and speed at the same time. Thus the particle remains, to some extent, undefined, and causality and necessity can no longer be fully established. Nevertheless, as the quotation from Heisenberg emphasizes, physics has to use the objective method, with all its elements if it is possible, but leaving out some if it is necessary, and its working is not impaired. Knowledge of external reality is immensely enlarged, even though it becomes less exact wherever a category has to be omitted. Moreover, the extent of the uncertainty itself should not be exaggerated. There is no need to turn to the subjective method for help in filling these gaps; even if it were possible, it would be unnecessary, for this uncertainty must not be equated with uncertainty in human affairs. The principle is embodied in a mathematical formula which keeps uncertainty within very narrow limits and which can be used like any other equation. In fact, causality and necessity are so effectively replaced by it that the fundamental characteristic of the objective method—its aiming at necessity—can be preserved. It is true that, since causality is abandoned, the scientist can only aim at a high degree of probability, but he must nevertheless try to make his formulae as reliable and the events as predictable as he possibly can—that is, he must approach necessity. Otherwise the technical application of, say, atomic energy would not be possible. The fundamental laws of thinking are not changed.

If one is not overwhelmed by the details of Kant's theory, but remains aware of its basic claims, the development of modern science provides, in fact, a striking confirmation of it. Modern physics, which shows most clearly the direction in which all sciences move, has led to the realization that the belief, still prevalent at the beginning of this century, that physics provides us with a direct and thus absolute knowledge, can no longer be upheld; that, on the contrary, all physical knowledge is 'suspended over an unfathomable depth'.* There are indications that, underlying the reality with which physics deals, there exists a primary reality; particular data such as the basic quantum of energy can be extracted from it, but they do not lead to understanding; the thing *per se* must be presupposed, it cannot be grasped. In modern physics, much is accessible, but not its foundation; the laws of thinking enable us, as Kant says, to deal with external reality effectively, yet they cut us off from absolute knowledge. 'Indeed, if we look more closely and examine the edifice of exact science more thoroughly, we very soon recognize that this edifice has a dangerously weak point, and this point is its foundation. The edifice lacks a basis which could be made safe in all directions against being shaken from outside or, in other words, there exists, within exact science, no principle which has both general validity and a sufficiently significant content as to serve as an adequate foundation.'†

* As Heisenberg says. See p. 99.
† M. Planck, *Sinn und Grenzen der exakten Wissenschaft*, 2nd ed. (Leipzig, 1947), p. 4.

3. The basic structure of Kant's theory of knowledge shows that it could be a help in theology. Kant wanted to make room for faith,* and as he proves that absolute metaphysical knowledge must remain unattainable, he actually does make room for faith by showing that it has its own sphere and task. Both metaphysics and unitary thinking can thus be prevented from usurping the task of faith and from invading and distorting its realm.

Yet many theologians reject Kant violently because they base their views mainly on his work *Religion within the Limits of Mere Reason*. Kant wrote this book when his powers were declining; it represents, to a large extent, a return to the ideas of his youth—a phenomenon not rare in old age—and it is dominated by the philosophy of the Age of Reason which he had outgrown, or even destroyed, in his main works, and to such effect that his contemporaries, who held the older views, called him 'the all-crushing'. This theological criticism, even if correct when applied to the work on religion alone, is therefore also misapplied; one cannot base the rejection of Kant on the consideration of a single minor work alone. His distinction between knowledge (meaning knowledge achieved by the conscious effort of thinking) and faith has remained valid, too. We shall return to it, as we have said, in the last chapter.

Thus we can now answer the question raised at the beginning of this chapter—whether our claim that Kant's teaching is of the utmost importance is contradicted by the fact that it has not been generally accepted. All the criticisms levelled against it are open to doubt; therefore the frequent rejection does not, by itself, disprove the validity of his teaching. The last word has not yet been spoken.

2

The categories of Kant which we have discussed so far are *the one and the many*, *cause and effect*, and *necessity*; and we have tried to show that they are still valid. The same could be done for

* See p. 173.

others, especially if we were to disregard their symmetrical arrangement.*

Let us give one more example which shows particularly clearly why it was essential to establish categories at all—the category *substantia et accidens*. The sense of this is that, to grasp an object, we must oppose to its essential characteristics the accidental qualities it possesses; we must recognize what it is (a table) and what distinguishes the particular object with which we are confronted from others of its kind (its size, weight, colour, etc.). Obviously, we are bound to think in this way. Today, this category may appear less important than some others; it often happens that, according to the preoccupations of different ages, different single categories are considered to be the essential ones. We shall see a similar shift in emphasis when discussing space and time. But in the case of the concept 'substance' this has happened because it removed, once for all, a great hindrance to the development of thought; it settled the old, unsolved problem of whether or not everything which exists is part of a unitary substance, and if so, what this substance is. For Kant shows that, since we are applying a category, such metaphysical questions are out of place; the concept cannot and must not be used, as it had been, to prove the existence of God or to explain the fundamental nature of reality. Thus this category elucidates the importance of all categories: it confirms that the thing *per se* cannot be grasped and that, unless this is realized, one is always in danger of mistaking conditions of thought for facts and of asking unanswerable questions which lead thinking astray. At the same time, it also shows how great Kant's influence has in fact been, in spite of the reservations to which we have referred; from the Middle Ages up to his own time this

* We have mentioned Kant's predilection for symmetry (p. 174). His table of categories is arranged in four groups; two consist of three single concepts and two of three pairs of opposites. (See *Critique of Pure Reason*, p. 113.) To understand the categories properly, it is advisable either to reduce the groups of three concepts to pairs of opposites (as we have done with the one and the many) or to concentrate on the opposites (such as cause and effect) which he enumerates within these groups. Necessity we have isolated, but it occurs in opposition to contingency, which leads to the opposition of necessity and freedom. This will be discussed later.

problem had played a prominent part in philosophy, but it has never been raised since.

As it is not our task, however, to explain Kant's theory of knowledge, but to explain its relevance to ethics, we shall assume that our discussion has by now justified our acceptance of Kant's basic teaching, and that the categories, being valid, support our description of external reality. Since categories have to be applied, they confirm that the knowledge due to them, though sufficient for all practical and scientific purposes, must remain relative because of its dependence on the laws of thinking. Kant's exploration of the working of pure reason elucidates what we have said about the working of the objective method.

This can also be seen in his approach to space and time, which we have only briefly mentioned so far and which he does not include among the categories, but deals with separately as forms of perception. In some respects, these concepts are similar to the categories; their task also is to make thinking possible, and although they are abstract, they cannot be derived from reality by the process of abstraction because, as we have said, they are present at all the stages of abstraction and are contributed by the working of our minds.* Therefore, space and time are, like the categories, concepts *a priori*; they are not derived from experience, but precede it. Yet they are different from the categories because they serve, not to connect thoughts (connecting, say, phases of an event by seeing them as cause and effect), but perception; they are the forms which make it possible. Previously perception had always been taken to be a direct experience of reality; Kant shows that it becomes possible because we place everything within space and time, so that it too is also based on laws of thinking. Only because we apply these forms to everything we perceive are we able to perceive at all. Thus space and time refer more directly to experience, and it will be a help to discuss them as well.

This contribution of the mind is probably more difficult to accept than the categories, and Kant takes great pains to make his claim convincing. He tries to prove it in several ways. There is, he

* See p. 116.

says, no experience of external reality without them; this reality must be perceived with their help; therefore, as we can say 'must', they are contributed by the mind and precede all experience. This is supported by another fact. Of objects we can think that they exist or do not exist, but we can never think that there is no space and no time, and while we can grasp external reality only so far as we grasp objects or events—that is, only so far as something exists or happens—we can think of space without objects and of time without events. Thus, while all other concepts denote certain things or events (even categories have to be applied to something to become meaningful; cause and effect, for instance, must become a particular cause producing a definite effect), space and time include all objects and events. Moreover, space and time imply the concepts of infinity and eternity; they cannot be separated from them in any way; but infinity and eternity are not given in experience.

Particularly important is Kant's reference to mathematics whose working, though usually taken for granted, is really an astonishing phenomenon. It only starts from reality, thereafter it is developed solely according to its own logic, a pure work of the mind, never checked by observation or experiments, and yet it proves the greatest help to the better grasping of reality. 'As mathematics withdrew increasingly into the upper regions of the mind of ever greater extremes of abstract thought, it returned back to earth with a corresponding growth of importance for the analysis of concrete fact.'* It is the most important tool of modern science. However, if space and time are contributed by our minds and form the basis of perception, then it becomes understandable that this pure work of the mind, elaborating its own contribution, should enable us to understand external reality better. Geometry, according to Kant, is the elaboration of space, arithmetic that of time; they provide the necessity which is absent in experience, and necessity, as we have seen, represents the perfection of the objective method.

Yet all these proofs, though convincing in themselves, have

* A. N. Whitehead, *Science and the Modern World* (Cambridge, 1947), p. 41.

failed to make the impact one might have expected. We shall therefore try to justify Kant's theory from a different point of view.

Undoubtedly the difficulties in accepting space and time as belonging to thinking are particularly great. We ourselves are bodies moving in space, so that size and distance are immediately real for us, and we live through days and years, growing older, so that history, too, is related to our direct experience. Of course, Kant's claim does not mean that space and time are mere illusions; they enable us to grasp reality and thus become part of our experience of reality; but it is still difficult to accept that they prevent any ultimate knowledge, that they do not belong to reality as it is in itself. How could anything be known with greater certainty than our bodily existence and the ageing which leads to death? We have mentioned that the knowledge that we and the world exist is absolutely certain,* and it is hard to imagine that space and time are not included in this knowledge. But it can be seen that our thinking—and even our lives—are impoverished and distorted if space and time are accepted as absolutely real.

In the Middle Ages, it was space (rather than time) which was identified with the absolute, and this led to the belief that this earth, because Christ had appeared on it, must be the centre of the universe. External reality was identified with the spiritual. So long as this belief was upheld, physics could not develop, and when physics did begin to develop, the belief led to that fateful struggle of the Church against science from which we have still not completely recovered because, the Church having now been defeated in this respect, we are strongly tempted to make science a substitute for religion. Just as too much was once claimed for religion, so we now claim too much for science. This false claim made for science has led, as regards space, to another distortion; infinity, a concept which is not given by experience and must therefore transcend it to become meaningful, is reduced to mere endlessness or vastness of space. Our lives are robbed of a dimension. To this we shall return.

* See p. 86.

Nevertheless, it has become easier than it was before to accept space as a form of perception, because physics has led to a questioning of the traditional idea of space. Unimaginable contradictions (that space is both infinite and limited) and unimaginable dimensions (making time a fourth dimension and creating a number of others) have been introduced, and even though these assertions, being unimaginable, have not influenced our thinking as such, they have made it thinkable that space is not absolute. But time has taken its place.

The focusing of attention on time has been, in our civilization, a comparatively late development. Up to the time of Plato Greece had no clocks; only then were even the sundial and the water-clock introduced; the consciousness of time plays hardly any part in antiquity. It comes into the foreground during the Middle Ages, when mechanical clocks announced every hour or even every quarter of an hour, but they were meant to remind man of death and had not yet much influence on his daily life. To a certain extent, the consciousness of time receded again in the Age of Reason, for the thinkers of this age aimed at timeless, at permanent results. Yet now we are obsessed by time, living by the clock, aiming at greater and greater speed and at saving time: time has become our absolute master. But something similar has happened as happened with space; time, taken to be absolute, confronts us with an entirely meaningless endlessness of time which replaces the concept of eternity.

The same danger, though in a different way, has also been revealed in philosophy—by those Existentialists who, like Heidegger and Sartre, base existence on the absoluteness of time. They are not concerned with its endlessness, but with the inner experience which this characteristic of our age produces; they see time as absolute because its course cannot be reversed, because everything which ever happened in time has become an historical event which can be neither denied nor undone. This is undoubtedly an important aspect of time and one which should be taken into account; but if it is accepted as ultimate knowledge, death becomes the absolute end of time for us; there can be no question of anything beyond. Accordingly, they have been driven to over-emphasize dread and despair and to neglect or undermine positive experiences; they have been fascinated by nothingness (which death thus seems to reveal) and made it the core of existence, and when some of them could not help trying to do justice to religious experiences, their attempts were forced. Heidegger has even returned to a kind of metaphysics, to 'fundamental ontology', which is just as dubious as the old metaphysical systems.* Their nihilism has remained more convincing than their attempts to overcome it, and this again reflects a rather common characteristic of our age. Once more our lives are robbed of the transcendental dimension.

All this illustrates that, though it requires a great effort to accept this part of Kant's theory of knowledge, the effort ought to be made. We have said that we are absolutely certain that we and the world exist and that this represents a challenge, because we also want to understand. This challenge is ultimately met by the impact of the absolute, but the experience of it requires the realization that space and time are contributions of our minds, for otherwise no room is left for any different kind of reality. If infinity and eternity are robbed of their meaning, we remain confined either to external reality or, in the case of Existentialism, to an internal reality which denies itself any way of approaching the absolute; consequently, if there is nothing else that matters, one of the two realities has to replace the absolute, and this we have found to be utterly wrong. We have to leave room for something beyond, and this means room beyond the space and time we know.

Of course, many people would object to this line of argument and insist that it is infinity and eternity which should be dismissed. They believe that these concepts cannot possibly signify anything but the vastness or endlessness of space and time, and that their transcendental meaning is nothing but a remnant of obsolete ideas which ought to be discarded. Yet this is contradicted by our experience. It is true that we cannot know infinity and eternity as

* For a fuller treatment see P. Roubiczek, *Existentialism—For and Against*, ch. VII.

such, but there are experiences which only make sense if we admit their existence.

The vastness of space is a challenge; man wants to be able to face its overwhelming impact and is therefore fascinated either by the old ideal of great conquests of land or by the new conquest of outer space. Speed, too, seems to enable man to become superior to space. But all these strivings, being merely concerned with the external aspect of space, do not finally satisfy him; they do not change the fact, to use Kant's words,* that 'the starry heavens above' consist of 'worlds upon worlds and systems of systems' and that this 'view of a countless multitude of worlds annihilates as it were my importance as an animal creature, which after it has been for a short time provided with vital power, one knows not how, must again give back the matter of which it was formed to the planet it inhabits (a mere speck in the universe)'. Thus, however, my stature as a human being cannot be safeguarded by subjugating some more space. It is only when I discover within myself an order of another kind which gives to the individual an absolute value, namely 'the moral law within' (or a similar absolute) that I am able to withstand the challenge of space, for the moral law 'exhibits me in a world which has true infinity' and thus shows that external space cannot be all-inclusive. 'The moral law reveals to me a life independent of animality and even of the whole sensible world.' In the sensible world everything is limited; even the vastness of space was realized only through the discovery of 'a countless multitude of worlds'—namely of limited celestial bodies; but the absolute, whenever we touch it, must reveal 'true infinity', not only because it transcends all we can possibly know, but also because we experience a reality of a different kind, which cannot be limited because this would destroy its very nature. Therefore my feeling of being crushed by the impact of that space which is the basis of perception can only be overcome by the impact of the absolute. We must attempt to overcome quantity by quality.

The endlessness of time, which Kant also mentions in this

---

* *Critique of Practical Reason* (transl. by T. K. Abbott; London, 1889), p. 260.

context, represents a similar challenge, for it seems impossible to ascribe importance to our own short lives when we compare them with 'the stellar systems, the limitless times of their periodic motion, its beginning and continuance'. The endlessness of time is experienced as its unceasing passage, and this constant slipping away of time makes its challenge felt within our lives, for time wasted is time lost and lost time cannot be regained. The course of time, as we have just said, cannot be reversed and is bound to lead to death. Therefore we feel the urge to make use of time by constant work, by attempts to experience or enjoy as much as possible, and again by speed. We feel that time should not be allowed to pass unused; if we are unable to use it properly, we try to kill it, to evade its threat. But all this, too, is of no avail; a human life, however active, rich or long seems insignificant when compared with the millions and millions of years preceding and following it; time's endlessness engulfs it. We can meet the challenge only if we arrive at permanent, absolute values which are valid once for all and thus not subject to time; the absolute alone, because it remains constant, has that 'true eternity' which can support us. In this respect, too, quantity must be overcome by quality.*

We may be inclined today to feel superior when we think of the mediaeval idea of the universe—a small, limited material realm safely embedded in the sphere of infinity and eternity; but it is a profound misunderstanding to deride it as a 'tight little cabbage-patch world'.† The astronomical picture was wrong, but the meaning of existence was safeguarded by true infinity and true eternity. The deadening influence of transferring infinity and eternity to the material universe where they become transformed into mere endlessness was foreseen by Pascal—the only thinker of the Age of Reason who was not enthusiastic about its new astronomy—for he realized that in consequence all existence, including human life, would be robbed of its significance. It is

---

* For a fuller elaboration of the different aspects of space and time see P. Roubiczek, *Thinking in Opposites*, ch. XI.
† F. Hoyle, *The Nature of the Universe*, p. 1.

true that the mediaeval idea also had its dangers; we have mentioned that the acceptance of space as absolute had disastrous effects; actually modern astronomy could help us to free the spiritual world of its misleading spatial framework and to understand such terms as 'above' and 'below' in a purely metaphorical sense. Yet this could only be achieved if we did not repudiate true infinity and true eternity—that is, if we recognized that space and time as we know them are forms of perception. We must leave room for our actual inner experiences, so that the impact of the absolute can make itself felt and be known.

Thus, however, even so far as it refers to external reality, Kant's theory of knowledge is important for ethics because it makes room for it. Any ethical teaching has to be based on a clear awareness of the scope of knowledge and therefore of the laws of thinking, and no ethics will be able to fulfil its task satisfactorily unless the nature of space and time is taken into account. In addition, Kant also clarifies the relationship of external and internal reality with regard to ethics.

We have said that a proper place for ethics has to be found within the general framework of philosophy, and that this can be achieved by accepting the two ways of thinking, because they include ethics in a way which allows for its necessary autonomy. But we have emphasized that ethical knowledge cannot simply be derived from, and identified with, internal reality—that it is based on essential knowledge which originates from the impact of the absolute. Ethics is therefore based on a transcendental reality which remains outside external and internal reality, although internal reality can open approaches to it. This 'outside', however, seemed so far to have no relationship to external reality, and if external reality were to remain isolated, the framework of philosophy would still be incomplete. But now the categories and forms of perception have disclosed that the apprehension of external reality itself makes it necessary that something outside it should be taken into account and left intact; this reality does not open the way to the absolute, but nevertheless provides confirmation of the need for an approach by another way of thinking.

Primary reality, though not directly accessible to knowledge, makes itself felt in both its knowable aspects. We have mentioned before that there are several consequences of the application of the objective method which show the need for the subjective method; these indications have been vindicated.*

At the same time, a possible misunderstanding is prevented: 'outside', from the internal point of view, could simply mean external. Ethics in general, like fundamental morality and conscience, presupposes that man is able to face himself, to recognize himself for what he is; he must see himself from a point of view outside himself. It was for this reason that we insisted that ethics cannot be based on internal reality alone, for there man may still remain confined within himself. This, however, could be misunderstood as merely demanding that we should be objective and use the objective method, but this method cannot satisfy the need of ethics either, because external reality excludes inner—and thus ethical—experiences. Yet this misunderstanding does occur, and it is therefore important, for this reason too, that external reality itself shows that the required 'outside' must transcend it.

The true merit of Kant is, however, that he does not remain content with revealing the negative limitation of external knowledge by investigating pure reason, but also explores the positive consequence of this restriction—namely the other way of thinking. He calls this kind of reason 'practical reason' because it determines action; this, in our terminology, means the grasping of internal reality by the subjective method. It is thus that he includes ethics.

3

Kant is concerned with the laws of thinking, with the question of how it becomes possible to say 'must' in the sphere of knowledge. This leads him to the realization that two ways of thinking exist, for there are statements containing 'must' which are entirely different from those concerning external reality—the statements

* See pp. 83–6.

based on the moral law. These have to be accounted for as well. Kant is once more the supreme realist: he does not question the absoluteness of morality, but starts from the fact that we experience it as absolute. He tries to find out how it is that this absoluteness is rooted in our thinking and how it is established. He investigates the contribution of reason in the realm of ethics.

Since we have discussed the impact of the absolute, we need not discuss this starting point of Kant, the more so as he himself does not try to prove it, but makes it convincing by showing the conclusions to which it leads. It will therefore suffice to sketch briefly his general attitude.

Again he is not concerned with psychology, with individual processes of thought, but with the scope of knowledge, with the foundations of thinking and its relation to the thing *per se*. The relation here is different from that in external reality because we are embodiments of the absolute; if the absolute exists, we must partake in it. This does not mean that we are enabled to know ourselves wholly in a direct way; even to grasp what characterizes us as individual beings we still have to employ pure reason which makes direct knowledge impossible. But we hear within us the 'still small voice' of the absolute and can thus know what it demands. In the words which we have used before: we are unable to answer the question 'Why?' in any fundamental context, even with regard to our own existence, but we do know absolutely that we ought to do the good.*

The obligation implied in this 'ought', however, has also a special content; we experience it as a definitive particular demand, and it is this demand which Kant tries to formulate. He calls it a 'categorical imperative'. It is categorical, because it is unconditional, not dependent on any further purpose; if we said, for instance, that we ought to do good in order to achieve happiness, we would, as we have seen, be committing the naturalistic fallacy. And it is an imperative because it does not refer to something which exists, but to future actions which are required. By emphasizing this difference so strongly Kant wants to show that

---

* See p. 14.

pure reason and practical reason (that is, statements containing 'is' and those containing 'ought') can exist side by side in complete independence of each other, even though the former leads to relative and the latter to absolute knowledge. With this complete separation we have disagreed, but for the time being we can disregard it, for we first want to discuss Kant's ethics by itself, and it is certainly true that the moral law is experienced as an imperative.

But is there really any need to formulate this imperative if it is a common experience; would not such a need contradict its absoluteness? Kant himself raises this question; if, he says, 'men are well able to distinguish in every case that occurs, what is good, what bad, conformable to duty or inconsistent with it, if, without in the least teaching them anything new, we only, like Socrates, direct their attention to the principle they themselves employ', it may seem that 'we do not need science and philosophy to know what we should do to be honest and good, even wise and virtuous.' But he answers convincingly: 'Innocence is indeed a glorious thing, only, on the other hand, it is very sad that it cannot well maintain itself, and is easily seduced' (pp. 24–5)*—by wrong impulses, by immoral wishes, by mistakes and distorted traditions. Ethics must therefore be philosophically developed.

The first version of the categorical imperative runs: 'Act only according to such a maxim that you can also will that it should become a general law.'†

This version expresses clearly and precisely one of the fundamental experiences we have when we become subject to an absolute moral demand; all such principles as the love of our neighbour imply that they should become general laws. It is also justifiable to say that the imperative defines a maxim, for we have seen that moral actions are guided by principles. A maxim, according to Kant, is 'the subjective principle of volition' (p. 20), that is, the principle which we accept, and the necessary task of the

---

* Page numbers in parentheses in this and the following chapter refer to *Fundamental Principles of the Metaphysics of Ethics* (transl. by T. K. Abbott; London, 1907).
† p. 48 of the original German edition, my own translation.

imperative is to make sure that we accept, not some arbitrarily chosen and possibly wrong principle, but the right one. Nevertheless, this version remains open to two objections. On the one hand, it is purely formal and says nothing about the nature of these actions. It is true that this accords with one characteristic of positive moral commandments which we have mentioned—that they must not be so definitive as to leave no room for personal decisions; yet the commandment to love our neighbour, although it does not tell us exactly what to do, still says much more about the attitude which is required, for it appeals to our feelings and arouses our inner participation, which the abstract concept 'law' cannot do. On the other hand, there are exceptional cases when a moral action cannot—or even must not—be made a general law; some moral actions are based on a particular situation which demands an individual decision, as in the case of mercy-killing. But a formulation which reaches for the very absoluteness of the moral law itself, of the law of thinking from which it springs, cannot be reconciled with exceptions.

For these reasons, Kant attempts to support the categorical imperative by introducing the concept of duty. But this concept only throws into relief both the merits and demerits of the first version.

Duty, for Kant, 'is the necessity of acting from respect for the law' (p. 19). Therefore this concept is important; it ensures that one of the main requirements of a moral action is realized: 'In order that an action should be morally good, it is not enough that it conform to the moral law, but it must also be done for the sake of the law' (p. 5). Thus the emphasis is put correctly on the motive; an action is only good, in the moral sense of the word, if it is done for the right reasons. 'Otherwise that conformity [to the moral law] is only very contingent and uncertain; since a principle which is not moral, although it may now and then produce actions conformable to the law, will also often produce actions which contradict it' (p. 5).

The importance of motives can be recognized even if an action appears to be good in itself. If, for instance, somebody jumps into the water to save a drowning child, his action lacks moral—as distinct from practical—value, if its motive is not moral, if it is done, say, for fear of being despised if the risk were not taken, or because of vanity, or the desire to be admired as a good or as a brave man. It would be wrong to say that such an admirable deed must be moral, whatever the motive. Certainly, it is better that the child be saved than drowned, but for the doer morality does not come into play, and if we interpret the word 'better' morally, we impute our own moral attitude to him. All the motives mentioned could also be satisfied by, say, killing men in war, without any consideration of whether or not killing or war can be justified. That the distinction should be made becomes more obvious, perhaps, in another example—if somebody helps an old person, ostensibly from moral motives, but in fact in the hope of earning or inheriting money, the help may still be good in itself, but he will not be acting morally. This will become apparent when his actual aim has been achieved, and misleading judgments could be avoided if motives were taken into account beforehand. It is essential that an action should be judged to be moral only if it is motivated by the moral law; otherwise morality itself is endangered.

But the concept of duty is also very general and much in need of further clarification. If the law to be obeyed is not sufficiently specified, duty may demand obedience to any law; moral quality then resides simply in being obedient. Such a misinterpretation has actually happened; Kant's concept has been interpreted as military duty. To accuse him of having this interpretation in mind is evidently wrong; he was one of the first to give the desire for peace a concrete shape by developing, in his book *Perpetual Peace*, the idea of a League of Nations. He never leaves any doubt that 'law' in this context means the moral law. Yet, in the course of events, the lack of further definition was of consequence; it may even have contributed to an attitude which led to the torturing of prisoners in concentration camps in the name of 'sacred duty'. The concept is important because, correctly understood, it points in the right direction, but it becomes extremely dangerous if misunderstood, and Kant's conception is again too formal to prevent misunderstandings. The more so as it meets both the objections which we have raised, but in the wrong way. It appeals to feeling and demands inner participation, but does not enable us to distinguish between justified and false convictions of certainty; and it does not allow for exceptions, though in this case exceptional decisions may be of particular importance because they enable man to reject what may be generally and often wrongly considered to be his duty. Therefore, the introduction of this concept does not really improve the first version of the categorical imperative.

Yet the final version which Kant develops is beautiful and entirely convincing. This time he says: 'Act so, that you treat humanity, in your own person as well as in the person of any other, always at the same time as an end, never as means only.'*

Here the two objections are met in the right way. The imperative is still general, as positive moral commandments must be, but it defines our attitude by arousing inner participation. It admits the one feeling which Kant accepts as truly moral—respect; and respect for the humanity in each of us appeals to a potentiality of our nature which might otherwise remain hidden. Love is still superior, but its acceptance is brought nearer by the impact which any new formulation of the moral law is bound to make. The more so as Kant remains supremely realistic; he emphasizes 'never as means *only*' because, in any society, man has also to be used as means—to produce goods or to do the work which is required to keep society alive. But for these very reasons it is particularly important to be told that such needs should never override the main consideration—that man is an end in himself, that the individual is of absolute value. Kant in this also takes account of the perhaps perplexing demand that we should love our neighbour *as ourselves*; respect for humanity is bound to mean that we must also respect the humanity within ourselves, and it is this respect which ensures that the apparently stern categorical imperative comes to life, that it can be fully experienced. Excep-

* P. 58 of the original German edition, my own translation.

tions are this time conclusively excluded; there is no morality which could disregard or circumvent this basic demand.

This final version of the imperative could be the starting point for a further elaboration of ethics; it could enable Kant to fill the gaps he has left and to prevent their misleading implications. But here his thought branches off in another direction; he returns, as we shall see in the next chapter, to metaphysical problems. The considerable merits of his ethics have been notably increased, but its shortcomings are not removed; they remain what they have been before. This, however, enables us to use them as a help to elucidate our own approach further, which we shall try to do by showing where and how far we follow Kant, and where and why we feel compelled to deviate from his teaching.

CHAPTER VIII

KANT II—MERITS AND SHORT-COMINGS OF HIS THEORY OF ETHICS

1

The merits of Kant's ethics can be recognized when we briefly review some of the other kinds of ethical teaching which have been developed.

One of these kinds has been dismissed before—that which makes the result of an action or its success the criterion of its moral value.* The oldest such teaching is hedonism which states that morality should be accepted because it is the safest way to happiness; and we have considered a modern version of it when discussing Fromm's theories. This teaching is useful because it distinguishes that form of happiness which is based on the realization of human values from other, especially from degrading, forms, and in this way hedonism can establish contact with morality. Yet to demand the good because it leads to happiness works against morality. Moral actions produce a particular kind of satisfaction, but this is not their purpose; they may require the facing of hardships and the making of sacrifices, even that of one's life; moral demands may constantly have to struggle against fear and despair. Thus ethics must allow the renunciation of all the forms of happiness taken into account by hedonism, which always aims at achieving the maximum of pleasure and at preventing pain. Hedonism is wrong because, as Moore has shown, it commits the naturalistic fallacy; it defines the good in terms of a different purpose, instead of accepting it as an end in itself.

The same objection applies to utilitarianism which is also rejected by Moore. This is based on hedonism, but might appear

* For this and the following see pp. 143-4.

more moral because it does not aim at a self-centred individual advantage; it demands what is useful for society—'the greatest happiness of the greatest number'. Thus it is concerned with one's neighbour and mankind, but it still makes morality a means to a different end; it deviates from hedonism only in so far as it sees in social usefulness the best way to secure pleasure and happiness for everybody. It is certainly no accident that utilitarianism led, not to a higher morality, but to materialism, for the useful is a lower value than the good; it is in fact that which is not judged morally. Thus the lower kind of happiness based on material welfare has become dominant, perhaps also because it offers itself as that kind which can be most easily defined, especially if one thinks in terms of the 'greatest number'. Social welfare in itself is an excellent thing and through it utilitarianism can also establish contacts with morality; but utilitarianism is bound to undermine morality in the end because of its wrong emphasis. In short, all the different forms of this kind of ethics are invalidated by committing the naturalistic fallacy, and their failure to lead to a higher morality confirms that this fallacy is detrimental to ethics.

In Kant's time, ethics was generally considered to be that part of philosophy which concerned itself with happiness, and it is undoubtedly his great historical merit that he restored the true meaning of ethics; from this point of view even the austerity of his morality appears justified. His achievement is still a help in fighting any distortion of ethics; but there is also another aspect of it to which little attention has been paid and which is probably even more important today. All these hedonistic teachings are based on what is usually called 'common sense', but common sense is a guide of doubtful reliability. It has two aspects: on the one hand it is realistic and practical and as such valuable; on the other it is the result of the popular assimilation of almost any convictions which have been generally current for some time, often simply a residue of obsolete beliefs or philosophies. In the latter aspect it is changeable; at one time it seemed common sense that there should be slaves, at another that money should buy indulgencies, more recently to allow the mentally deranged to be killed to relieve society of a useless burden. The valuable realism of common sense therefore needs to be protected against prejudices and customs, which can only be done if a valid philosophy is developed independently. That this should happen is particularly important for morality, which so easily deteriorates; we have referred to Moses, Socrates, Buddha, Jesus as men who made a fuller realization of the good possible, and they were not motivated by common sense. Kant restores morality by showing that its fundamental demands, though appealing to all men, have nothing to do with—and frequently contradict—accepted conventions. He justifies the exceptional deed which, though generally rejected, is nevertheless needed to make the good real.

This justification is mainly based on a difference between the objective and subjective methods which Kant elaborates and which is essential for ethics—that general validity is achieved differently in each reality. In external reality, general validity is established if there are no exceptions to a law; a scientific theory must be altered or replaced if a single exception is discovered. In internal reality, a single individual may hold exceptional convictions which contradict those of everyone else and yet he may be right. Kant gives an example to which we have already referred in a different context.* It may be possible to assert, he says, that 'there never have been actions which really sprang from such pure sources' and that 'the world has hitherto never given an example' of pure friendship. Faced with such historical probability, common sense would conclude that it is nonsensical to demand such a friendship. But Kant concludes: 'Even though there might never yet have been a sincere friend, yet not a whit less is pure sincerity in friendship required of every man' (p. 29)—and we cannot possibly doubt that his conclusion is in conformity with ethics. Even if pure friendship were quite the exception, the demand for it would nevertheless be generally valid.

Hume supports a different view, but it only helps to show the correctness of Kant's conclusion. Hume claims that actions are right when they arouse in the majority of mankind a sentiment of

* See p. 95.

moral approval. If this were so, the actual development of morality would be difficult to understand, for new moral departures are at first rejected by the majority and only understood and accepted by later generations, as the example of Socrates shows.* It is a basic characteristic of morality that we have to obey conscience even though it may contradict what everyone else believes, and even our own previously held beliefs.

All these arguments show that ethics cannot be based on the results of our actions; morality is only secure if we aim at the good itself. Thus they point towards the kind of ethics which Kant develops—an ethics which is concerned with intentions, with the motives of our actions. This is confirmed by a reservation which has to be made with regard to the results: we must, if possible, consider the likely consequences of what we do, for we shall be responsible for them, but the feeling of responsibility transcends the desire for happiness or usefulness. Thus this reservation contradicts hedonism and utilitarianism and stresses the importance of motives. Moreover, there are situations, as we have said, when it is impossible to predict the consequences of different courses of action, and then we have to rely on what we believe to be good and right; contradictory guesses as to what will or might happen would make us unable to come to a decision at all and thus also prevent moral actions.

Another type of ethical teaching emphasizes the formulation of moral laws and the necessity of obeying them. This is probably the original form of ethics, because it sprang from religion and at first based its authority on direct divine commandments. But we have pointed out already that, though a commonplace, it is correct to say that to obey rules for the sake of rules is wrong, and this remains true even if the laws themselves are the right ones.† Acceptance of this teaching has two main falsifying effects. On the one hand, it may lead to what Fromm calls the 'authoritarian conscience'; in this case laws which are imposed from outside are obeyed because they are generally accepted, without being tested by one's own conscience. On the other hand, morality may be

* See also pp. 154–6.   † See pp. 91–2.

identified with outward compliance with the law, without regard to whether or not it is obeyed for the right reason. Both attitudes tend to lead to complacency because, since it is easier to do what one is told or what is customary than to decide for oneself, self-satisfaction replaces inner conflicts; or to pride, because the appearance of being moral enhances reputation. In either case, desire for safety is the ulterior motive, and this surrender to the naturalistic fallacy destroys the possibility of those exceptional actions which we have just found to be important. But even the predominance of the laws themselves, apart from the probability of their producing a wrong attitude, distorts ethics, because laws reduce both the scope of, and the need for, personal decisions; they eliminate the need for an 'area of the unprescribed'.* The more so as this kind of ethics is bound to concentrate on the creation of further laws such as those of marriage which have been mentioned, which are meant to regulate the application of morality. Once more, the importance of Kant's emphasis on motives becomes obvious.

This time, however, a stronger reservation must be made. Our investigation has led us to include principles which, when accepted, represent necessary laws; these laws give us guidance and also enable us, by their challenge, to make actual what would otherwise remain a merely potential ethical self. These principles must not be disregarded. They may be transcended by individuals who are so possessed by the necessity of doing the good that they cannot but act morally; such men need neither laws nor ethics, but we have said that such a perfection is rare.† Ethics, therefore, must be developed with the help of principles. It is true that to safeguard their ethical nature they must be obeyed for the right reason, and that, as we have seen, the principles and laws themselves must be challenged, tested and chosen, all of which points again to an ethical teaching based on motives. Nevertheless, principles and laws must be admitted as well.

The position of laws is different when ethics is based on religion and when belief in God and His grace enter, but even then laws do

---

* See p. 131.   † See p. 97.

not disappear; their position is only clarified—neither ethics nor religion should be founded upon laws alone, but both must include them. Some forms of Christianity wrongly over-emphasize certain laws (such as those regulating the relationships between men and women), but opposition to this emphasis should not hide the fact that Christianity, although it aims at transcending the law, does not simply abolish it. The Old Testament is not rejected, but fulfilled. Again, single individuals may transcend the law, but in general moral laws have to be acknowledged. There are attempts to make them superfluous, but both St Paul and Luther, after establishing that faith and nothing but faith matters, are obliged to explain that this means neither passivity nor licence, and to support their plea by castigating vice and demanding virtue. Laws have to be relied on as an initial stage on the way to faith and to correct errors so long as a complete surrender to faith has not been achieved. This applies even more to non-religious ethics which does not offer the opportunity for such a surrender.

Kant elaborates the kind of ethics which concentrates on motives and intentions and thus on the right kind of moral attitude. In the preceding chapter, when discussing duty, we have seen that he does establish the importance of motives, and why. But he also takes over what is essential in that kind of ethics which concentrates on laws.

An ethical teaching which dealt with motives alone could be misleading. This can be recognized when Kant goes so far as to extol, above everything else, the 'good will':

Nothing can possibly be conceived in the world, or even out of it, which can be called good without qualification, except a Good Will. Intelligence, wit, judgment, and the other talents of the mind, however they may be named, or courage, perseverance, as qualities of temperament, are undoubtedly good and desirable in many respects; but these gifts of nature may also become extremely bad and mischievous if the will which is to make use of them, and which, therefore, constitutes what is called character, is not good. It is the same with the gifts of fortune. Power, riches, honour, even health, and the general well-being and contentment with this condition which is called happiness, inspire pride, and often presumption, if there is not a good will to correct the influence of these on the mind, and with this also to rectify the whole principle of acting, and adapt it to its end. . . . Thus a good will appears to constitute the indispensable condition even of being worthy of happiness (p. 10).

From all we have said it can be seen that this statement in itself is justified. It agrees, in particular, with what we have said when discussing conscience, for conscience gives us the definitive certainty of acting in accordance with the good will if we want to do what we believe (even erroneously) to be good.* But we have also seen that this certainty, if it is not controlled by a clear awareness of what is good can be utterly misleading, and to praise the good will can be similarly dangerous. For of what use are good intentions if they do not lead to any action at all, or if they lead to the wrong kind of action? Yet Kant makes sure that the good will is guided in the right direction; the book which is introduced by the statement just quoted deals to a large extent with the categorical imperative and thus with the attempt to exclude errors with the help of the moral law.

The final version of the categorical imperative shows the fruitfulness of this combination. As imperative it both demands action and ensures that its motive is ethical, namely respect for man as an end in himself; and as categorical it establishes a law with the necessary universality, because it does not allow of any exception. It gives expression to the moral law itself; no principle can possibly deviate from it. Kant thus makes it convincing that morality has to be accepted as absolute and this is probably the main merit of his ethics.

The importance of the imperative can be appreciated when we consider the Ten Commandments in its light, for it helps us to understand why their moral part belongs to absolute morality. Some of these laws, for instance the prohibition on stealing, can appear as merely social demands. But in fact they define the fundamental moral attitude: we must not violate humanity in other persons, and this we do if we despise parents, tell lies, steal or commit adultery, and by these degrading actions we also violate humanity in our own person. The moral commandments

* See pp. 161–2.

of the Sermon on the Mount go one step further; they mainly prevent the violation of humanity within ourselves, so as to make us capable of love. To hate the enemy or to think of adultery need not have any external consequence, but such thoughts invade, degrade and isolate us. All these commandments ensure that we fulfil the moral law by respecting humanity in every man, which can only be achieved if we accept every man as an end in himself.

When we remember how little has been added to fundamental morality throughout the ages, Kant's achievement will not be underrated. Yet the fact that he does not make any further use of the final version of the categorical imperative in the building up of his ethics leads to shortcomings.

We have said that this version arouses our inner participation by appealing to our feeling of respect. This appeal is undoubtedly essential and should never be omitted, but respect alone does not go far enough. There are many feelings which have to be overcome (such as hatred) or disciplined (such as joy) or awakened (the right kind of love) if morality is to become dominant; and respect, being probably more closely connected with an intellectual approach than these other feelings, is certainly not among those which need guidance most strongly. It can hardly be distorted by passion, as love frequently is, but neither can it produce on its own the full involvement which devotion to a moral cause requires. To demand respect begins in the right direction, but is no more than a first step, and this demand does not therefore in itself eliminate the shortcomings of Kant's ethics.

Kant, emerging from the Age of Reason and witnessing a wrong reaction against it, namely the rise of sentimentality, distrusts feelings too much; he fears that they are—with the exception of respect—unreliable and misleading and should therefore be excluded altogether. The categorical imperative provides us with an excellent criterion for distinguishing between justified and false convictions as to what we ought to do, but only after these have arisen; it does not awaken that immediate response of our potential ethical self which could by itself lead to a moral action, as can the commandment to love our neighbour. Kant shows the reasonable aspect of morality, but only makes a beginning as regards bringing it to life.

As he is concerned with the laws of thinking which are dictated by practical reason, he says: 'All moral philosophy rests wholly on its pure part. When applied to man, it does not borrow the least from the knowledge of man himself (anthropology), but gives laws *a priori* to him as a rational being.' (p. 4). To acknowledge that the moral law precedes experience—which is why it is absolute—is of the greatest possible importance, but the rejection of any reference to man's nature excludes the ethical self, and this makes any response to the moral law difficult to understand. What Kant actually omits becomes obvious when he later says: 'There are many minds so sympathetically constituted that, without any other motive of vanity or self-interest, they find a pleasure in spreading joy around them, and can take delight in the satisfaction of others so far as it is their own work. But I maintain that in such a case an action of this kind, however proper, however amiable it may be, has nevertheless no true moral worth ... for the maxim lacks the moral import, namely, that such actions be done from duty, not from inclination' (p. 16).

This radical rejection of inclinations, a consequence of the exclusion of man's nature, is again in part important; inclinations tend to fluctuate and may thus be unreliable; this is the reason why ethics has to be developed. Of course, if our inclinations contradict the demands of the moral law, they should be suppressed; and even if the demands of duty and those of inclination coincide, the latter, being changeable, are insufficient to ensure that we behave morally. This applies whenever duties such as those expressed in the different versions of the categorical imperative prevail; but does it also apply to love? Certainly, love of our neighbour has to transcend the especial inclination we feel towards people we like; yet once this has happened, love must involve our whole being and cannot be separated from inclination. Duty may have to struggle against inclination, but love fails so long as it is merely experienced as duty; love must include our inclinations and transform them.

All these shortcomings of Kant's ethics, however, do not invalidate it; they only disclose gaps. Thus, in contrast to the other teachings which we have discussed, his kind of ethics—based on motives and admitting laws—should form part of any ethical teaching. But his shortcomings indicate that, to make ethics more complete, another approach to it should be taken into account, and they even show, by the nature of the omissions, how the gaps may be filled.

2

Kant establishes clearly the need for the two ways of thinking and shows many of their characteristic consequences, such as the distinction between relative and absolute knowledge and the two kinds of general validity. Yet he does not entirely clarify the distinction between external and internal reality, for he narrows down internal reality to morality only, and morality to its reasonable aspect. What he says about this aspect should never be disregarded in ethics, but the incompleteness of his grasp of internal reality leads to and explains a corresponding incompleteness in his ethical teaching.

This main gap in his philosophy is the reason why, instead of continuing the elaboration of ethics, he turns in a different direction and asks what metaphysical conclusions could be based on the moral law. As the fullness of internal reality is lacking, morality has to be supplemented in an external way. He tries to prove that, in order to make sense, morality makes certain metaphysical assumptions necessary. With his *Critique of Pure Reason*, as has been mentioned, he wanted to destroy absolute external knowledge to make room for faith; but his *Critique of Practical Reason* elaborates morality in such a way that it tends to become, as a result of asking these metaphysical questions, practically a substitute for faith.

The metaphysical assumptions themselves are made compatible with Kant's rejection of metaphysical systems by being stated as postulates. These are not based on concepts *a priori* and do not allow us to say 'must'; they 'are not theoretical dogmas, but suppositions practically necessary'* which do not precede knowledge; they are added after knowledge has been achieved. That which is postulated is a logical conclusion suggested by the moral law and known only through its practical—that is, moral—consequences; it can be assumed to exist, but cannot itself be known. Since, therefore, postulates cannot form the basis of a metaphysical system they do not logically contradict Kant's philosophy; but they nevertheless show where its weakness lies.

There are three postulates: of man's immortality, of the freedom of the will, and of the existence of God. Each of them throws light on what is missing.

Of most direct importance for ethics is the freedom of the will. Here a problem has to be faced—the problem, of course, that external causality does not allow any exceptions and thus cannot admit any freedom whatever, while morality is only possible if man, by his will, can freely cause actions which, as they take place in external reality, contradict the all-inclusive necessity established by the causal law. Nevertheless, morality must presuppose freedom; without it, we could not possibly be responsible for our actions, and the categorical imperative would be meaningless if it did not imply that we are able to do what we ought to do.

Kant describes this contradiction admirably. He takes as an example 'a malicious lie by which a certain confusion has been caused in society' and says:

First of all, we endeavour to discover the motives to which it has been due, and then, secondly, in the light of these, we proceed to determine how far the action and its consequences can be imputed to the offender. As regards the first question, we trace the empirical character of the action to its sources, finding these in defective education, bad company, in part also in the viciousness of a natural disposition insensitive to shame, in levity and thoughtlessness, not neglecting to take into account also the occasional causes that may have intervened. We proceed in this enquiry just as we should in ascertaining for a given natural effect the series of its determining causes. But although we believe that the action is thus determined, we none the less blame the agent, not indeed of his unhappy disposition, nor on account of the circumstances that have

* *Critique of Practical Reason*, p. 229.

influenced him, nor even on account of his previous way of life; for we pre-suppose that we can leave out of consideration what this way of life may have been, that we can regard the past series of conditions as not having occurred and the act as being completely unconditioned by any preceding state, just as if the agent in and by himself began in this action an entirely new series of consequences . . . The action is ascribed to the agent's intelligible character; in the moment when he utters the lie, the guilt is entirely his. Reason, irrespective of all empirical conditions of the act, is completely free, and the lie is entirely due to its default.*

I have quoted Kant here at greater length than usual for several reasons: partly because the passage shows how we actually do think; partly to emphasize how much of his philosophy has to be accepted despite all the objections which are to follow; but mainly because the difference between the two ways of thinking—and between a psychological and an ethical approach—is once more made very clear; which also makes convincing the need for them both. With regard to freedom this difference is further clarified when Kant says: 'This freedom ought not, therefore, to be conceived only negatively as independence of empirical conditions. The faculty of reason, so regarded, would cease to be a cause of appearances. It must also be described in positive terms, as the power of originating a series of events'—for freedom must enable man to perform moral actions within external reality. 'And thus what we failed to find in any empirical series is disclosed as being possible, namely, that the condition of a successive series may itself be empirically unconditioned',† and to recognize this obviously requires a different kind of thinking. What Kant calls 'empirical' refers to external reality, as grasped with the help of categories which establish causality and necessity; but since freedom must be admitted as a positive faculty, it demands that way of thinking which is based on what we actually experience.

But Kant goes further than that. He does not rest content with accepting the contradiction and thus the two different approaches which represent the same reality under different aspects (as we

* *Critique of Pure Reason*, p. 477.   † *Ibid.*, pp. 476 and 475.

have done when distinguishing between external and internal reality). He wants to show 'that this antinomy rests on a sheer illusion, and that causality through freedom is at least not incompatible with nature.'* He therefore develops the 'cosmological idea' of an 'intelligible world'—that is, of a separate world disclosed by reason and accessible only to intelligence; of a world which exists 'outside the series of appearances (in the intelligible), and therefore is not subject to any sensible condition, and to no time-determination through an antecedent cause.'† This explains 'the necessary supposition of independence on the sensible world, and of the faculty of determining one's will, because moral actions can thus be done 'according to the law of an intelligible world'.‡ Freedom of the will is made a postulate in order to enable Kant, not only to introduce another way of thinking, but also to claim that freedom belongs to another world.

Here again, we can accept Kant's argument up to a point— that reason, by establishing the moral law, shows that we possess freedom and that its conditions cannot be understood in terms of the world of sense perceptions; we have said that internal reality opens approaches to the absolute. Yet it is not convincing that freedom therefore proves the existence of a separate different world which manifests itself only in reason and the moral law and is accessible only to intelligence; for if the absolute exists, it cannot be confined to a realm of its own; it must penetrate everything. Nor can it be said that we, as moral agents, are 'outside the series of appearances' and no longer 'subject to any sensible condition, and to no time-determination'. We experience freedom as real, not only because our actions must take place in external reality and thus belong to it as well, but also because we, who intend them, continue to live in this world, even though some of our motives may arise because of an experience of the absolute. That we find ourselves in a world which is apparently completely determined by causality and yet are able to produce actions at will is an astonishing contradiction, and it is

---

* *Critique of Pure Reason*, p. 479.   † *Ibid.*, p. 475.
‡ *Critique of Practical Reason*, p. 230.

astonishing just because we so fully enter into the world of appearances; for freedom affects our whole person, including all our senses, feelings, urges and thoughts, and all our relationships to other persons and to objects. Therefore, even though freedom is grasped with the help of a different kind of thinking, it cannot be merely 'intelligible'; since it affects our whole being, it must be understandable in terms of internal reality—as in fact it is, if we pay attention to that part of internal reality which Kant neglects.

Once freedom becomes directly and entirely real to us, it is one of our richest and most significant experiences, so that we cannot help becoming involved in its demands. There are, of course, different degrees of the awareness of freedom; we may take it for granted, without making it fully conscious; or we may deny it and believe in determinism, though even then the consciousness of freedom does not entirely disappear, for we constantly assume that we are able to cause actions, even if only by moving from one place to another. In fact, every endeavour presupposes freedom, whether it aims at material goods or scientific achievements or ideals; but none of these endeavours need necessarily be accompanied by a conscious realization of freedom. Kant is right that it is the moral law which forces us to become fully aware of freedom; when we realize that the moral law means that we are able to do what we ought to do, we can no longer escape the knowledge that we can and should use that freedom which the moral law discloses. It has by then become impossible to say— with those who believe in determinism, and some psychologists— that we are as we are and cannot help it; despite all external and biological or psychological compulsions and other restrictions on our exercise of freedom, we know for certain that, fundamentally and in the last resort, we are responsible beings who possess freedom, even if in particular cases some of the obstacles to its exercise prove insuperable. Thus, however, our whole being and not only reason has become involved. We are no longer content to aim for, or be satisfied with, affluence and a comfortable life, nor to concentrate on intellectual endeavours alone, nor to pursue other ideas or ideals which do not directly appeal to our freedom; we also want both to exercise our moral freedom and to live according to the good. We feel the urge to transform and fulfil ourselves by making if not all then at least some of our ethical potentialities actual within and in the face of the world. It is through this fullness of experience that 'the moral law within' enables us to face the challenge of 'the starry heavens above'.

This, then, is the contradiction which Kant illustrates when he says that the origin of a wicked lie can be explained as the necessary consequence of the liar's nature and circumstances and that we yet judge that he is guilty, without doubting his freedom. We actually watch the interaction between a world which appears to us to be determined by causality and a world of free persons. But this interaction does not unify our knowledge; we must still see reality under these two aspects which cannot be reconciled because each of them is an aspect of the whole reality. The experience of freedom merely confirms the validity of the internal aspect. There is no other way but to accept this dichotomy. In external reality we must aim at necessity and cannot accommodate freedom, for otherwise we could not understand the world in which we live; in internal reality we must start from freedom, for otherwise we could not understand ourselves. It is true that we also experience the impact of the absolute (to which we shall return in a moment), but this does not provide us with explanations or solve problems; essential knowledge, as we have said, is an additional knowledge. It still leaves the two aspects of reality intact and we cannot dispense with them. The glimpses we get of a more fundamental truth do no more than force us to realize that neither external nor internal reality can be identified with primary reality; they do not entitle us to believe in a separate 'intelligible world'.

The reason why Kant makes freedom a postulate is indicated by his use of the word 'empirical' in its customary narrow meaning; in this respect he does not go beyond Hume. 'Empirical' should mean 'based, acting on observation & experiment, not on theory', but it has been narrowed down to mean 'relying solely on experiment',* so that it now usually means 'verifiable by material evidence' and refers to external reality alone. But our existence, after all, is not only verifiable as external; we apply observation and are thus empirical and not theoretical when we scrutinize inner experience, for we try to distinguish that which reliably discloses internal reality from wrong reactions or mere fancy. Inner experience, properly scrutinized, can be valid evidence. But for Kant, who wants to derive ethics entirely from reason, any empirical enquiry into man's nature appears by definition ruled out. He therefore disregards the ethical self, and has to postulate a different basis for ethics outside man. He is afraid, of course, that consideration of man's nature would blur the boundaries between morality and psychology, and we have seen that his fear is justified; psychology does tend to explain morality in a wrong way. Yet when the ethical self is acknowledged, the distinction can still be made; the absolute moral law which makes the potential ethical self actual must needs still remain outside psychology which is concerned, not with what is unconditionally valid, but with relative conditions and functional connections. Even Fromm, although he accepts the moral law in practice, feels bound to deny its absoluteness.†

We come up once more against Kant's distrust of feeling. Our knowledge of values and especially of the good is ultimately based on feeling. No definition of the good can really convey what it is or what it means; unless we have actually experienced and felt it, we shall not understand more than rules of conduct. But that kind of feeling on which the good is based is obviously something very different and needs to be distinguished from the kind of feelings which are awakened by particular occasions. These are the feelings with which Kant deals, such as the pleasure which arises when our inclinations are satisfied or the disappointment we feel when they are not satisfied, or the feeling of being

* Both definitions from *The Concise Oxford Dictionary*.
† That Kant goes too far can be seen when he even excludes anthropology (see p. 206) which can make an important contribution. Buber, for example, correctly calls his *I and Thou* 'philosophical anthropology', and it is this kind of anthropology which discloses the ethical self.

crushed by 'the starry heavens' or saved from despair by the moral law, and also the feeling of elevation which the passage referred to itself expresses. It is true that all these feelings are not conducive to knowledge; they merely accompany action and thought and can be misleading. His mistrust of inclinations is also justified, for these need not be moral at all and they can change at any time in any direction; they may be immoral, and if they are the feeling of satisfaction may come from the success of a wicked lie. But there is also the other kind of feeling which gives us knowledge of the good and which could be called 'feeling as an organ of knowledge'.* Kant appeals to it when he expects us to respond to the categorical imperative or to want to do our duty, but he does not pay attention to it. He only accords a special place to respect, but respect is not quite of the same kind; it is part of the moral attitude, but does not clarify it, as the sense of the good or of what is right does. He sees no need to satisfy more than reason, and reason alone can be appeased by abstract postulates, but not for long; so long as one of the main sources of experience is not tapped, we remain unsatisfied.

Kant is also concerned in this context with another problem which we have mentioned before—that the logical separation of statements about what exists from those about what we ought to do cannot be final if any unconditional moral obligation is to carry conviction. He feels strongly that this apparently 'unbridgeable gulf' should be bridged, but he fails to bridge it, and thus the insufficiency of the postulates is revealed even more clearly.

In theory, the claim that the 'ought' of the moral law is rooted in a different intelligible world could solve the problem, for the intelligible world seems to conform to what we have called the absolute. But there is an essential difference between the two. Kant's way of interpreting the moral law makes the absolute logically possible, but does not make it accessible to experience. Thus the absolute becomes unreal. We are not challenged by an impact from outside, nor torn by a conflict between contra-

---

* For a full description of these two kinds of feeling see P. Roubiczek, *Thinking towards Religion*, ch. v. We shall also return to them in ch. x, sect. 2.

dictory facts—experiences which we have found to be a condition of the emergence of essential knowledge. For our ethics it is this knowledge which, without offering further explanations, bridges the 'gulf' because it reveals the existence of facts which are, at the same time, demands which we ought to obey.* Kant, however, wants to go further and explain. The result is that we remain confined to that part of internal reality which he takes into account—to reasonable morality—and he adds only an abstraction to it in order to guard us against external reality and to reassure us that reason can be trusted. Thus the supposition of an intelligible world does not allow for—it rather insulates us against—the very experience which could make the absolute real for us. This intelligible world does not establish the 'outside' which is needed. We have said that Kant makes room for it,† but as the postulates replace it by abstractions, it does not become as real as external reality and cannot transcend it; and since the ethical self is excluded as well, what we ought to do remains entirely dependent on the moral law. The gulf between facts and commandments is not bridged.

The insufficiency of abstract logical conclusions is confirmed by the other two postulates—of man's immortality and the existence of God. These do not directly refer to ethics, so that we need not discuss them in detail, but only so far as they increase the dangers of Kant's one-sided approach to ethics.

That man is immortal and that God exists are beliefs of Christianity and other religions, but to support them by postulates—that is to give them the status of highly probable and therefore reasonable conclusions—only gives to both these claims the appearance of arbitrary assumptions. A believer would proclaim them as truths; as postulates they remain unreal because they are reduced to abstract ideas. God becomes, as Pascal feared, the 'God of the philosophers'—a mere hypothesis which has no power of conviction and does not convey what it really means, in terms of experience, to believe in the existence of a being who transcends understanding and on whose power and grace we

* See pp. 143–4, 164.   † See pp. 190–1.

nevertheless depend. Immortality and God, if they are to become real, have to be accepted because experience forces us to embark on the adventure of faith and perhaps to surrender to it; otherwise they remain, at best, a consolatory accompaniment to existence. The intelligible world is meant to represent the world beyond, but the only part of it which we can accept as real is the moral law on which the postulates are based, and not the postulates themselves.

Since, however, when presented in this way, it is the moral law alone which we find confirmed by experience, Kant is in effect, contrary to his intentions, replacing faith by morality. But can morality replace faith? Faith must transcend the moral law which is recognizable by reason alone; it must answer the question of where morality comes from, why it carries obligation, and thus it must include the absolute. It means belief in things unseen which, because they cannot be fully known, have to be accepted by an act of faith. Kant wanted to make room for faith and does so by his theory of knowledge, but after having achieved what he intended he blocks the way to faith again, because he only succeeds in making the moral law real. The postulates merely exalt it, so as to give it the appearance of being a proper subject for faith. Yet morality itself is endangered by this because its absoluteness, when supported by abstractions and not by experience, also appears a mere assumption.

Ethics is not concerned with faith; in fact morality can thrive despite—or even because of—constant conflicts and doubts. But if absoluteness is claimed for it at all, it cannot simply rest on an assertion. It arises within and through experience; therefore a way must be left open for the absolute to make its impact felt, even if it is not, or not always, fully realized and openly acknowledged. The surrender to faith may never occur, but an experience which allows for the possibility of being enlarged is obviously more fruitful than an experience made narrow by a false sense of security which rests upon abstractions. Kant was right when he wanted to make room for faith, because that and no more is what philosophy can and should do; if it attempts more, it will always be prone to create a unitary way of thinking and an all-inclusive metaphysical system, both of which Kant has shown to be a distortion of knowledge even though he encourages them by his postulates. We must remain content to base ethics on his theory of knowledge, because knowledge arrived at by the conscious effort of thinking must not be allowed to masquerade as direct knowledge of primary reality and the absolute; it must not usurp the place of faith. Otherwise we shall claim to know more than we are entitled to claim.

All this shows that a further kind of ethics is still needed, in addition to that based on motives and principles. It is most important to scrutinize our motives and be guided by principles, but since the scrutiny can only be undertaken after the motives have arisen and since the principles must remain formal, we also need an appeal which can awaken our potentialities in such a way that they give rise to moral actions, for we have many—and by no means only moral—potentialities. In other words, we need ethical aims which give purpose to our striving. Of course, these aims must not be established in a dogmatic way; the 'area of the unprescribed' has to be preserved to allow us to come to our own decisions; but these decisions should be provoked by ethical alternatives. We must not forget the motives, for an aim which is good in itself may, as has been seen, be desired for the wrong reason and thus become immoral. For this reason, too, aims must not become dogmas, but even so they can create experiences in a more concrete way than either motives or laws. Ethical experience must become as rich as we have found freedom to be, but it must also give content to freedom.

This further kind of ethics can be established when we consider internal reality in its fulness and pay attention to those parts of the subjective method which Kant excludes. For this method also contains a way of making judgments which enables us to recognize values. These represent an important part of internal reality, and it is evaluation which, though rarely taken into account, offers a basis for the additional ethical teaching which is still needed. Ethics—as we shall try to show in the following chapters —should also be founded upon a knowledge of values.

We did not mention values when we described the subjective method by comparing it with the objective method because the latter offers no equivalent, but we said that the subjective method is in need of further elaboration. To this task we shall now turn, for evaluation is one of the main elements of the subjective method. This form of thinking is just as natural to us as any of its other basic forms; we constantly have to decide what is more or less agreeable or useful, or what is better or worse, or right or wrong. To judge the value of things and events or actions is as unavoidable a part of everyday life as the attempt to discover causal connections. Ethics therefore has to include it.

Kant touches upon the problem of values, but does not deal with it directly, except in his *Critique of Judgment*; there, however, he only takes it up with regard to teleology (which belongs to the realm of pure reason) and to aesthetics, neither of which concerns us here. From now on, therefore, we have to leave Kant behind, even though his concepts of 'end' or 'purpose' and of 'purposefulness', which he introduces in his third Critique as 'regulative principles', will still be of use later. In this critique he also tries once more to bridge the gulf which separates existence from obligation—that is, to reconcile statements containing 'is' with those containing 'ought'—but it is only by going beyond Kant and including values in ethics that this gap can finally be closed.

CHAPTER IX

VALUES—THEIR NATURE AND APPLICATION

1

Our intention is to discuss ethical values. Since, however, philosophy has hardly concerned itself of recent years with values, we have first to create a basis for this further kind of ethics. This means that we must investigate the process of evaluation itself and the different kinds of values which exist, in order to be able to discern and to understand those values which are important for ethics, the more so as all values are closely interconnected.*

'Value' is one of those basic terms which cannot be fully defined. We hope that it will be clarified by the following analysis of what happens when we recognize and establish values and by the description of the values themselves. But there are a few general characteristics which apply to all values, whether lower ones, such as agreeableness or usefulness, or the highest ones, such as goodness or truth, and we shall begin with the consideration of these before entering into the discussion of details. In this way, some possible misunderstandings can be eliminated right from the beginning.

A value expresses the significance—great or small—which man ascribes to matters related to a particular activity or experience or to his life in general and thus provides him with guidance for his behaviour. (In natural science, the term is sometimes used in a

---

* It did not seem helpful in this context to go back to Plato or Aristotle or even Kant. In our century, ethical values have been thoroughly investigated by two German philosophers, Max Scheler and Nicolai Hartmann, but these are, so far as I know, the only major attempts in this field. Their works contain important and helpful details, to which I am indebted, but they seem to me unsatisfactory in their dealing with some of the fundamental questions. Therefore a new start has been attempted in this book.

different sense, but this will not concern us here.) Values do not exist as objects in space and time, but are established by judgments —by judging things, qualities, events or actions from a personal point of view. They therefore contain both subjective and objective elements. These are differently related to each other in the different kinds of values, but the following basic relation always exists.

On the one hand, evaluation belongs to the subjective method. Thus values require our personal participation to come into being —that is to become more than abstract concepts. Something must be valuable to us (or the opposite), otherwise we get to know facts and not values. A thing is not useful of itself, but for the purpose for which we need it; saving a life or taking a life are simply events unless we recognize the one deed as good and the other as evil. Similarly, if there is to be any justification for calling such an everyday event as a sunset beautiful, it must be seen as such. Therefore values are not expressed by factual statements, but by judgments; our personal participation and the conclusions derived from it are of the essence.

On the other hand, although personal participation is required to bring values into being, they refer to something which is objective. The fact that our judgments can be mistaken makes this clear; something may be quite useless even though we think it useful; it is the saving of a life which is good and not our judgment of the act which makes it so; and beauty does not lie entirely in the eye of the beholder, but resides in the object as well. Our value-judgments about things, about human behaviour and even about works of art can be right or wrong, which shows that values possess a foundation which is independent of us.

Both the subjective and objective elements have always to be taken into account, for it is the placing of an undue emphasis on either of them which easily leads to misunderstandings.

Because of the subjective elements, it is frequently claimed that values are purely subjective and therefore potentially different for each individual, merely, in fact, 'a matter of taste', and that they cannot therefore be discussed. This is true of one of the different kinds of values which we shall distinguish later, as when we say that something is agreeable or pretty; but it certainly implies a considerable underrating of human intelligence to extend this attitude to all values, particularly to moral ones. Calling murder evil is not a matter of taste.

Because of the objective elements, we tend to identify an embodiment of a value with the value itself, or at least to consider the embodiment as an integral part of the value. Many people believe, for instance, that it is not only just to punish criminals, but that the concept of justice is indissolubly connected with the punishment of criminals; for them this simply is justice; thus this particular realization of an embodiment of it represents the value itself. That such an identification is wrong becomes obvious when, as often happens, the significance of a value is doubted because opinion concerning one of its embodiments changes. Those who identify justice with punishment deplore the disappearance of justice when the idea of punishment gives way to the intention to help and reform the convict. Others deny the permanence of all moral values because certain actions (such as defending either one's own honour or the honour of one's country in the war), which were once considered as highly moral, are no longer accepted as moral at all. Similarly, changes in the customs governing marriage may make us doubt the value of marriage itself, or we may deny the importance of beauty when a work of art, once admired, is later dismissed as bad. Such views, however, distort the relationship between a value-judgment and its object.

The misunderstanding is due to the fact that values do not exist independently in the same way as things; they must be embodied to be experienced; we cannot know goodness or beauty in the abstract. Since they have to be embodied, we often aim at the embodiment and not the value; when saving a child from drowning, we think of the child and not of goodness. We only become aware of the value when we judge what we have done, which may happen afterwards as here, or beforehand when we have to choose between different plans leading to future actions. But the embodiment itself (the punishment of criminals, the beautiful painting, the saving of the child) is not the value nor does it form part of it; an embodiment has value and must be judged if the value is to be recognized. Values are canons of judgment; through their application we become aware of certain qualities in the action or object; and these in their turn produce in us an appreciation of the values which are embodied. Our power of appreciation may increase or decrease, or we may err, but that does not affect the value itself. The value of friendship, for instance, will not be diminished if we happen to have trusted a false friend. Therefore we shall have to distinguish the values from their embodiments.

There is, however, a borderline case. Some of the positive qualities of man, such as courage or firmness, are usually called values—partly because they always seem positive and partly because they are similar to values in that they must be embodied to become more than abstract concepts. They can be included in value-judgments of actions, as when we say that a deed was courageous, but the qualities themselves, if present, have to be acknowledged as belonging to the doer's character and they are therefore embodiments of values; strictly speaking, they should not be called values, but virtues. Yet the word 'virtue' does not convey the meaning it once had, but has rather acquired misleading overtones, which is probably the reason why it has been replaced, even in contexts where its opposite 'vice' can still be used without hesitation. Thus it would probably be too pedantic to insist on the distinction between values and virtues, and we shall include the latter among the former. Only love—which is often called the highest value—will be kept separate, for reasons which will become obvious when we discuss it.

Another general characteristic of values can be recognized when we consider a difference between external and internal reality which we have not yet mentioned—the different meaning which the term 'negative' has in each of the two realities.

External reality we know only so far as we know something; obviously, things of which we have to say that they do not exist (such as a square circle or a unicorn) or laws which have been disproved do not refer to anything real. The negative opposite of existence—nothingness—does not correspond to any part of external reality. It would be embodied in complete emptiness, but emptiness can only be conceived within the framework of something which exists. We have said that we can think of empty space; nevertheless, the mere possibility of its external existence creates difficulties in physics, even though it is still made recognizable by the existence of celestial bodies. Not long ago, a theory was based on the assumption that the apparently empty space is filled with an invisible and undetectable ether. This theory has now been abandoned; instead equations are used which cannot be translated into common language. We should not be misled by such expressions as the negative electric pole; this stands in opposition to the positive pole, but both exist in the same way; positive and negative are merely names for different qualities. Negation, in external reality, has a purely logical function; it can help us to show what is incorrect, to limit what exists, or to proceed in the process of abstraction. But the negative as such is not real.

In internal reality, on the contrary, the negative refers to parts of this reality. Here negation creates and represents a real content which exists. In the realm of feeling, for instance, pleasure is positive and pain negative, but both are equally real. A negative feeling, such as hopeless despair, can even become so overwhelming that it destroys all positive feelings. Nothingness, too, corresponds in this sphere to a real experience; I can feel completely annihilated because of the emptiness of my life; it is due to such experiences that nothingness has become one of the fundamental concepts of Existentialism. On the other hand, emptiness can also be made a way towards unlimited receptivity; I empty myself of all thoughts, feelings and desires, in order to achieve a union with the transcendental—an important factor in mysticism.

This relevance of the negative is most obvious in the case of values. There are always corresponding positive and negative values, such as useful and useless, good and evil, right and wrong, and they are equally real; the negative quality does not only indicate the absence of the positive quality, but very definitely the presence of the negative quality. Any value is grasped by seeing both its positive and negative forms; the positive value implies the corresponding negative one and is clarified by it; they are both forms of the same value and depend on each other. We must apply both or neither.

We should therefore dismiss the illusion that we could concentrate on the positive values alone and disregard the negative ones.

In imagination we feel sure that it would be lovely to live with a full and rich awareness of the world. But in practice sensitiveness hurts. It is not possible to develop the capacity to see beauty without developing also the capacity to see ugliness, for they are the same capacity. The capacity for joy is also the capacity for pain. We soon find that any increase in our sensitiveness to what is lovely in the world increases also our capacity for being hurt ... If we choose to minimize pain we must damp down human sensitiveness, and so limit the source of possible delight. If we decide to increase our joy in life we can only do it by accepting a heightened sensitiveness to pain.*

It is true that a positive value may, in the end, transcend the negative one completely; we can think, for instance, of pure goodness. But to understand and experience it fully, we must have known evil. If somebody constantly points out that everything is good or bound to work for the good and we notice that he is unaware of the power of evil in our world, we shall be inclined to dismiss his view as unrealistic.

In the sphere of values, moreover, negation can help us in two ways to discern what exists, for here negative statements have two different meanings. If we say, for example, that something is not useful or morally good, this can mean either that it is useless or evil, or that we should apply another value—that, say, our judgment of a picture should not be based on the assumption that it ought to be useful or have a moral purpose, but that it should be evaluated by a scale of values which defines degrees of beauty or meaningfulness.

One of these two meanings always applies and we should be aware of both because, unless we want to introduce another kind

* J. Macmurray, *Reason and Emotion*, 2nd ed. (London, 1962), pp. 46–7.

of values, the denial of a positive value does not simply dismiss it, but supports its negative opposite. We are inclined to believe that negation enables us to remain neutral and to escape commitment —that if, for instance, we disregard ethical values, we can simply avoid these values altogether and rely on psychological arguments instead. But we have already seen that the denial of unconditional moral standards undermines morality; to explain morality in terms of its psychological (or historical or sociological) elements, even though these have their own importance, replaces genuine conscience by obedience to custom and thus leads towards immorality. We can also think of truth in this context, although we shall only discuss it later,* for we have seen that the tacit agreement to admit only what is relative actually means that nothing can be finally trusted, so that, in the last resort, nothing is ever really true; we are left hovering in the void. Similarly, the denial of responsibility does not merely mean that we manage without this concept, but it contributes—together with the other denials—as much to the growth of nihilism as does the acceptance of nihilism itself. It makes no difference that we may only have wanted to be more cautious or empirical in our judgment, or to avoid the need to make a judgment; we do not escape commitment by cautious or sceptical negations. Every negation of a positive value supports or establishes the corresponding negative value.

This function of negation has little significance with regard to minor values, such as agreeableness, but its importance grows in proportion to the importance of the values we are concerned with. It is therefore essential for ethics.

The need for a clear decision may often be hidden by the fact that negation can refer to different degrees of values, as in such phrases as 'not very useful' or 'hardly good'. Yet this reference to the higher or lower degree of the realization of a value is something entirely different. It points to a further characteristic of all values.

Since each value has a positive and a negative form, we are

---

* See ch. XI, sect. I.

bound to arrange everything—objects and events, actions and experiences, and even the values themselves—in scales, according to the degree to which every item contributes to, or prevents, the realization of a particular value. Anything we evaluate tends to take its place in such a scale more or less automatically, so that we are not only confronted with the values themselves, but also with corresponding scales of values.

All values lead, more or less distinctly, to the building up of such scales. Different commodities have different prices and different qualities; we must obviously be aware of both scales—of their value in terms of money and also in terms of usefulness—and compare them carefully when we want to buy what we need. There are scientifically developed scales setting out the different qualities of metals to enable us to choose exactly the right one for various purposes. In the moral sphere, we are rarely confronted with a clear-cut choice between good and evil, but frequently with one between better and worse; there are conflicting loyalties, there is 'the lesser evil'; thus our decisions have to be based on knowledge of the different degrees of value, and it is essential that this knowledge should be as clear and correct as possible.

At the same time, we have to be aware of the fact that these scales of values may contradict each other; this is part of their nature and should be acknowledged and accepted. Such contradictions can be seen even if we are dealing with the same kind of objects from a similar point of view. When, after the introduction of oil, the value of coal for the purpose of heating is reduced, the price of coal may nevertheless go up. The same things can always take diametrically opposite places in different scales of values. Air is indispensable for our lives, bread most important, and toys and jewellery are inessential; but air costs nothing, bread is cheap, and the most inessential things can be most expensive. At the same time, a beautiful piece of jewellery may be comparatively cheap, and an ugly one, perhaps overloaded with diamonds, very expensive. The diamonds themselves can be seen as useful if precious jewellery gives us pleasure, or if we want to invest money, or cut glass, but they are useless if we are starving in a part of the world where we cannot sell them. Actions which are helpful for progress in our career may have little or no moral value or even be immoral. These contradictions should be kept alive, for they can help us to come to the right decision; we must make up our minds whether we prefer advancement or integrity.

In this respect, there is once more an important difference between external and internal reality. If two scientific theories contradict each other, a serious problem arises, as can be seen from the great exertions made by some physicists to resolve the contradiction between the general theory of relativity and the quantum theory. Einstein, indeed, devoted the last decades of his life to this attempt. In the sphere of values, contradictions are the natural rule; our examples show that no scale is invalidated if it is contradicted by another, and that no problem arises with regard to the scales. On the contrary, any attempt to unify the scales by basing them on a common denominator falsifies our judgment; it is just as wrong to judge harmless pleasures in the light of a rigid morality as it is to expect that moral behaviour should be useful for our material welfare and rewarded by success in our profession.

In fact, at least one attempt at such a unification—valuing everything in terms of money, thus making money an all-inclusive scale—enjoys, though perhaps unconsciously, a wide measure of acceptance: but this only shows how dangerous such unifications are, for we are led to overlook that a scale of this nature is bound to be one-sided and limited. Obviously money cannot measure truth, goodness and beauty; but even usefulness for a special purpose, as our examples of oil and coal, of air and bread show, must still be decided in other terms. Yet once this scale takes hold of a man to such an extent that he wants to earn more and more money, because he judges everything first of all by the amount of money it brings, he will finally forget the end altogether, and thus destroy the value of the means as well because it no longer serves a valuable end. He will neglect, and by this neglect gradually undermine, all those ends which cannot be accommodated in his scale— human relationships, morality and all the higher values—not to mention his enjoyment even of those minor pleasures which the money was originally meant to provide. This kind of unification of contradictory scales of values must, in the long run, become destructive.

Nevertheless, since we have to choose the scale which we should apply, we need also a hierarchy of values, in spite of all the contradictions to which they give rise. The values themselves have to be evaluated and therefore grouped in a scale. Whenever values conflict, they reveal their relative importance, and this fact should be taken into consideration as well. We should know, for instance, the relationship between our actual needs and what we desire only because it gives us pleasure; if we concentrate too much on pleasure, it is likely to escape us. Circumstances may arise in which it is impossible to act with love and be at the same time polite and obliging, and we must choose between the two. In fact, the order of values which we accept influences—or at least ought to influence—our lives more than does anything else. This order mainly depends on our choice of what shall be dominant in it, whether money or a good conscience; the idea of success as conventionally interpreted, or a genuine commitment to a deeply felt higher value. It is true that many people avoid such a decision by dividing life, as we have mentioned,* into separate compartments, and living by different standards in each—ruthlessly pursuing success in their career, while trying to be decent and humane in the private sphere. But this is obviously not a satisfactory solution because, though many who adopt it may prosper in their careers, their lives gradually become warped and degraded by such double standards and the scale of the lower values becomes dominant. The lower values are stronger than the higher ones, for they are supported by our natural selfishness; it is the 'still small voice' which has to be deliberately developed and strengthened. Thus the humanity in our own person as well as in the person of others suffers. Once more the negative, this time the non-acceptance of a binding order of values, instead of helping us to remain neutral, produces commitment of the wrong kind.

* See pp. 7–8.

This need for a hierarchy, however, can lead to another distortion of evaluation. It is important that any such hierarchy should not become too rigid and all-embracing a system, as our example of the unitary scale based on money proves, as well as the example of all bureaucracies. We have said that morality and beauty must not be made dependent on each other, nor should moral values, even if dominant, interfere with harmless pleasures. The element of contradiction between the different scales of values must always be kept alive, and this means that the overall scale which groups the value-scales themselves must also be open to contradiction by another scale which, in certain cases, must be given preference. Yet a fundamental order is nevertheless necessary; otherwise a preoccupation with minor values will tend to obscure issues which we know to be more important for us, and the demands of career or practical success will jeopardize our integrity.

These general characteristics of values will be further clarified when we come to add to them the particular characteristics of the different kinds of values. But we are now in a position to discuss the relation of evaluation to internal reality, and we shall do this first because it will ensure that we appreciate the different kinds of values correctly.

2

When investigating the interdependence of the two realities, we have said that internal reality, to become real, has to be embodied or expressed with the help of external reality—that we must be interested in something, love somebody, or see justice or injustice done. Our feelings, too, to be known or to lead to knowledge, have to be related to an object.*

External reality, however, is adapted to being grasped by the objective method and therefore will, so to speak, put up a strong resistance against being used in this way by the subjective method —against being made to express, not itself, but internal reality. The necessary transformation is brought about by evaluation.

* See pp. 118–19.

The regulative concepts which Kant introduces—'end' or 'purpose' and 'purposefulness'—point in this direction and show how the gap is bridged. He calls them regulative (and not categorical) because we are not bound to apply them; we can describe a table, say, without referring to its purpose, and in certain contexts, when it is for instance a question of transport, we shall be satisfied by this description. But we must obviously think constantly of ends and purposes and they are therefore of great importance. Once we apply these concepts, however, external reality is no longer grasped only as external, but also as related to ourselves; we still have to use the objective method to find the right means to our end, but the object is no longer seen entirely as objective; it is subordinated to our need. Purposefulness, to a greater or lesser extent, connects large parts of external reality with internal reality; sometimes actual objects are even included in internal reality. We may have planted a tree to protect our house or garden from the wind, or to improve the view; but once we come to know it well, enjoy its shade, experience its beauty, watch its growth, it becomes part of our inner life. Something similar can happen with a piece of furniture or any other object; its purpose leads us on to appreciate its other values.

This transformation of external reality can also be illustrated by one of the examples mentioned before—the scientifically developed scales of the qualities of metals. The degrees of the scale are ascertained objectively, but once we want to use metal for a certain purpose, an essential difference arises. The purpose is chosen independently of the scale; an engineer, to serve the chosen purpose, may require a metal which is very hard and stands high on the scale, or a soft one which stands low on it. In this way, a new evaluation arises which subordinates the objective scale to the subjective approach. Or to give another example, taken from biology: it seems that certain organs have been developed to serve certain purposes, even though no conscious value-judgment could have occurred—that lungs, for instance, were developed because animals moved from water to land and had to adapt themselves to different conditions. But the greatest efforts have been made to exclude all terms referring to purpose or value, even if they seemed to offer the simplest explanation, for these terms are bound to endanger objectivity because they belong to the subjective approach and lead to anthropomorphism. Only if they can be dispensed with can biology be made an exact science; therefore the appearance of new organs is now explained with the help of causality—as being produced by mutations, although the causes of these are still unknown and have to be accounted for as happening by chance.

The main work in breaking down the resistance of external reality to the application of the subjective method is done by the many available scales of values, especially if we pay attention to the contradictory scales. Even in the sphere of objects, these scales cover external reality with a network of manifold relationships which make it accessible to a quite different approach; by including the same object in different scales, these objects are, as it were, made amenable to a different treatment. In the case of the tree, for instance, we appreciate the agreeableness of its shade, the usefulness of its wood, fruit and position, the beauty of its different shapes in the different seasons and years, of its foliage and blossom and its relationship to its surrounding. The facts are set out in such a way that they can be used within the context of the subjective method and be changed into that form which embodies internal reality. The greater the number of different values we appreciate in this way the more the single details of any object will become clear, and these details, in their turn, will make clear why we evaluate things as we do and how we should evaluate them. The net covering external reality will become increasingly reticulated so that less and less can escape through its meshes, and thus external reality will become conducive to the knowledge of values.

The scales of values are also important for the development of feeling. Clarity of feeling is essential in this context because, as we shall see, both the lowest and the highest values are indefinable and their appreciation therefore depends on our sense of value. Yet feelings become clear when we develop, through an awareness of differences and details, a wealth of differentiated feelings.

Feelings can be very sweeping; a single feeling such as joy or hate can completely overwhelm us and will then colour and falsify all our thinking. In the sphere of values we often content ourselves—in cases when we are hardly involved as well as in those when we are overwhelmed—with such exclamations as 'How wonderful!' or 'How awful!', but if feelings are to lead to knowledge, we must obviously be able to differentiate and discriminate. The scales of values, by increasing attention to details and contradictions, therefore serve simultaneously the development of feeling and knowledge. To this we shall return when discussing the different kinds of values.

How the many contradictory scales work can be seen from the following example, which it is hoped is faithful in its representation of this aspect of the actions described, even though it is very much simplified in others.

Four men each start a business of their own. They share a common first aim, namely to become rich if they can, and they use the same means and methods to make their activities serve this purpose; but in their ultimate aims they differ entirely. The first man simply wants to become rich; he finds the idea of wealth satisfying, although he hardly knows how he would make use of it; he enjoys having money; it gives him self-confidence. The second wants to make money in order to be able to build up an organization or a new industry; he wants to create something, to contribute to technical progress, to discover better methods of production. The third wants to save up enough to be able to retire early and devote himself to things which really interest him —to reading, the study of literature or music, to seeing the world. The fourth does not desire riches for himself, but wants to be able to help others, to fight misery and poverty, to do what he believes to be morally good.

These four men will have to apply a scale which evaluates means according to their suitability for earning money in business. This scale will in practice be the same for all of them, but if we want to evaluate the different aims which they have chosen, it is evidently insufficient, so that other scales will obviously have to be applied. Each of these will throw light on particular aspects of their endeavours and thus bring into the open more and subtler differences within the scales of values, which will lead to a better knowledge of the values themselves as well as of internal reality. Roughly speaking, the following evaluations will have to be made:

1. The means have to be evaluated, as we have just said, according to their suitability for serving the desired end—namely, to make the business lucrative.

2. If different means can serve the same end, they have to be evaluated, too, so that one can choose between them. Men can become rich by honest work, speculating on the stock exchange, marrying a rich woman, or by gambling or crime. In making the choice between these different means, other scales will obviously be taken into consideration—personal inclinations, concepts of achieving satisfaction, and most probably moral values.

3. The end itself has to be evaluated according to its capacity to serve the further achievement which it is meant to serve. This applies to all the men except the first. An industrial enterprise could be built up by working as a manager; some of the aims of the third man who wants leisure could be achieved by choosing a modest, simple way of life; other people could be helped, as the fourth desires, by some such activity as being a doctor. If these three men choose to enter business, they make a choice based on their evaluation of wealth, but they have probably considered the values just mentioned as well, and they may also have evaluated their own abilities.

4. Every man harbours many different desires, and therefore these have to be evaluated too. Wealth—and the power which it usually brings—are very tempting; if some of them choose other final aims, they must have decided that these are of higher value.

5. All this shows that different scales of values come into play, so that these scales themselves have also to be evaluated. Each of the four men must decide what it is that is most important to him and should determine his behaviour—whether wealth and power,

or practical achievements, or the development of personality, or trying to do good.

6. When they reach, or fail to reach, their aim, they will probably look back and consider whether or not both their aims and the means which they chose to achieve them were chosen correctly, and this may lead to a correction of the original value-judgments.

The last point shows that an increasing differentiation between values can hardly be avoided, for the need to take stock may occur at any stage in the careers of these men. The first, who wanted nothing but to become rich, may recognize that he has become a slave to his money and is failing to appreciate pleasure or joy; he overrated the value of wealth. The second may have been misled by his love for individual freedom; as manager of a large organization he might have achieved more. The third may find either that he will never be able to retire or, when he does, that he has lost the ability to understand and enjoy those things to which he had wanted to devote himself; he had a wrong conception of a rich man's life and leisure. He should have chosen an activity directly connected with his interests. The fourth may find himself involved in growing conflicts between the demands of business methods and conscience; he ought perhaps to have developed his ethical self as a teacher or doctor or social worker. Or any one of the four may realize that he would have done more justice to himself had he chosen a quite different final aim and entered, say, politics or the Church or the university, or if he had devoted much more of his time to his family and his friends.

At the same time, the fruitfulness of being concerned with values may show itself as well, for the correction of previous value-judgments, though disappointing in some respects, can transcend the disappointment. The more scales these men are forced to apply, the more the external reality with which they have to deal will become, so to speak, transparent and reveal internal reality, and so their new knowledge may give them greater satisfaction than the successful realization of their original intentions could ever have done. Another kind of experience can become so strong that it opens to them another dimension of life which is richer and more rewarding than anything they could have imagined before.

Of course, all these choices and evaluations may not become fully conscious, and they will not be as clear-cut as they have to be in our abstract example. But unless these four men become dulled to values, which is also possible, some such processes will happen and, in any case, if we want to understand their behaviour we have to become conscious of the values they apply. The small part which values have played in ethics is due to a wrongful neglect of this need. In the end, a further effect of evaluation will undoubtedly make itself felt, though perhaps again in a less distinct form than our example suggests.

Since the four men are forced to pass through several stages of evaluation, they are gradually driven towards including higher and higher values. This can be noticed whenever values are applied. Even mere usefulness easily leads on to the question 'What is really worth doing?' when the choice is not merely one of means for a particular end, but between different ends, as, for instance, when we have to choose between different kinds of careers before we can choose between types of education. Such a choice, however, will certainly imply the question 'What is really good?'. A so-called realist may retort that he simply wants happiness, but this will force him to choose the kind of happiness he wants, either in one of the ways the four men did, or by choosing the fulfilment of particular individual wishes, or a good family life, or a respected position in society, or friendships and close human relationships, or moral satisfaction. He may remain selfish without being aware of it, but others will notice it and he will notice it in others, and once more some conception of goodness will enter and determine his judgments. In other words, sooner or later we shall be forced to include the highest values and to choose what we consider to be good or true or right; it will prove difficult to stop evaluation before this stage has been reached.

In this way, the reality of these values will make itself felt. We have mentioned the resistance of external reality to the application of the subjective method; but there is also something which we could call resistance within each reality which is significant and of great help. In external reality such a resistance is obvious; if a theory is false, experiments will disprove it; what is externally given will resist misinterpretation. In internal reality the resistance is less obvious, but it will be experienced more and more strongly the more we advance in the application of values. Experience will teach us where our value judgments went wrong; our own subsequent satisfactions and disappointments will show that we cannot make such judgments arbitrarily. There seems to be something in things, in events and actions which we could described as waiting to be discovered by evaluation, an existence of dormant qualities which apparently desire to be brought into the open and willingly respond to such an approach; if we judge wrongly, the object of our judgment resists such a transformation. An unspoilt landscape, for instance, seems to respond if we look at it with an eye receptive to beauty; its beauty seems to be there to be discovered; but we feel some kind of resistance if we try to persuade ourselves that, say, an industrial townscape is beautiful when it is not. Similarly, if we do something which we feel was not quite right, for instance exploit the weakness of another person for the sake of advancement in our career, we may convince ourselves for some time that it had to be done and was therefore right, but the more our sense of values is awakened, the less secure we shall feel in this kind of judgment. Thus the higher values which may at first appear merely abstract gradually become as real as things or actions themselves; in the end, if we still try to insist on a wrong judgment, we shall feel a resistance as strong as if we were banging our head against a wall.

The great significance of the values resides in this fact—that they make internal reality completely real. At the same time it is of their very nature that we can and must choose between them; they enforce choices; and thus their reality removes all doubts about another essential inner experience—freedom of will, which means freedom of decision and action as well as freedom of choice, for choice would be meaningless if it could not have consequences. We have referred to this freedom many times and hope that its existence has been accepted by now;* but it is the inevitable acknowledgment of values which finally confirms the reality of freedom. For value-judgments show that freedom has two different forms, and these make us understand what we actually experience as freedom so clearly that we cannot but accept it.

We could call these two forms, somewhat paradoxically, 'freedom of choice' and 'choice of freedom'. If we are free, we must obviously be free to choose, but we can either make a choice which really sets us free or a wrong choice which enslaves us. Freedom means acting in full accordance with our true nature without any hindrance. This, of course, raises the question of what our true nature is; but this question will be answered through the experience of the values we choose. If we choose, for instance, money or power, this kind of choice enslaves us again, because it forces us into actions which do not allow us fully to realize what we, as human beings, in fact potentially are; the stronger such desires as that for money or power become, the more impossible it is for us to give more than rudimentary expression to anything else in our nature. Those who misinterpret freedom as licence will become slaves to the addictions which they allow themselves to indulge. Something similar will happen if we do not exercise our freedom to choose; we shall then be entirely subject to our instinctive urges. We can become free only by acting in such a way that the positive potentialities of internal reality are made actual, for thus, as we have seen, we are set free—that is, we must not only choose, but also choose correctly.

In other words, there is both a 'freedom from' and a 'freedom to'. This means that freedom is not only negative, but also positive—not only that the bonds of necessity, however powerful they are, cannot bind us completely, but also that we should make proper use of our freedom. Freedom is thus more than a mere denial of determinism; it opens the way, as we have tried to show, to great richness of experience. I have, however, chosen to use

* See pp. 6–7, 40–1, 86, 98, 140–1.

different names, partly because these are perhaps less clumsy than saying 'from' and 'to', and partly because they indicate the actual content of each form of freedom and thus make the difference between them clearer.

The more obvious of the two forms is the freedom of choice. We have mentioned many experiences which leave no doubt of its existence; it will therefore be sufficient to refer to some of these very briefly. If we want to lift an arm or to stop reading this book, nobody will convince us that we are not free to do so at any moment, and this confidence is not as trivial as it may seem, for it is of the same kind as that experience of freedom which is the basis of moral decisions. Moreover, lack of freedom of choice would make any discussion meaningless; if we could only hold views which were determined by external or psychological factors, nobody could ever hope to convince us by arguments, not even of determinism itself, for the acceptance of any conviction, if it is to be significant at all, must be based on a conscious attempt to choose between truth and falsehood. We shall not understand man unless we start from this sort of freedom.

The other form, the choice of freedom, makes sure that freedom can really be exercised. In the sphere of ethics, this freedom is based on the acceptance of the elements mentioned so far—the moral law, moral principles and motives, the ethical self; and it is thrown into relief and made particularly clear by evaluation. Of course, freedom is not restricted to the moral sphere; there is political freedom which, as in the case of freedom of thought and speech, will overlap with moral freedom, and there are natural, artistic and religious potentialities which, when brought into the open, set man free. But here we are not concerned with these and we can disregard them because the ethical appeal, as has been mentioned, forces us most directly to become aware of our freedom. This appeal, moreover, forces us also to face our immoral potentialities, because we must struggle against them, and therefore no part of our being is disregarded; if, on the contrary, the immoral potentialities are allowed to gain the upper hand they lead to enslavement, for they prevent some of our moral potentialities from ever becoming known to us. To make freedom real, we must therefore not only choose, but choose those values which give the right content to freedom, by enabling us to give the fullest expression which we can possibly achieve to our ethical self.

The significance of the choice of freedom can also be understood if we follow another line of thought. When we look at man from outside, we are bound to look for necessity and thus to assume that his character—which we tend to accept as constant—is to be regarded as a cause of the events in which he is involved. In fact, as soon as other people and society are taken into consideration, we have to think in terms of causality, and this seems to exclude freedom. But if a person has made his choice of values, he is gradually transformed by them and will therefore, at some point, enter as a different cause into the chain of events because he has been changed by the use he has made of his freedom. Thus, through its second form, freedom can be seen at work even from outside.

How this choice of freedom should be exercised will be seen as we now proceed to the discussion of particular values. But we can already recognize the two main reasons why values can actually fulfil our expectations.

On the one hand, since there are so many values and scales of values, their clarification appeals to the many potentialities of our whole being; they stimulate us to exercise our freedom and elucidate and enrich our moral experience. We are able to acknowledge different demands on different levels; duty need no longer bar the way to love. At the same time, they also appeal to both reason and emotion; they can be discussed as well as felt; and they thus lead to those distinctions within the sphere of feeling which we have found necessary.

On the other hand, values can reconcile statements referring to what exists with those referring to what we ought to do. This may, at first, sound surprising, for values are norms of judgment and behaviour; they therefore seem to be abstract and to lack existence and, moreover, they are not formulated as demands. Nevertheless, the norms, when accepted, make potentialities actual and give rise to actions, so that what they entail becomes real by being lived, and their inner reality is confirmed by the resistance which we encounter when making wrong judgments. At the same time, existence is reconciled with obligation, because when a value is experienced as positive this makes it desirable and thus raises the demand that it should be made real; these demands become obligations when we experience the reality a value acquires once it has led to an action.

The notion of value, excellence, or goodness carries within it the notion of worthwhileness, passing into obligatoriness. In recognizing anything as excellent we at the same time recognize it as worth having, worth doing, worth being or pursuing, as imposing an imperative of action or of respect and admiration.*

But to be able to use our choice of freedom correctly, we have to distinguish between different kinds of values.

3

The world of values confronts us with an astonishing fact. Although values contain—and are constituted by—subjective elements which defy definition, we find in this sphere a high degree of general agreement and of certainty. Hardly anybody will deny that courage, nobility or firmness are admirable; there may be disagreements, in particular cases, as to their actual presence and genuineness, but not about the values themselves. This confirms the reality of values; yet in spite of this fact, and even though we constantly make value-judgments, we are little aware of what we actually do when making them because, as we have said, the process of evaluation and the laws of thinking on which it is based have not attracted sufficient attention.

We have begun to explore this sphere by describing some of the general characteristics applying to all values. In addition, we can discern particular characteristics because there are, in the main, three kinds of values. To distinguish between them, we can once more use Kant's regulative concept 'end'. The three kinds are:

* M. Ginsberg, *On Justice in Society* (a Pelican Original, 1965), p. 20.

Values, *their nature and application*

1. Purely subjective values, such as agreeableness. These serve an end which can only be appreciated by the individual concerned and therefore cannot be either described or defined.

2. Relative values, such as usefulness. These evaluate means according to their suitability to serve an end, and they can be defined by the purpose they serve.

3. Absolute values, such as goodness, which are sometimes also called intrinsic values. These serve no other purpose, but are ends in themselves; they can be described, but not fully defined.

The purely subjective values are of no direct significance for ethics, so that they require only a brief discussion. But they have to be distinguished from the other kinds, in order to enable us to describe these, and also to make the necessary distinctions between different kinds of feelings.

In one form or another, these values refer to qualities which make things agreeable or disagreeable, to likes and dislikes; they are purely a matter of individual taste and cannot therefore be disputed. The well-known example 'I like sugar in my tea' is a good instance of such an indisputable value-judgment, but it is valid solely with regard to these values; we shall see that it is wrong to use it as a support for the claim that all values are 'merely a matter of taste', as has been done. Yet within the sphere of taste—and only there—it is obviously only I myself who can decide what is agreeable for me and what I like—whether it be sugar, a particular colour, or a certain tone of voice—and my judgment has to be accepted because I cannot describe my reactions in any other terms, nor state any reasons for them which could be discussed. It must be remembered that the word 'subjective' is not used here in the sense it was in the phrase 'subjective method'; we call these values 'purely subjective' because they are not accessible to any methodical investigation. To a certain extent, happiness also belongs to these values, but not entirely, for we have seen that striving for it forces us to consider other values as well.

This characteristic of the purely subjective values has two consequences. On the one hand, since any value-judgment requires personal participation, these values accompany all value-judgments; any experience of a value is either agreeable or disagreeable. This applies, for instance, to courage and truth as well as to good and evil. The purely subjective values must therefore be known, for otherwise they could hide—and thus falsify—the difference between all other values. On the other hand, just because they tend to blur the boundaries between the different values, they will have to be dismissed when we come to distinguish and discriminate between these.

This is confirmed and elucidated by the feelings to which the purely subjective values give rise. Before we enter upon a discussion of these feelings, however, it is necessary to remind ourselves that any abstract philosophical discussion suffers from the disadvantage that it must treat all experiences as if they were fully conscious, which is by no means the case. This difficulty can be overcome, as has been mentioned before, if the reader, instead of viewing these discussions as more or less interesting ideas, will translate them into terms of his actual experience. This is particularly important when we deal with feelings, for in their sphere experience is most direct and therefore less easily apprehended in terms of abstract thought. It is undeniable that the differences between feelings are at the start rarely conscious, and that feelings can hardly be produced at will; nor are they often susceptible to being managed. But our appreciation and understanding of feeling will grow through consistent effort.

The experience of a purely subjective value gives rise to an undifferentiated kind of pleasure and pain, which makes me concentrate on my own feeling, while in all other cases, even though my personal participation is stronger when higher values are at stake, I am drawn away from my own person and concerned with the values themselves. When I enjoy the sunshine, I am enjoying myself; when I want to do something useful, I concentrate on my task; when concerned with right and wrong (when injustice has been done to someone else, for instance), I may forget myself completely. If, however, I direct attention towards my feelings, clear evaluation will become difficult, for neither pleasure nor pain (that is, neither liking nor disliking) is a criterion. The more important values—for instance the good—may demand the foregoing of certain pleasures, such as those of a comfortable life, and yet lead to other pleasures by the inner satisfaction they produce. On the other hand, I may well recognize the value of a particular virtuous man or of a work of art and yet so thoroughly dislike them that merely seeing them is painful to me.

Pleasure and pain, moreover, accompany all our more particularized feelings; there is no feeling—be it joy or sorrow, love or hate, exuberance or despair—which is not either pleasurable or painful or a mixture of the two; but differences between pleasures and pains cannot be ascertained except in connection with the experiences which they accompany and thus they themselves cannot help in the making of distinctions. They do not tell us anything about the nature of the particular feeling with which they occur; a sudden, overwhelming stroke of good luck may at first be just as painful as a bad shock, and melancholy or sadness can be pleasing. In fact, we can easily be misled. My pleasure may be noble or it may be mean, my pain either moving or despicable; something very harmful, such as some forms of tuberculosis, can produce a pleasant euphoria, while something helpful, such as the treatment it requires, may lead to great pain.

We are naturally inclined to increase our pleasure and to reduce our pain; if we indulge this tendency and try to achieve pleasure at any cost—a course which usually makes us particularly sensitive to pain—the predominance of these two feelings will obscure all other differences. The effect will be the same if (as may also happen) a surfeit of pleasure makes us generally insensitive and coarse. To strive for higher values is often difficult; if we overemphasize the desirability of increasing pleasure and avoiding pain, we may be tempted to abandon all more demanding aims.

We are therefore entitled to say that the purely subjective values, since they focus our attention on pleasure and pain, have to be transcended, even though they must be known in order to avoid falsifications of the other values.

It is true that, with the help of other values, even the purely subjective ones can become more articulate, so that our reactions can be compared with the individual reactions of others, and then they can contribute to a fuller understanding of these other values. Likes and dislikes, if we acquire some detachment, can give to moral experiences greater objectivity, as when, for instance, we dislike punishment and yet feel compelled to punish. Good taste, in essence inexplicable, is capable of development and can lead to a fuller knowledge and appreciation of beauty. In general, however, we should give to pleasure and pain less attention than we are usually inclined to do, and develop our feelings in a direction which leads, not towards pleasure and pain, but beyond them.

The difficulty of speaking in the abstract becomes particularly obvious here. We do not mean that pleasure and pain could or should be disregarded when they are the direct outcome of experience, as when a wound creates intense pain and a relief from such a pain great pleasure. These are strong emotions by themselves, not by-products of others, though even they should not be over-rated; we must not reject a treatment which promises relief because it is painful. Nor are we speaking of joy and sorrow; of course, joy is pleasurable and sorrow painful, but these are emotions of a different nature; they correspond to the relative values and will be discussed in the next chapter. We refer rather to that pleasure and pain—or to those likes and dislikes—which, more or less as a physical sensation, as a nerve-reaction, accompany all experiences and feelings. This distinction will be easy to appreciate if, say, pleasure accompanies an experience which we know we ought not to enjoy (as when we do harm to a person we dislike and enjoy doing it), but the distinction will be difficult if pleasure and experience do not contradict each other (as when an experience of friendliness gives us pleasure). Nevertheless, for the reasons mentioned, even then it is important to sharpen our awareness and to distinguish what is essential from what could be misleading, so that, for instance, we do not break off a friendship when it ceases to be a pleasure and begins to demand sacrifices. It has perhaps already become obvious that this discrimination can be achieved.

When we bear these points in mind, we can probably understand that the phrase 'to develop our feelings away from pleasure and pain' makes sense. We can develop feelings in different directions; we can use the object as an occasion for indulging our feelings and then pay attention merely to the feeling so produced, to our nerve-reactions and our state of mind; or, in contrast to this, we can allow our attention to be absorbed by the object and by our experience of it. We can either dwell on our feelings or try to understand what they tell us. (The former way leads to sentimentality which will be discussed in the next chapter.) We move in the right direction when we begin to forget ourselves, because then the cause of the feeling—namely the significance of the object—will have become dominant. We must learn to feel in terms of the object. The following two examples may show that such an effort is possible.

1. 'Suppose we are listening to the playing of a violin ... These sounds we may be aware of as pleasing, but, when we are rapt in music, we cease to be conscious of the pleasure of the sounds, and are conscious of the music only as a continuous melodious meaning.'* Only the latter attitude will lead to an understanding of music, and it can be deliberately developed if we are musical.

The preceding reservation has to be made because the sense of values, as mentioned before, must always be presupposed in evaluation; there is what Scheler calls a 'value-blindness' which can make an individual totally unable to appreciate some particular value, including even moral values. Both forms of freedom are limited, not only by the possible restrictions of our power to choose and to act which we have discussed, but also by our inability or failure to recognize some of the options open to us. The elaboration of values is important for this reason, too: it can help us to realize further values and thus give us more scope for choice.

* J. Oman, *The Natural and the Supernatural*, 2nd ed. (Cambridge, 1950), pp. 174–5.

2. A different facet of the same kind of experience can be seen in the case of so-called 'romantic' love, where the lover wants to be in love, not with a person, but with love itself. It is a vague emotion which he tries to support by finding some object for it; and since it is only his own feeling which matters, it can be attached now to this, now to that person; the partner is not really important because the lover is apt to see the person whom he happens to choose in the light of his desire and as adorned with certain preconceived qualities, in order to increase either the pleasure or the pain (for it is frequently unhappy love) which he wants or happens to feel. In this case, pleasure or pain may be transcended by ecstasy or despair, and the lover may also, for periods, forget himself; yet, since he is still dwelling upon his feelings, this kind of love will not lead to any knowledge; it will falsify his value-judgments and basically intensify a wrong pre-occupation with his own person, with his state of mind and his emotions. By contrast, someone who is really in love with a person and resists being misled by a false ideal may acquire knowledge both of the person loved and of himself, and thus correct and develop his value-judgments.*

This transformation can be achieved when we apply the other two kinds of values.

---

* One could, of course, also refer to poetry to illustrate this 'feeling in terms of the object'. This is, for instance, particularly striking in the case of Rilke who was opposed to the re-printing of his early poems because these were still too much concerned with expressing his feelings—and this makes clear how successfully he used his feelings in his later poems to deepen knowledge of the objects he then represented.

CHAPTER X

RELATIVE AND ABSOLUTE VALUES

1

The relative values, according to our definition, evaluate the suitability of means for particular ends. But two kinds have to be distinguished. First, those (such as usefulness) which directly judge the means by its purpose, and second those (such as courage) which, even though not directly dependent on a purpose, should nevertheless be judged in the light of the purpose which they do in fact support. The latter are the virtues of which we have said that they will be included among the values; they will be discussed in this context, but separately.

When speaking of these values, we have always given usefulness as an example, because it is the clearest one. But any aim which we might want to achieve—whether to enjoy ourselves or to entertain others, to educate ourselves or others, to help somebody, to live a good married life, to serve the community—have their related means which we have to judge by their fitness for the aim. And even when we have no intentional aim, but merely experience feelings which we like or would avoid, such as joy or sorrow, love or hate, we shall frequently want to relate them to causes, in order to know the means by which we could kindle the feeling again or avoid it, and we shall evaluate them accordingly. Thus relative values show most clearly how indispensable evaluation is; for whatever we experience or do leads us to judge, with the help of relative values, the means we have to apply to attain a chosen end. This is just as inevitable as the development of science out of practical needs.

It is here, however, that one could doubt whether there is such a fundamental difference between the scientific approach and evaluation. One might ask whether the practical usefulness of a

247

means cannot be ascertained scientifically. But we have shown already, when discussing scientifically developed scales of qualities of metals, that this objection is invalid, for how we use such a scale still depends on the purpose we have chosen, and the choice is made independently of the scale.* Even usefulness is established on the basis of a personal decision, although the objective qualities of the means have to be taken into account.

Naturally, the relative values determined by practical purposes refer to external reality, but this does not interfere with their belonging, as values, to the sphere of internal reality, for their application only confirms the two claims we have already made. On the one hand, since the purpose is chosen according to our need or desire, the resistance of external reality to the subjective method is broken down because external reality is subordinated to our choices. On the other hand, the choice of ends is bound to include more and more of internal reality, because it requires an evaluation of these ends too, so that we are continuously driven to the application of more values and scales of values. It will make a great difference, for instance, whether we want to achieve something which is useful for ourselves or useful for others. Higher values will enter into the value-judgment—perhaps only unconsciously, creating an uneasy feeling, if we care only for ourselves (for nobody can remain quite unaware of, or un-influenced by, what is generally thought of selfishness), or to be consciously accepted if we care for others. In both cases, different means still have to be judged according to their fitness to serve the chosen end, but in each case the value of usefulness appears in a different light, and this will lead to further distinctions, to the evaluating of the moral qualities of a man's motives and aims. Once begun, however, the consideration of moral values can hardly remain restricted to one particular instance.

The most important point which arises from the distinction between the three different kinds of values is the need to be clearly aware of the relative values. Purely subjective values cannot be

* See p. 230.

disputed; absolute values cannot be defined; the relative values are the only ones which can be defined—namely by their purpose. Therefore we should insist that they really are defined, and this requires a clear evaluation of the purpose as well. It is lack of definition of the relative values that most frequently leads to confusion in this sphere, and it is this kind of confusion which, either by distorting or by discrediting the whole realm of values, tends to corrupt our lives.

Consider how this applies, for instance, to television. Seen merely as a means of communication, television is an astonishing achievement of science and technology, a fact now perhaps too much taken for granted. But this aspect is not the only one to be taken into account; we should go on to ask which of its actual functions is truly useful. Should it be used only for the trans-mission of news or also of drama and music? Should it be a means of general or political education or of entertainment as well? What kind of information is useful and what kind of entertain-ment is valuable? Should criticism and the propagation of unorthodox views be encouraged or restricted? Unless we define the means by its purpose and evaluate the purpose, we are in danger of becoming mere addicts of television as an end in itself, and then the lowest of the values—that is, the lowest kind of entertainment—will prevail, and the merit of every programme will be assessed on this level. If this happens, it is bound to lead to a corresponding deterioration in the programme and to an under-mining of the feeling of responsibility on the part of their pro-ducers who naturally try to do their given task well—namely to awaken the fullest possible response. In other words, relative values are reduced to purely subjective values and this, as we have seen, works against any proper development of sensitivity and knowledge. In this way, one of the great inventions of the mind is made to contribute to its corruption.

This, of course, is a rather obvious example, but it may help us to become aware of other similar distortions. However fascinating the technical achievements of our age may be, we must avoid being bewitched by a mere means, whether it be computers or rockets or the whole range of instruments which make the exploration of the moon and outer space possible. We obviously cannot help admiring such achievements. Nevertheless, evaluation must also concern itself with the end which is meant to be served by these astonishing means and ensure that the real end is seen and correctly evaluated. Otherwise we shall be unduly influenced by misleading emotions.*

The main problem at the present time is probably the evaluation of natural science itself. We often hear it asserted—by a number of scientists and by even more laymen—that science is concerned with truth and nothing but truth and that every kind of scientific investigation must be pursued whatever the consequences. This would make scientific knowledge an absolute value, for it is only these which can be accepted as ends in themselves. But is this evaluation of science justified? We shall discuss the concept of truth in the next chapter, but an essential point can already be made now.

The preceding assertion can be supported in two ways. First, it seems justifiable to demand that scientific investigation should not be subordinated to practical ends. Many experiments which were made for purely scientific reasons and with no regard for their possible usefulness—such as the splitting of the atom—have unexpectedly led to very great practical achievements, and these would never have materialized if an immediate practical purpose had determined research. Second, it would obviously be wrong, even if it were possible, to stop the advance of science; its successes in every sphere of life speak for themselves; non-scientific considerations should not therefore interfere. But does this justify the exemption of the scientist from all responsibility for what he is doing? Today scientific research is practically the only human activity which is not judged morally because it is accepted as having absolute value, and this has given rise to many grave

---

* Cf. the following report which certainly reveals a widespread attitude: 'The United States public wants Americans to land on the moon, not out of scientific curiosity, or even a sense of adventure, though that comes into it. They want to get there before the Russians do.' (*The Times*, 23 October, 1968.)

problems for which no solution seems to be in sight. A different approach may thus be worth trying.

We have said that all value-judgments contain objective and subjective elements. Science cannot be accepted as embodying—or aiming at—an absolute value on either of these counts.

When we look at scientific discoveries objectively we have to admit that, whenever possible, they will be used for a practical purpose and thereby subordinated to a different end. Discoveries, after all, usually lead to inventions. The assertion that science must be pursued as an end in itself because it is in this way that practical purposes are best served admits, at least implicitly, a relative aspect of science. But many scientists reject responsibility for the practical application of scientific discoveries, partly by distinguishing sharply between pure and applied sciences (and often disparaging the latter), partly by leaving responsibility to those who are concerned with practical affairs. Yet can anyone deny responsibility for what he is actually doing? The scientist may at first be unable to guess the possible consequences of his achievements, but these will become obvious at a later stage and then, owing to the specialization of science, he may well be the only person who can fully understand what is at stake. Leonardo da Vinci destroyed the flame-thrower which he had invented because he feared that it would do too great harm to mankind. A further complication is that, to a large extent, scientific research has become team-work so that any individual decision may seem irrelevant; when many refused to develop the atomic bomb, others took their place. Yet some of those who supported its construction, for instance Einstein, felt remorse when it was too late. These are extremely difficult problems. The supporters of the bomb could say that to oppose its construction would have prevented the development of atomic energy for peaceful purposes, but obviously no such problem can be solved unless the relative value of science as a means for other ends is taken into consideration. If, however, science were accepted as a relative value, the scientist could no longer deny responsibility for what he is doing, and since responsibility can only be felt by the individual, the team could not be used as an excuse for evading it.

A scrutiny of the subjective elements leads to a similar conclusion. The conviction that the scientist himself has no responsibility for the application of science contributes to his natural inclination to disregard the consequences of his activities, and he is encouraged to do so by the general belief that science embodies an absolute value. Subjectively, this belief would be justified if he were searching for truth for its own sake, or if he experienced this search as an expression of his desire to help his fellow-men. But his motives seem in fact to be different.

Two eminent scientists may speak for many. At the 115th annual meeting of the British Association for the Advancement of Science Professor A. V. Hill is reported as supporting the view of Sir Edward Appleton; he agreed 'that the chief and most effective motive of scientific endeavour was curiosity and adventure, not philanthropy. They deceived themselves, although not perhaps others, if they pretended it was. And its chief reward was not power or fame for themselves, nor the satisfaction of benefit to others, but the joy of the artist in building a beautiful discovery on skilful and elegant experiment, or of the adventurer and explorer who got there first'.* This statement, replacing one kind of self-satisfaction by another, explicitly denies that the relative or practical value of science has any influence on the motives of the scientist; it obviously presupposes that science is an end in itself, for only thus could this emphasis on purely subjective values appear satisfactory. But, as we have seen, meaningful discussion of subjective values is impossible. Sir Edward Appleton himself also says: 'The desire to know does not need any greater justification than the pleasure—the inward excitement—which attends its satisfaction.'† He thereby feels relieved of any responsibility; but are these motives sufficient for us to agree that he need not feel responsible? Such statements only confirm what was

---

* In a vote of thanks, not included in the Society's publication of the proceedings. Quoted here according to *The Times*, 3 September, 1953.
† *Science and the Nation* (Edinburgh, 1957), p. 36.

said more than three hundred years ago by another eminent scientist—Pascal. When he looked back on his scientific activity, he declared that he had been motivated, not by an unselfish search for truth, but by a selfish 'lust for knowledge', though in his case the discovery destroyed any feeling of satisfaction.

Thus both the objective and the subjective elements contained in this particular value-judgment confirm that science should be judged as a relative value, because the equating of science with an absolute value as well as the introduction of purely subjective values result in the omission or distortion of essential facts. This does not in itself solve the problem, nor does it mean that a clear-cut solution can be found. The main difficulty is the two demands concerning science with which we have agreed—that pure science should not be subordinated to practical considerations and that the advance of science should not be hindered. Nevertheless, we can see that a discussion based upon the relative aspect of science could lead beyond the present impasse without endangering either pure science or science in general.

This different approach is neither startling nor utopian, but for this very reason it could help to rectify the present situation. Naturally, since the prevalent attitude is the result of a development which began centuries ago, the most we can hope for is that this change of attitude could introduce a different development which in its turn will need time to make itself felt.

Whether we like it or not, a choice between different kinds of research is constantly being made, and it has to be made because the capacities of the human mind and the financial resources of any state are limited. But so long as every scientist feels entitled to claim support for any experiment or observation which has become possible, just because it has become possible and regardless of the consequences, one of two things will happen. Either support will tend to be given to the one whose obsession seems the most fascinating or adventurous, even if more urgent needs of mankind have to be neglected; or science will actually be considered as relative by those who finance it and support will be given because a particular line of research promises certain practical results; but since the scientist himself does not admit this kind of argument, he will be unable to ensure that his discoveries are not used for ends which he abhors. Both developments are happening today in the exploration of outer space, which enjoys the most costly support of all scientific endeavours, and the prevalent convictions among the scientists as well as the general climate of opinion which exempts scientists from responsibility allows them to accept support for whatever reasons it may be forthcoming—which means, in effect, that they disregard any military potentialities of the results. Or, to mention other examples in which research for its own sake is probably the only driving force—is the discovery of new particles really worth the staggering amount of work and money which it demands, and should considerable resources, badly needed for research into food production or the causes of cancer, be diverted to radio-astronomy? All these problems could be approached in a more rational way if science were recognized for what it is: if it were seen as belonging to the realm of the relative values, for these demand consideration of consequences and thus responsibility for them. After all, this is already done, and with beneficial results; quite a number of useful lines of research are supported because of their practical usefulness, though probably not as lavishly as those mentioned. But the scientists who deny their responsibility would have to change their attitude, so as to be enabled to give unselfish advice to those concerned with science. Pure research would go on, but the fields where it should be pursued would be selected by more reasonable methods than is the case at present.

The problem is not confined to natural science; it also arises in those disciplines which we have discussed, especially in sociology when it is combined with psychology. Dahrendorf says:

Very possibly tomorrow's sociologist will face as difficult a conflict of conscience as today's nuclear physicist. One need but think of the none too distant possibility of keeping totalitarian governments in power with the assistance of sociological insight—or of 'human relations in industry', as the current phrase goes, whose implicit goal is often to prevent strikes and wage demands without regard to their legitimacy . . . Because the postulates of sociological analysis are likely (if not certain) to be misunderstood both inside and outside the discipline, the sociologist must leave the comfortable refuge of his logical righteousness and take a moral stand ... As a science, sociology is still in its infancy; but already—contrary to the wishes, although often not to the practice, of sociologists—it has developed capacities for curtailing freedom that as recently as half a century ago were conceived of only in utopian fantasy.*

Undoubtedly the problem is difficult; the splitting of the atom, in combination with molecular biology, both based on researches for their own sake, have contributed to some alleviation of the suffering due to cancer and may lead in some cases to its cure. On the other hand, it is true that any beneficial discovery can be misused. Nevertheless, the pursuit of pure research has obviously got out of hand, and the control which the suggested different approach could provide is badly needed. In the long run, moreover, this introduction of a new rational element—by no means arbitrary, but recognizable as justified—could also lead to unforeseen beneficial consequences.

Similar considerations apply when we move to those values which could be called virtues. These are different because, as we have said, they are not directly dependent on particular ends; they only give support to the pursuit of them. But because they do this, they too must be judged in the light of the ends they serve, and this makes them relative values. Dangers arise if they are mistakenly accepted as absolute; in this respect there is no difference between them and the other relative values.

One such value, for instance, is courage, which is undoubtedly the condition of a great many valuable endeavours, and yet a relative value, for it can serve good or bad ends, and is only good if it serves a good purpose; otherwise it may be foolish or criminal. To mistake courage for an absolute ideal leads to the common admiration for great conquerors or great criminals and allows us to overlook the senselessness of their acts and the brutality and killing that go with them. We isolate a single aspect, thus distorting reality, and dwell on it in a sentimental way, thus distorting feeling. And, more seriously, this wrong interpretation of the

* *Essays in the Theory of Society*, pp. 67, 98, 101.

ideal provides even the worst kind of adventurer with followers, if only he is daring enough. The relative value, because it has been endowed with absolute claims, tends, wrongly, to turn into a purely subjective value for, if it is to appear absolute, it must not be defined. A valuable concept is thus made to serve corruption and destruction.

The same can be said of most other values of this kind. Firmness is generally, and often rightly, accepted as admirable, yet it is hardly so if one remains firm in pursuing a decision which one knows to be wrong. The boundaries between firmness and obstinacy can obviously only be drawn if firmness is seen as a relative value—as dependent on the purpose it supports. We have already seen that duty, in many ways a helpful or even indispensable concept, is in need of a clear definition in terms of its end; otherwise it can be used to encourage evil.* Even respect has its relative aspects; to respect every man as an end in himself must not mean that we respect every aspect of his behaviour or all of his decisions; we should treat the traitor or criminal as a human being and not merely as a danger to society who is simply to be eradicated, but that does not mean that we should not reject what he does. Respect is closely related to awe, and the positive aspect of awe can hardly be overrated; it is the condition of any experience of the transcendental, the absolute, of God. Yet admiration for a great conqueror, such as Napoleon, or for a man who ruthlessly uses power, such as Hitler, can also awaken something akin to awe, as can confrontation by extreme wealth or the effort to comprehend the significance of astronomical numbers, of light years and distances. Another virtue is obedience, and obedience to the moral law is highly desirable; but that kind of obedience which is the basis of what Fromm called 'authoritarian conscience', or submission to the wrong kind of authority, is not. The same applies to loyalty. Thus all these values are not ends in themselves, but must be judged in the light of the purpose they serve.

In fact, there is hardly any more dangerous error than to mistake a relative for an absolute value, for this is at the root of all

* See pp. 195–6.

fanaticism. Nationalism offers a clear example. Acceptance of one's nationality as a relative value can be good; if a man sees his belonging to a nation as part of his natural and social endowment, he may even draw advantage from it and make it the basis of some noble achievement. Certainly mankind would greatly lose if all differences between the nations were to disappear. But, in order to make his nation an absolute value, the nationalist endows it with all the qualities generally considered admirable, regardless of their applicability, and makes some particularly cherished quality the highest of all and the sole prerogative of his own nation. 'Faithfulness' becomes German, 'fair-mindedness' English, 'logicality' French. His own nation is given the appearance of being ultimately the best, while the bad qualities are divided among the other nations; this makes them enemies of the good, which, in turn, easily leads to making them enemies of the nation. All nationalists disregard two facts: that any national character can only be described with the greatest difficulty and most unreliably, and that any nation is only part of mankind and therefore relative to the whole. This aberration may merely lead to complacency, but even then further distortions of judgment occur. A man is born a member of a nation; he cannot help it and should not, therefore, make it a source of pride; yet praise of the nation makes him, too, seem praiseworthy and absolves him from special efforts to prove his worth. By transforming a mere fact into a merit, he strengthens the purely subjective values, is able to enjoy them and to indulge his emotions. But nationalism tends to become fanatical and lead to evil actions, and complacency can easily change into fanaticism in times of crisis, and then the dangers become obvious. Since the nation has been accepted as an absolute value, all moral restrictions are swept away; any action in the service of the nation and against the enemy appears to be justified. In particular, respect for the single individual—inside and outside the nation—is abolished; the basic commandment is changed into 'thou shalt kill when thy country demands it'.

Making the same kind of error, fanatical communists regard their materialistic ideal of happiness to which their social order

should lead as absolute, although happiness is obviously dependent on the individual nature of man; thus they despise the
happiness of the single individual and become ruthless, regarding
each of the single demands of their programme as absolute, to be
imposed by absolute dictatorship. Capitalism may usually be less
fanatical, but if it is accepted as a guarantee of the ultimately best
order, material possessions are made ends in themselves, and this
kind of materialism also prevents a full development of personality, so that it can easily lead to fanaticism whenever communism is opposed or fought.

All mistaken absolutes divide men and lead to a disregard for
human beings, which in all extreme cases allows us to kill them.
How great the dangers are can be seen even when fanaticism is
lacking. Most of the relative values have been accepted, at one
time or another, as absolute and have wrongly been made the
basis of morality—of a pseudo-morality based on power, on hero-
worship, on the concept of duty, on obedience—and thus have
distorted or destroyed whatever could be accepted as truly moral.
Today we watch attempts to base morality on science, but the
identification of science with absolute truth must in itself also
lead to a disregard for man, because the objective method is
bound to be impersonal. In the end, only utilitarianism is left
intact—a poor substitute for morality.

One condition of arriving at such wrong results is the impression that the chosen quality is 'great'. It is the great conqueror and
the great criminal who are admired, and the nationalist sees his
nation as great. (Minor facts or actions are easily seen for what
they are.) Greatness is needed because it arouses strong feelings,
and strength of feeling can make anything appear absolute. A
further brief discussion of feeling will therefore contribute to a
clarification of this problem.

2

When discussing inclinations, we have distinguished feeling as an organ of knowledge from occasional and misleading feelings, and later we have said that discrimination in this sphere is dependent on the application of many values and scales of values and the realization of the differences between them, for this enables us to develop a greater wealth of feelings.* Whenever this discrimination is lacking, a single strong feeling (such as desire or hate) easily becomes sweeping and dominating, and this creates the conviction that its object is absolute. If we want to discern that kind of feeling which is an organ of knowledge, we have to be aware of this false absoluteness.

The distorting influence of lack of discrimination can be seen on two levels.

(1) Comparatively harmless is the blunting of feeling by sentimentality. Since such shades of feeling defy definition, we are once more facing here the difficulties of any abstract discussion; but the word is now commonly used in a derogatory sense, and if we accept this sense, we can always ascertain that two basic tendencies are at work.

On the one hand, sentimentality inclines a person to adopt conventional attitudes, to feel what he thinks he is supposed to feel on certain occasions, without fully relating his attitude to the particular, individual experience or situation. On hearing that someone has died, for instance, somebody is likely to remark 'How sad!' and we sense general agreement among the hearers, including ourselves, even though none of us knows exactly whether this particular death was really sad or a relief from unbearable suffering. In the last war, a soldier was greeted as a hero though he might have experienced far less danger and hardship than the civilians who welcomed him. If we see children playing in the street we may feel like exclaiming 'How charming!' when they are in fact up to some mischief which is not at all charming.

* See pp. 214 and 231–2.

This means that when we feel sentimentally we do not fully consider either the actual event or the real person nor our relationship to these, though at other times we may well be aware of them; we simply conform to an accepted pattern of feeling. Our feeling may be genuine—sincerity and sentimentality need not contradict each other—but it is not fully a response to our immediate, particular experience.

On the other hand, a person prone to sentimentality tends to dwell upon his feelings. In general, as we have said, our feelings are determined by their objects; our attention is focused upon the object and not upon the feeling itself. In a sentimental state of mind, however, we indulge our feelings, are proud of them, or pity ourselves because of them; we exploit them in order to enjoy them. Even a feeling of melancholy or of being wronged can be enjoyed in a sentimental way. We also try to prolong the feeling beyond the occasion which gave rise to it, so as to remain in the mood we like (or pretend to dislike) for a long time. The first tendency—observance of conventional feelings—supports this attitude, for it loosens the relationship between the feeling and its actual object; the object has to be pushed into the background so as to allow us to emphasize the feeling itself. 'When we enjoy our feelings, we are feeling unreally or sentimentally. When we feel really, we enjoy the thing itself, not the feeling.'*

The result to which sentimentality leads is that our capacity for feeling will become weak and sterile; weak because we must not permit any experience to become strong enough to control the feeling, and sterile because, if we want to enjoy the feelings we know, we cannot permit our experience to develop them further. It is this imposition of limits which gives the wrong impression that we are confronted with something ultimate. In fact, we thereby only confine our experience to purely subjective values and do not develop feelings beyond pleasure and pain, and this prevents feeling from becoming an organ of knowledge.

(2) On the other level, the distortion of feeling is much more

* J. Macmurray, *Freedom in the Modern World* (London, 1932), p. 152. Cf. also his book *Reason and Emotion*, chs 1–3.

serious. The second tendency of sentimentality—indulging one's feelings—is still present, but the purely subjective values are replaced by a relative value which is mistakenly accepted as absolute, and this mistake once again becomes extremely dangerous because it leads to the subjugation of thinking by feeling.

All the examples we have given in this context can illustrate the effects which such a misuse of relative values has. We have found that it is at the root of fanaticism, and the common factor in all fanaticism is a disregard for the individual. This disregard runs counter to a component of human nature which is at least dimly felt; therefore it has to be supported by a strong feeling and this feeling, to remain strong and unshaken, has in its turn to be protected against possible attacks of conscience. This is done by abstract thought which, however, in such cases is not, in the last resort, founded upon knowledge and conclusions derived from experience. The extreme forms of both nationalism and communism, for instance, are bound up with systems of thought which in the case of communism, at least, may be very elaborate, complex and logical; but these systems have been first conceived under the influence of a dominating feeling in order to support and justify it, and only later provided with a theoretical basis. If courage is mistakenly accepted as an absolute value and leads to hero-worship, the effect will be the same; and we have seen that even a commitment to duty, if wrongly interpreted, may have similar consequences. Thinking becomes determined in such a way that it cannot but interpret reality in favour of the feeling which it serves.

Relative values give rise to occasional feelings, that is to say emotions which are reactions to particular situations—such as joy, anger, grief, fear, interest, desire, disgust.* These go beyond pleasure and pain in that they do not refer to some generalized reaction accompanying all other feelings and experiences, but to single distinct feelings, to special states of mind. They are not in

* Here the word 'emotion' comes naturally to mind and we shall use it whenever appropriate, but without insisting on a differentiation between feelings and emotions, because these words are not used in a clearly different way.

themselves conducive to knowledge, but can lead to further discriminations if we learn to feel in terms of the object. (To this we shall return in a moment.) Once a relative value is accepted as absolute, however, a single object is elevated to the status of the highest value, and thus the desire for it is bound to become so strong that all other emotions become dependent on the wish to achieve it. For devoted revolutionaries, for instance, all joy and grief, interest and fear—outside a narrow and often despised private sphere—may become as nothing if the demands of the revolution lack fulfilment. Their feeling develops into a passion and makes any further discrimination impossible.

The supremacy of one particular feeling and the subjugation of thinking are brought about by imposing upon reality a black and white pattern which distorts the world even further. All other feelings must be made either wholly positive or negative, for only then are they sufficiently undifferentiated to produce no further thoughts, but simply uphold the system which supports the obsession. Any fanaticism therefore needs an 'enemy'. In this way attention can be directed away from the shortcomings of the system and the many facts which cannot be accommodated within it; attacks upon 'Jews', 'Imperialists', 'Communists' have to be resorted to and often play a more important part than the fanatical belief itself. Even belief in science, if it becomes exclusive, produces this blindness; the word 'unscientific', a justified negative value-judgment within science, which outside it should only be used as a factual statement indicating that something belongs to a different sphere, is used as a value-judgment, in order to discredit everything which contradicts the required belief.

The loss is twofold. Thinking, it is true, can be highly developed or rather driven into intellectual extremes, but is prevented from fulfilling its task properly because it has to support one special conviction at all costs. Its development, however elaborate, remains useless; kept strictly within the boundaries of the dominant feeling, it merely transforms external reality in such a way as to remove all obstacles which might interfere with that feeling. At the same time, any conscious awareness of what is being done must be avoided, for this could lead to a critical appraisal; the total distortion of thought has to remain hidden, so as to make the system appear objective. Feelings, on the other hand, since they are restricted to supporting a black and white pattern, lose touch with the qualities of the object experienced and make any more subtle differentiation within the sphere of feeling impossible. No fanaticism, therefore, ever allows the desire to distinguish between feelings to be awakened, for such a desire is inimical to its own existence. The fanatic is caught in a vicious circle.

To break out of this circle, however, becomes possible if the occasional feelings are allowed to unfold properly, even though they are not in themselves, as has been said before, conducive to knowledge.* In some cases, they are even misleading; when we are happy we tend to see everything through rose-coloured spectacles, while despair makes everything seem gloomy and threatening. In other cases, they may be helpful; a stimulation by some interest, for example, encourages us to acquire more knowledge than we would without it, and joy or even disgust can have a similar effect. But in these cases, too, the feeling itself does not convey knowledge; it only supports or hinders its acquisition. Nevertheless, if the multiplicity and diversity of such feelings is not suppressed by a dominant feeling, we can learn to feel in terms of the object, which makes us more and more able to react to any impression or experience in a different way and to increase the wealth of feelings. When we are thus enabled to discriminate, we also discover a different kind of feeling which is conducive to knowledge. Any false absoluteness can be transcended because the feeling which is an organ of knowledge can be heeded as well, and this makes us accessible to what we have recognized as the impact of the true absolute.

To develop feelings instead of falling under the spell of any one of them can be helpful because the wealth of different single emotions which arise naturally—and which therefore can be developed instead of being disregarded—is very great indeed, for whatever interests us, appeals to us, or maybe displeases us,

* See p. 214.

necessarily awakens our emotions. We have to bear in mind here the simplifications which the poverty of our language dictates. We cannot avoid, for instance, using the word 'joy' to cover a wide range of emotions, but the joys we actually feel differ according to the experiences which occasion them—looking at a rose, meeting a friend, playing with a child, being successful in our profession, being able to help someone—and they will also vary according to our state of mind. Even those emotions of joy which appear to be very similar—the joy arising from looking at a rose, or a sunset, or a work of art—differ considerably, and each will vary at different times. If, therefore, we do not dwell sentimentally upon all our joys as if there were no diversity, nor suppress the diversity by a dominant feeling, but remain open to the special impact of the particular occasion, our appreciation of the wealth of different single emotions can grow constantly.

It is this wealth which matters, because it leads to the interaction between thinking and feeling. Since there is hardly any impression or experience—hardly any thought—which is not connected with feeling, these different emotions accompany all our thought, influence it and are, in their turn, influenced by thinking. This interaction between thinking and feeling is natural, for every feeling, so long as sentimentality is avoided, tries to force its way into consciousness; if we feel, feeling directs our attention, and we usually want to know what makes us feel as we do. Thinking, however, makes us aware that feeling reacts to evaluation and the different kinds of values, and thus we also become aware of the absolute values and of that feeling which enables us to know them.

Feelings which contribute to the acquisition of knowledge are love of one's neighbour and such feelings as responsibility, trust, compassion or guilt, and in a different way faith, which will be considered later. We call this kind of feeling an organ of knowledge because, as has been seen, the absolute values can only be fully understood with its help; although they can be elaborated by thinking, knowledge of them is finally based on feeling. It has certainly become clear by now that knowledge of the good, if rational thought alone is employed, can be quite unreliable; it is reduced to a mere collection of rules, and these can harden into rigid laws which may even produce cruelty instead of love. That we are justified in emphasizing feeling in this context is also made clear by the existence of conscience: the promptings of conscience are first felt and only afterwards translated into thought. Feeling as an organ of knowledge, however, is not simply inwardness, but is awakened by the impact of the absolute; and it has to be consulted because the absolute remains beyond reason. It must act as a mediator so that we can clearly discern that knowledge which we have called essential.

This kind of feeling corresponds to the absolute values; it will therefore be clarified when we come to discuss them. But we can state beforehand why these values solve the problem discussed in relation to feeling—why, unlike all other values and feelings, they cannot lead to false absoluteness. Its clearest expression is fanaticism, and we have found that a characteristic of all fanaticism is disregard for the individual. The absolute values, as we shall see, are interconnected; all of them therefore partake in the nature of the good; they imply that love of man which is demanded by goodness and they never trespass against the demand of the final version of Kant's categorical imperative—that the individual should be respected and treated as an end in himself. If, nevertheless, we meet a fanaticism which seems to belong to this sphere—if, for instance, morality hardens into rigid laws and produces cruelty—we can be sure that the value has been distorted, that only part of it has been grasped and that this part has replaced the absolute value itself. The danger here is that the absolute value can be reduced to a relative value and the feeling to an occasional emotion. But a full understanding of the absolute values and the corresponding feelings makes such a distortion impossible.

At the same time absolute values do not exclude other values or scales of values, but increase their number and thus the wealth of different feelings which are possible. We have said that false absoluteness is always created by the elevation of a single object, idea or principle to the status of the highest value, and that this suppresses most of the required distinctions and consequently the need for discrimination. Once we reach those values which are in fact the highest, however, discrimination is not abolished, but demanded; goodness, for instance, is expressed by such general commandments as that we ought to love our neighbour, but these only become real when they are actually applied in various situations and embodied in a variety of actions, and thus they require the application of many scales of values. We have emphasized that essential knowledge is an additional knowledge which neither solves nor abolishes problems; similarly the absolute values are added to the other values without making them superfluous. Moreover, the absolute values are not only interconnected, there are also tensions between them, and these ensure that no single feeling can become too sweeping.

All this will be more fully explained later. Yet to make it possible for feeling to develop in the right direction, a further mistake has still to be avoided—thinking must not inhibit the development of feeling. This mistake usually finds expression in the claim that the end justifies the means—or, more explicitly, that a good end justifies the employment of bad means. But this principle is fundamentally wrong.

Why this is so can be understood if we scrutinize our experience. The means is what we actually do and thus fully know; therefore it always exercises a stronger influence than the end which, more often than not, is far away in the future, and an abstract idea. It may or may not ever be achieved, and even if it is, the influence of the means may have transformed it beyond recognition. Marxism, to take an obvious example, certainly aims at an ideal future society free from bondage; to create it, a period of dictatorship is introduced as a means, but this dictatorship forms the actual experience of the men involved and influences them so strongly that it becomes extremely difficult to abandon it, and this makes all its successes serve totalitarianism which is very different from the end originally envisaged. Nor are anti-communist or idealistic strivings any more free from such dangers once bad means are accepted; even in Plato's Republic similar flaws become obvious. Thus it is not only practically, but also morally wrong to justify means by the end, for this is bound to lead on to the using of man as means only.

Underlying this mistake there is always the same kind of wrong thinking—man believes that he knows more than he is possibly able to know, which contradicts Kant's teaching. The use of bad means can only appear justified if one believes that the end is fully known and if it is accepted as absolutely certain and absolutely good. Only then can man feel entitled to enforce it and even to kill for its sake; if he believes himself in a position to know how the greatest happiness of the greatest number could be achieved, he will believe himself justified in destroying the happiness and even the lives of a smaller number. He will probably remain confirmed in this belief, too, because the employment of a bad means (force or killing) cannot contribute to a better knowledge of an end of a quite different nature (happiness). Any further development of knowledge and feeling is blocked and wrong absoluteness creeps in once more because, as with all the other mistakes, a single object or idea is seen as the final embodiment of the highest value and as representing the whole value. This makes any real appreciation of this value impossible, even if the end itself is good. Since the absolute cannot be grasped either in itself or completely, we need many embodiments of the absolute values to give us access to it and enable us to grasp as many facets of it as possible.

Of course, in practical life we are not always able to avoid using means which are not entirely good and may be very dubious; there is the problem of the 'lesser evil'; but this makes it even more imperative to recognize that using bad means is nevertheless wrong, so that the evil is at least known for what it is.

3

When we turn to the absolute values, we are again confronted with a surprising fact. Whereas in the case of the relative values we have to attempt to discover and to apply as many as possible, the number of the absolute values is limited. According to tradition there are three—truth, goodness and beauty—and the validity of the tradition has been confirmed in so far as all attempts to introduce further absolute values have failed.

In the sphere of relative values it would be wrong even to try to map out the whole of their realm or to draw up a list of all of them.* Since our sensitivity has to be increased, its growth must not be hindered; we must constantly be able to make new and often quite unexpected value-judgments. We should never be satisfied with any mere assertion that something is valuable, for this would prematurely end evaluation. Good health, for instance, is undoubtedly most valuable; but if we do not ask questions which go beyond it, we shall either make health an end in itself and thus most probably undermine it, or at least we shall neglect other endeavours through thinking too much about it, or not realize that, to make it truly valuable, we still have to make proper use of it. Similarly, an overrating of happiness or even too exclusive experience of it can have paralysing effects. Any recognition of a relative value ought to be made a starting point, so that we are led in the end to the most important values of all—the absolute values.

The number of the absolute values is small because they are ends in themselves and can never become means; but they still need means to become real. Like all values, they become real by being embodied, and the embodiment is achieved with the help of means and ends. Thus they do not exclude, but on the contrary demand, the application of other scales of values; relative values and the corresponding occasional feelings have to be put into their service. The number of the absolute values can be small because they are not concerned with details of how they come into being, but with the essence of the single objects which embody them. Their task is to become or to determine the purpose by which the relative value serving them is defined, and practically

* Of course, many more values than those mentioned could have been discussed, but as this book is concerned with the foundation of ethics, examples had to suffice.

268

any relative value can be transformed by them. We have mentioned that the significance of usefulness changes when, instead of thinking of ourselves, we want to do something which is useful for others, and pleasure, in itself a purely subjective value, acquires a very different meaning when we think of either creating or destroying the pleasure of others. Natural desires can be purely selfish or can transcend selfishness, and the absolute values, being ends in themselves, also create a desire which demands satisfaction.* Therefore these values have to provide us with a basis and framework to enable us to make a judgment— with an understanding of our desires and of whether and how far a relative value has actually been employed and determined in a way which agrees with their demands. Since we can only grasp single facets of the absolute, these values which give access to it have to ensure that, in any of its embodiments, it really is a facet of the absolute which we grasp.

A different relationship between relative and absolute values is disclosed by those relative values which are virtues. Some of these are more frequently and more clearly positive than negative and thus form a kind of transition between these two kinds of values. At the same time they can also form part of the feeling which is an organ of knowledge; humility, for instance, or compassion and trust can lead to a state of greater awareness which contributes to the knowledge of the good. But as values they are still relative. Compassion would be wrong if it led to the condoning of brutality; humility has to be distinguished from submissiveness and this requires reference to the authority which inspires it; and trust can be misplaced. If, however, the relative value is justifiably established as positive, the corresponding feeling leads to a greater knowledge of the absolute value. The two spheres overlap, because the nature of the value differs from the nature of the feeling.

The boundaries between the relative and the absolute values

---

* This is another reason why hedonism is insufficient; as it does not admit absolute values, it cannot take into account that these values satisfy a desire which they themselves create.

should therefore not be drawn too rigidly. Nevertheless, this transitional region still only shows further ways towards the absolute values and must not invade their sphere, for they themselves remain different. This can be recognized in the failure of all attempts to establish other absolute values, for the proposed additional values have been taken from this region. The failures confirm how distinct the absolute values are and clarify what absoluteness in this context means.

There are four such additional values which are of more than passing significance—nobility, justice, love and holiness.

The attraction of nobility is probably its vagueness; it can be used simply as a term of praise and when thus used it exemplifies what is a constant temptation in the realm of values—namely to justify ourselves when we rest content with merely asserting that something is valuable; it adds a certain lustre to our satisfaction. There is no doubt that the appreciation of any valuable character or endeavour is enhanced if we can see it as noble, and lack of nobility diminishes its value. Emphasis on nobility can also be important when, as often happens, morality tends to become a narrow-minded or philistine attitude. Yet the idea of nobility can be determined either by the ideal of the great hero or superman, as it was by Nietzsche, or by magnanimity or by devotion to Christian ideals. Thus, however, it is a relative value because it depends on this further determination and cannot be made an end in itself. It is similar to the absolute values in that it cannot be defined; it appears as a felt 'something' added to another value-judgment; but the absolute values, though they cannot be defined either, can be described and thus become ends. Mere vagueness is no criterion. In this case the mistaking of a relative for an absolute value may not seem to do any harm, but this is an error, for it hides the impact of the absolute. The absolute values force us to face reality because to accept them is always difficult; we are constantly assailed by experiences and theories which make us doubt that anything absolute exists. Nobility, however, when severed from ideas which can be either doubted or held up for admiration in their own right, makes it easy to accept a vaguely

lofty aim without questioning or even clarifying it. This leads us
into sentimentality—into indulging the feelings which any such
appeal, whatever its sources, arouses in us. Nobility, in other
words, if not seen as a relative value, can be reduced to a purely
subjective value.

Thus nobility illustrates what is a constant danger in this sphere
—that the mere fact that a value cannot be defined makes us overlook the essential difference between pure subjectivity and conclusions reached through the proper application of the subjective
method.

Justice belongs more clearly to the transitional region just
mentioned.

Instead of good and evil we could also speak of right and wrong;
in some cases the former wording, in others the latter will be
more telling. The difference between these two pairs of concepts
cannot be entirely defined, but it can be recognized in individual
cases. It may be right to hang a murderer, but this is obviously not
a good action in itself; it may be good to tell a person a lie to
spare him unnecessary suffering, but this is not quite right. Such
distinctions should be constantly explored to clarify our conception of the good; a morality which is not confronted with
justice may become soft and lose its distinct character. Justice
itself, however, is not an absolute value. The starting point of
justice and morality is very nearly the same, but justice has to be
legally enforced and to be expressed by laws; and though some
of the laws are founded upon morality and try to enforce it, the
laws themselves are not moral because they must be obeyed for
no other reason than that they have become laws; legal demands
are satisfied when laws are obeyed whatever the reason for obeying them. Thus they lack one of the main conditions of morality—
that even a deed which is in itself good only becomes moral if it is
done for the right reason. Therefore, some of the laws, by merely
giving support to existing but unjust social conditions, can also be
immoral.

Moreover, the concept of justice implies that it must not be
influenced by anything outside itself, especially not by love, which

could falsify it. Thus strictly interpreted it is even an end in itself, but as such it can become cruel and destructive. This throws into relief that all absolute values, since they exclude any disregard for the individual, are actually permeated by love, and it is for this reason, too, that justice cannot be included among them. In the sphere of feeling, justice can contribute to knowledge, as part of a character it can be a high virtue, but in the sphere of values we still have to recognize it as relative because it must be judged in the light of the higher virtue of love, and only the absolute values pass this test.

Love itself, however, is not a value; it transcends all values because it must not be based on a judgment. We should love our neighbour unconditionally, whatever our value-judgments tell us about him; we may judge his shortcomings but not him as a person. To this we shall return after our discussion of the absolute values, because then the difference between these values and love will be more easily seen.

Holiness transcends the sphere of values for a different reason: it presupposes faith. Hartmann gives a clear definition of holiness: 'Those objects are holy which on account of their inherent worth must be loved to the uttermost but never touched, feared absolutely but never hated.'* Yet absolute values lead to what can only be called a meeting with the absolute; we experience its reality and are touched by it, and thus we also touch it. This becomes clear if we think, for instance, of a profound experience of the beauty of a landscape. We do not feel fear either; probably we experience awe, but then fear has been modified and robbed of its sting. Holiness is accepted—and can be loved to the uttermost —only after the absolute has been experienced as transcending all human evaluations; the absolute values remain a way towards it.

The reason why there are three and not more or less absolute values can be recognized when we remember what we have said about the objective and subjective methods, for they indicate that there are three—and only three—major operations of thinking which make us accessible to the impact of the absolute.

* Nicolai Hartmann, *Ethics*, vol. 1 (London, 1932), p. 13.

(1) Truth. To grasp truth, we must obviously break through the surface of reality and try to get hold of its innermost nature. This direction of striving is characteristic of the objective method by which we endeavour to achieve a more fundamental knowledge of external reality and to advance from the mere knowledge of objects and events to the laws which determine them. But we have said that knowledge of these laws is achieved by contributions from internal reality and is thus relative;* if we want to discover truth, therefore, we have finally to leave the objective method behind and to use the subjective method. This creates a certain ambiguity in the understanding of truth; it seems possible to interpret it either as a purely factual statement about external reality or as a value, as the truth by which we live. This we shall discuss. Yet the way towards truth corresponds to the objective method, for it is concerned with what creates or determines the world as we know it.

(2) Beauty. This is a concept which has lost much of its deeper meaning and is often identified with mere prettiness, a purely subjective value. As absolute value it should mean that an important content has found full expression; the content must be important, so that it can appeal to our most profound feelings, and it must find a form which expresses it so distinctly that it can become an object for the feeling. Beauty in this sense means the complete concord between form and content; it arises when we succeed in finding a form—either by experiencing or creating it—in which external elements bring to life and embody any of the essential facets of our inner experience. This, however, corresponds to the working of the subjective method, for we have said that internal reality, to become real, must be embodied.†

(3) Goodness. To understand man himself we must, as we have said, start from freedom. Awareness of freedom transcends the scope of the objective method and is brought about by the subjective method, but freedom itself, as distinct from the awareness of it, transcends the subjective method too, because it must be freedom to act; if it could not lead to external actions, it would be

a sham freedom. Thus a third way towards the acquisition of a fuller knowledge is opened. The two methods are so different that they can never be united; so long as we apply them, we only understand either external or internal reality. But our actions include both realities, because inner motives produce external events, and thus we are enabled to experience the unity of the absolute. We still cannot grasp this unity directly, for our thinking remains dependent on the application of the two methods, but we are given and can accept that additional knowledge which we have called essential.* Goodness corresponds to this way from freedom through action to understanding.

Whenever successful, these three operations of thinking lead to experience of the absolute values, and thus values which lack this basis cannot be added to them. But, since these values are the results of such different approaches, we must not, as is sometimes attempted, try to unify them. Tempting as it may seem, we cannot simply say with Keats 'Beauty is truth, truth beauty', for to do so would be to mistake for an abstract general truth what is in fact, in its context, the perfect evocation of an impression. Although the unity of the absolute makes itself felt, even the absolute values disclose only different facets of it.

In experience, it is true, they are interconnected and are not as clearly distinguished as they have to be in our abstract investigation. This is most obvious in the case of goodness because, to be acceptable, it has to be based on truth, and however much the concept of beauty may have been robbed of its meaning, there is still no other word to describe the impression of, say, a perfect friendship, an enduring love between man and woman, the repentant sinner, the father who welcomes the returning prodigal, or any great and costly sacrifice. Truth may seem to stand apart, but we shall only be able to find our way through the jungle of fascinating ideas or ideals with which life confronts us if we apply the test of goodness; no fanaticism, however idealistic, could ever have seemed acceptable if this test had been applied. We shall also see that the truth which is a value must convince us by 'shining

* See pp. 126–7.

in its own light', and this means beauty. Beauty itself presents a more difficult problem because it has no obvious relationship to goodness; strangely, in art, a perfect expression of evil can be beautiful. But if beauty touches upon the absolute, it must obviously be founded on truth; and it can arise, as we have just said, in an embodiment of goodness.

Nevertheless, the three absolute values have to be distinguished clearly, because it is the tension between them which protects us from the error of believing that we have grasped all that can be grasped. Humanist idealism sometimes includes the absolute values and rests satisfied with them, making either the ideal of the good or of beauty or both the basis of a teaching that is meant to proclaim truth, usually a modified Platonism.* In this case the transcendental is excluded. But can the absolute values be understood without it? The facets which the different values show are ultimately contradictory; truth may go far beyond morality, as when a final insight forces a man to sacrifice human relationships or even his own life; beauty can make us aware of the reality of evil and its persuasiveness, and thus threaten morality; and goodness, when it has become fullness of love, may reach apparent absurdity, leading to a consummation which resembles self-destruction more than fulfilment, distantly reflecting the crucifixion. Tensions of this kind constantly arise, both between the values and, as we have seen when discussing mercy-killing, within the sphere of the single values. Such tensions show that these values, though absolute as values, do not give us final knowledge but lead on to further questions. We must never overlook that, since values are established by judgments, they open up further vistas—on that which is being judged.

But before asking such questions, we must now try to say more about the absolute values themselves.

---

* A recent example: Iris Murdoch, *The Sovereignty of Good over other Concepts* (Cambridge, 1967).

CHAPTER XI

TRUTH, GOODNESS AND LOVE

1

The clear limitation of the realm of the absolute values has an important consequence for ethics. Since means and ends have to be employed, many values not themselves ethical can become ethical, but they are recognized as such by their being rooted in and serving the absolute value of the good. Some values, such as the virtues discussed, are more directly related to ethics than others, and it would be possible to go on describing a number of ethical values in greater detail, especially if the negative values were included for contrast. Yet such an attempt will not be made here, because this book is concerned with the foundations of ethics; its task is therefore different—namely to show the criteria by which ethical values can be recognized. This indication of the essence distinguishes, as we have said, the absolute from the relative values, and thus we are entitled to proceed now to the absolute values themselves.

Of the three absolute values, beauty is not directly connected with ethics and we shall therefore not include it.* But we have to discuss not only goodness—the value on which ethics is based—but also truth, for goodness must in its turn be based on truth to be acceptable. Truth is thus the most basic of the values and has to be discussed first. (It is also basic to that beauty which is an absolute value.)

We have emphasized before that the absolute values cannot be fully defined; in this respect they are similar to the purely subjective values; but unlike the latter they can be described and to some extent elucidated, and more can be said about them than is usually admitted.

---

* For a fuller discussion of beauty see P. Roubiczek, *Thinking towards Religion*, pp. 152–9, and *Thinking in Opposites*, pp. 156–8.

In the case of truth, probably the first question which comes to mind is why truth should be considered a value at all. I have argued elsewhere that there are two kinds of truth which should be distinguished, and that it would perhaps be even better to distinguish them by different names—correctness and truth. A few remarks may suffice to explain the nature of the difference discussed more extensively there.* Truth has also to be distinguished from truthfulness which is a virtue and must be judged by the end which it serves—love of man or self-righteousness. Truthfulness is therefore a relative value and not under discussion here.

The kind of truth for which the scientist strives is true or correct so far as he knows, but open to change. It is discovered with the help of the objective method and characterized by what we have said about the results so achieved, namely that we acquire certainty with regard to ascertained facts, but not in the deeper region which could give us understanding, for there we remain dependent on changing theories. Of ascertained facts we are accustomed —and of course entitled—to say that these are true; it is obviously true that a stone robbed of its support will fall or that we must starve if we stop eating. But the noun 'truth', though much abused, still makes us expect more than is ordinarily meant by the simple statement that something is true; it implies both knowledge of facts and that understanding which we have called existential and which makes sense in terms related to our experience. A comprehensive encyclopaedia, even if it contained all currently ascertained facts and the theories explaining them, would hardly appear to us as a repository of truth. This kind of truth which the noun leads us to expect cannot be reached by the objective method, the scope of which, moreover, is also limited by the laws which Kant's theory of knowledge discloses.

But this other kind of truth undoubtedly exists—a truth which is not merely true so far as we know at the moment, but forces itself upon us as ultimate and which, once we have recognized

---

* See P. Roubiczek, *Existentialism—For and Against*, pp. 101–2 and 182–4. For the following discussion of truth see also *Thinking towards Religion*, ch. VII, and *Thinking in Opposites*, ch. IX.

and accepted it, can no longer be shaken by doubts nor ever change. In a flash of insight—which may follow a gradual development or a long struggle—we sometimes know for certain that we have touched upon final truth; we are struck by an impact of the absolute and are given essential knowledge. Here knowledge of facts and the understanding just mentioned depend on each other; to accept the existence of the transcendental, for instance would be meaningless unless we knew what kind of experience is meant by it, and the understanding of ethics would not make it real, namely binding, if it could not be based on facts. This truth, however, which alone really deserves to be called truth, is a value because we ourselves must judge, in the light of our experience, whether or not it is absolute; its absoluteness can only be confirmed by our own experience. It is the truth by which we live and must therefore become our own; it is confirmed if we feel committed to it.

Certainly, knowledge of external facts also strongly influences our lives, as today's scientific and technical achievements make clear. But, confronted with these, we still have to decide what kind of influence these general conditions of life should be allowed to have on our attitudes. Therefore they have to be seen as relative values, for it is only in this way that we can judge and transcend them, which we must do if we want to make personal and moral decisions and thereby define our attitude to the world. We actually admit the absolute value of truth into our lives whenever we feel any need to give meaning to our existence; it influences us more than the other values because it governs our conception of the kind of persons we ought to be. With its help we can transform external conditions and relative values into means of achieving self-fulfilment.

This, however, raises the problem of all essential knowledge. Since it is based on an impact of the absolute, it cannot be brought about by a conscious effort of thinking, nor is it capable of any logical or material proof. Truth, therefore, 'must shine in its own light';* it must coerce us into accepting it and be so self-evident

* H. H. Farmer, *God and Men* (London, 1948), p. 18.

that it would be nonsensical or dishonest to dismiss it, for if we denied it we would be denying what we know by experience to be true. But this leads to the question which we have had to ask several times before: how can we, if we have to rely on inner experience alone, ever distinguish between justified and false convictions of certainty? Yet if we accept truth as a value, we are able to see that much of what we have already said provides us with criteria of truth.

Truth as a value is based on our judgment and thus the organ by which we grasp it is, in the last resort, our sense of truth. This sense can mislead, but it can also be tested, for we must see truth in the right context. The possibility and importance of this test can easily be recognized whenever certainty is experienced. On the most irrational level, for instance, a lunatic may be firmly convinced that he rules the world or is persecuted by everyone (and a slight tendency to such lunacy is hidden in all of us); but he has lost the context of society, he has become unable to establish the right contact with the world in which he lives. On the highest rational level, a mathematician may consider his findings to be the nearest approach to absolute truth, but this is also not the context in which truth can be discovered, because mathematics is purely formal and has to be applied to acquire significance, while truth must give us direct knowledge of a content—that is, of both facts and their meaning.

Therefore the right context for truth is the world of free persons. These two conditions—the personal approach and freedom—are equally essential. We must be concerned and involved as the individual persons we are, because it is the subjective method which opens approaches to truth; and truth must appeal to us as persons, because it must strongly compel our attention and influence our lives, so that our sense of truth is stimulated into action. At the same time we must be free because otherwise, as has been seen, any discussion—and thus also the search for truth—would be meaningless.* We have to be able to detach ourselves from the conditions which determine our lives—at least to such a

* See pp. 40–1.

degree that we can change our minds when confronted with evidence which contradicts our beliefs, whatever the conditions which gave rise to them.

We can never hope, however, to know the absolute completely, even if our sense of truth responds correctly to its impact; we have emphasized that we grasp only facets of it. This means that we can never know absolute truth in its fullness. But this very short-coming provides us with another test; each facet must belong to the same kind of truth; to be true, each partial truth must partake in the whole truth. Even if the limitations of our knowledge prevent us from achieving more than a glimpse of absolute know-ledge, its fundamental oneness, although it can be neither fully grasped nor translated into concepts, must be seen and felt in all the separate glimpses. This is well illustrated by the example which we have used before, by Plato's assertion that it is better to suffer wrong than to do wrong, for if we were compelled to dismiss it as false, our whole conception of existence would have to be changed. A facet of truth is not simply a detail of knowledge which could be easily omitted or replaced without otherwise affecting that knowledge; it implies a comprehensive order and brings us into touch with the foundations of existence, so that all the facets must be interconnected. They confirm, in their partial way, the one truth by which we live.*

The sense of truth is part of the feeling which is an organ of knowledge, and the nature of feeling offers a further criterion. Feelings cannot be preserved for any great length of time; there-fore truth must be experienced always anew, and the new ex-perience must be a vivid experience, for mechanical repetitions or obedience to rules merely kill feelings. Abstract formulations of results which have been achieved, philosophical or religious statements, expressions of wisdom, works of art can help us to remember truth; they preserve the knowledge once acquired and make it possible for us to pass it on or for a new experience to lead

---

* For this reason a different name for scientific truth seems desirable, for if this impersonal knowledge is accepted as a different kind of truth, all truth may be distorted.

us farther, but any such knowledge of truth loses its significance once it is no longer understood in terms of living experience. All established forms of truth, if they no longer evoke a new experience, can become a dead burden; a ritual or worship, originally conveying an impact of the absolute, can become an empty ceremony; a work of art, if no longer appreciated, reveals nothing; the best deed, if dictated by rules alone, will become meaningless; the Bible can become a dead letter. No single facet of truth can be regarded as something which we rely upon possessing for ever; it must awaken our feeling—our sense of truth—constantly afresh and be tested by new experiences. If it is a facet of truth, it will re-emerge triumphant, but we have to take the risk of finding that it does not withstand such a scrutiny.

For the same reason, truth must be embodied in such a way that it can be lived, and it has to be lived to become entirely real. A mere proclamation of truth is insufficient; our belief in the truth which a mystic professes, for instance, will be severely shaken if we discover that he evidently desires power and luxury, even though there may be truth in what he proclaims. Truth as an absolute value must strike and convince us so strongly that we commit our lives to it.

This explains why a new truth so frequently needs a personal sacrifice before it becomes powerful; it needs the witness by whom it is made moving, compelling, even terrifying. Buddha had to renounce his worldly position, Confucius could not remain a minister of state, Socrates had to die, Christ had to go to Calvary, Christian martyrs in a non-Christian world knew the needs of their faith, and so did the early Reformers (and in countries where the Reformation succeeded its Roman Catholic opponents) who went to the stake. In the absence of the possibility of proof, a new truth becomes convincing when we can see personal participation. Socrates—the best example for us, because he was a philosopher—could easily have escaped, but he saw and explained that this way was barred to him. He had to bear witness that his new conception of truth mattered to him profoundly, that he was deeply involved in those general human

281

principles which transcended loyalty to a particular city-state; otherwise his sayings would have seemed no more than interesting speculations among many. In the absence of proof, it is life which has to show that we either do or do not believe; for Socrates to escape would have meant that he did not rely on what he taught and his teaching would therefore have been invalidated.* If weakness of character or lack of courage prevent a sacrifice demanded in the service of truth, the insight is not thereby proved false, but not in this way are new truths brought to life nor others convinced that they ought to be accepted.

It hardly needs to be said that this does not apply to that kind of truth for which the scientist works; because here there is the possibility of proof and the proof supersedes the witness. Galileo's recantation, though certainly not admirable, did not hinder the advance of physics.†

Yet even sacrifice itself is not a proof; men have given their lives for the most atrocious causes, from the crusades to Nazism. But Socrates himself indicates a further criterion—the importance of doubt. To appreciate this properly, we have to return for a moment to our distinction between external and internal reality and the two methods, for doubt plays a different part in each.

The objective method allows us to ascertain facts which are well-nigh absolutely certain, but the laws of thinking make these facts entirely external and prevent full understanding of them. It is no accident that the word 'fact' is derived from the Latin *facere*, to do; we have to do something to create facts and thus we remain outside them. The method therefore culminates in theories which only achieve approximations to facts, for they contain

---

* The book *In Solitary Witness*, mentioned on p. 64, gives a more recent example: Franz Jägerstätter, a simple farmer, who recognized that the Hitler state was immoral and anti-religious, refused to join the army or to serve the state in any other way, knowing that his action was bound to lead to his execution. His friends and the Church tried to dissuade him, pointing out that his action would have no practical effect, but he insisted that the personal sacrifice was required, because the truth he knew could not be made visible in any other way.

† For a fuller discussion of Galileo's decision see P. Roubiczek, *Thinking towards Religion*, pp. 144–5, and also K. Jaspers, *The Perennial Scope of Philosophy* (London, 1950), p. 9.

speculative elements.* Both the ascertained facts and the approximations have to be tested by doubts, in order to make sure that the facts have been correctly established and that the speculations are fruitful and not misleading. But as the results of this method can be tested and proved by observation and experiment, doubts are simple steps in the advance of external knowledge; they can do their work easily and can be conclusively confirmed or refuted.

The subjective method has to deal with immediate experiences; certainty is therefore a question of 'either/or'; we either gain it or not. Yet just because the experience is immediate, both justified and false convictions of certainty can appear equally certain. Thus doubt is here an important instrument in the sorting out of certainties; any conviction must be exposed to doubt again and again, because only a full and repeated experience of doubt can confirm that we have gained essential knowledge, namely that knowledge which is only fortified by doubt. The mere fact that we doubt is already a sign that we are able to move in the right direction; no fanatic will ever admit doubts which could shake his belief. Yet to make such a use of doubt is difficult; the subjective task of doubting is bound to confront us with further problems.

On the one hand, doubt may not be pushed far enough. Strong convictions, even if they are not fanatical, make us prone to avoid exactly those doubts which matter, and if we at the same time raise other doubts, we can easily overlook or disregard such an omission. Nationalists, for instance, may be very critical of their government, of the actual performance or of the state of mind of the nation, yet never doubt that their nationalism is justified. On the other hand, doubt can go too far; practically everything can be doubted, especially the validity or existence of the absolute values, and thus even justified convictions may be undermined. We have to be accessible to the impact of the absolute, and this requires our collaboration; we have seen that moral principles only become absolute when we accept them. This applies to all essential knowledge, for we have also shown that we can discredit or circumvent any experience, and doubt can be used to do so.

* See p. 76.

The danger of doubting too much needs particular attention because doubt, anathema in other ages, is greatly admired today and often pushed farther and farther for its own sake. It is, in fact, a very tempting attitude to adopt; so long as we doubt we seem to remain superior to all believers and even to our own experience and conscience, because we cannot be taken in; our intellectual capacity seems to become limitless. In this respect, we still accept Descartes' teaching—which is otherwise usually rejected—as the beginning of modern philosophy, because he made it a duty to doubt everything which can possibly be doubted. This, so it seems to us, is the origin of any acceptable philosophy. But it was already Kierkegaard who pointed out that doubt, in Descartes' time, was only fruitful because there were regions which doubt could not reach, which were considered as being beyond doubt, such as moral standards; doubt merely removed unjustified credulity. In our age, however, everything has become open to doubt, so that it can shake the very foundations of existence. This prompted Kierkegaard to return to Aristotle's definition of the origin of philosophy—that it begins with astonishment; he saw that positive results must spring from positive experience. Naturally, too easy credulity must be avoided, but the equally important need of philosophy—which aims after all at positive results—is to know when to cease doubting and to accept, so that we can recognize any valid evidence provided by inner experience and any justified convictions of certainty.

But where should doubt stop? Since we must constantly employ the test of doubt, we cannot and even must not draw a precise line between what should and what should not be doubted. But if we bear in mind the distinction between the objective and subjective methods, we can, to a considerable extent, differentiate between correct and false doubts, for most of the destructive doubts make use of external elements in order to undermine inner certainties, as has already been seen in the case of fanaticism which rests on the support of external systems. This needs no further elaboration, for what is to be said here has been said in chapter II, when we discussed the unjustified undermining of belief in absoluteness by history and psychology, and in chapters IV and V which explained the differences between the two methods. The objective method should never interfere with internal reality; on the contrary, it should disclose the boundaries of external reality so as to make us aware of internal reality, in which the subjective method alone can give us knowledge. If used in this way, it can be seen that each of the two methods starts from a basis of fact: just as the objective method must start from a given external reality, so the subjective method has to be based on what is given in internal reality. It is this indestructible basis which has to be uncovered, and this can only be done by the repeated testing of inner experience. We have found that it is senseless to doubt the existence of reality and this applies to both its aspects.

It is true, however, that in internal reality it is a more difficult task to discover what cannot be doubted; inner doubts may be wrong or we may cease to doubt too soon. Yet truth has to be experienced always anew, and if this is done, the criteria we have discussed enable us to judge our convictions with growing reliability; we become certain that some single experiences disclose facets of truth and can dismiss the fear that our convictions could be wrong. We can no longer doubt that we have been given essential knowledge. Moreover, there is a further criterion, of a different kind, which in practice, though not in theory, can be finally conclusive—the interconnection between truth and goodness. For goodness can be tested by action.

2

Kant has shown that final certainty is based on concepts *a priori*; since our knowledge is limited, we can say 'must' only when we are able to rely on laws of thinking. In ethics, he has elaborated these laws by showing the *a priori* basis of the moral law, and he also often presupposes the absolute value of certain aspects of the good, as in the final version of the categorical imperative (for only absolute values are ends in themselves), or when he says that sincerity in friendship would be demanded even if it had never existed (for such an appreciation of sincerity cannot be derived from experience alone). He does not explicitly embark on the investigation of the absolute values themselves, but his teaching can also be applied to these; the understanding of them shows that they are absolute because they precede experience. Goodness can best serve to exemplify this fact; we shall therefore discuss it first with regard to goodness and only afterwards with regard to truth.

All that has so far been said about truth applies to goodness as well. The absolute cannot be known completely in this sphere either; we are thus only able to grasp facets of goodness (in our own impulses and in the actions of others), but these will be necessarily interconnected in such a way that they become recognizable as parts of the same basic value. Proof still remains impossible, so that the good, too, must shine in its own light. Since it refers to action, the right context for it is the world of free persons, and it has to be embodied and lived. The fact that proof is impossible means that feeling—the sense of goodness—plays an essential part, and this, like all feeling, cannot be acquired once for all, but must be experienced afresh each time. The task of doubt also remains the same.

In the sphere of goodness, however, it can be more easily seen that some of these criteria point to an *a priori* knowledge. The new embodiments which are constantly needed can be recognized as representing the good because the good itself does not change and remains independent of the way in which it is made real; we can ascertain whether or not an action is good precisely because goodness is not derived from the particular embodiment, but precedes it. Yet when we meet the good—in a verdict of conscience, in a character, in an action—it is familiar to us; we recognize it even if we meet it for the first time and have no previous knowledge of it. This does not simply mean that we then understand the meaning of the word, with which we are bound to be familiar, but that the good makes sense in terms of experience, as a well known part of our lives; it gives expression to something we already know without fully realizing that we know it.

The promptings of conscience clearly imply that knowledge of the good is presupposed; they do not tell us what the good itself is, but apply it to our actions or omissions. We have seen that to have a bad conscience, too, is based on the realization that we ought to have satisfied the demands of goodness. Looking back on a particular situation in which we failed to do good, we may be unable to imagine what we ought to have done or what else we could have done, but we nevertheless know that we fell short of our actual obligation and should have done better, and this shows that, even if we do not have any distinct idea of the higher value, we still know of its existence.

Moreover, we cannot hope to acquire this knowledge by conclusions drawn from something outside the absolute values; just as the acknowledgment of freedom has to be a starting point for the subjective method, so these values, being interconnected with freedom, must also be its starting point and be understood directly. They must be known beforehand because they are ends in themselves, and only something known can be made an end; and since they are given beforehand, we must accept them as they are. Like all concepts *a priori*, they impose upon us a necessity which entitles us to say 'must'. This is confirmed by two further aspects of the good.

On the one hand, any moral commandment is founded upon the value which is to be realized by obedience to the commandment. That we ought or ought not to do something presupposes the positive or negative value of that which is to be done or should not be done. It cannot be the other way round; obligation does not create values; it arises precisely because values have a reality of their own; we are asked to act in accordance with a known value. Otherwise Kant could not have demanded sincerity in friendship even had it never existed. The absolute values are *a priori* laws of the corresponding kind of experience.

On the other hand, and for this very reason, the absolute values are the most objective of the values. This may sound surprising because, since they cannot be defined, their knowledge is entirely dependent on the subjective method and on that feeling which is an organ of knowledge. When this method opens approaches to the absolute, however, the resulting impact takes the form of a confrontation with an absolute value which thus discloses a reality independent of internal reality. This can again be seen most clearly in the promptings of conscience; if allowed to make themselves properly felt, they cannot be influenced by our inclinations or wishes; they have necessity. The experience of an absolute value is objective because, in its absoluteness, we meet the absolute itself.

The meeting with the absolute—and thus with something which is given *a priori*—is the crucial point; if it is not acknowledged and accepted, the absolute values disappear. There is always the danger of their being reduced to relative or purely subjective values, for they carry with them their own temptations leading in this direction. These we have already mentioned. The truth by which we live is often replaced by the other, less exacting kind of truth, by correct factual statements or by science, which robs the truth which we are discussing of its foundations; beliefs then become merely a matter of inclination. Morality is understood as mere obedience to rules, which makes it less problematical, but deprives it of depth. Beauty is identified with attractiveness or what is pleasing and thus loses its own peculiarly demanding quality. These interpretations are the more tempting because they can—and frequently do—establish some positive values which are worth striving for; they only become harmful if they are meant to replace the absolute values. But we can recognize that these interpretations are false, because all such attempts to dismiss the absolute lead to distortion of experience.

Once more, goodness shows this best because it is that absolute value which is, at one and the same time, in some respects most certain and in other respects most open to misapplication. It can be recognized more reliably, yet also distorted more easily than the other absolute values, and both these possibilities elucidate the common nature of all absolute values.

On the one hand, goodness is most certain because it refers to our actions. Therefore it can be fully elaborated, for actions need principles, obligations, values—in short ethics; morality and ethics are an elaboration of the good. All that we have said about these—that is, the greater part of all preceding chapters—explains the meaning of goodness, so that there is hardly need to say more about it. Only goodness is accessible to such a systematic elaboration. For truth metaphysics sets out to achieve the same, but we have seen that all-inclusive metaphysical systems have failed.* Beauty is elaborated in aesthetics, but this part of philosophy has remained highly unsatisfactory. Moreover, as we have to act upon our knowledge of the good, it can be more directly and conclusively tested than the other values, namely by results; if we do what we believe to be good we discover in subsequent experiences what our conviction really means and implies.

This becomes clear when we remember that ethics cannot be based on the success of our actions; success and failure are not ethical criteria. The result for which we strive may—but need not—conform to our intentions, and a failure to achieve what we intended makes it particularly obvious that the good is independent of ourselves. When discussing the experiences of the four business men we have seen that what is achieved can be quite different from what is expected, and that even success may prove disappointing and failure deeply satisfying. Such contradictions can correct and amplify our knowledge of what is really good, because they confront us with a direct experience of the value itself. As always, we must not expect perfection or complete avoidance of error, but—with goodness and not with the other values—we can learn to establish a very close and revealing connection between our beliefs and our actions. An appearance of goodness can hide very different—indeed immoral—intentions and motives; but our conscience will hardly be misled indefinitely if we are honestly concerned with goodness. In our own actions as well as in those of others, the true nature of an action, whether evil or good, tends to make itself felt.

On the other hand, however, goodness is in some respects the least secure of the absolute values. It refers to activity and can

* See pp. 13–14.

become translated into moral laws, and since activity is so important a part of our living, it can come to appear sufficient by itself to give content to the whole of our lives. Do we need more guidance when we want to know how to live? But we have had to point out more than once that moral laws, if accepted as binding without regard to our personal participation and without being tested again and again, can easily petrify into hard rules, estranging us from real goodness. If moral rules appear self-sufficient, the effect is to overemphasize personal activity and the possibility of acquiring merit. But very important experiences and insights are, after all, given to us—often in a most unexpected or even inexplicable way—without our activity bringing them about; in fact, as we are ignorant of them in advance and therefore cannot aim at them, they are not the result of our activity. These experiences require a willingness to receive, open-mindedness, passive acceptance, endurance of suffering. An overemphasis on activity bars the way to this kind of sensitivity and to our readiness to listen, and these are also needed because, as we have said, morality cannot itself produce that complete involvement which is necessary to make it a living force.

Goodness is insecure, too, because there is no escape from conflicts between contradictory moral principles and loyalties—from conflicts, that is, which cannot be resolved once for all. This has been seen in the case of mercy-killing; in an individual case we may convince ourselves that one of the principles overrides all the others, but this will rarely give us complete satisfaction, nor will the decision represent a final solution applicable in all similar situations. It is true that there seems to be an answer; it has been said that in such conflicts (when we can satisfy only one of two or more conflicting demands which are all moral in themselves) morality is safeguarded because, if we honestly want to make a moral decision and face all contradictory arguments, whatever choice we actually make satisfies all demands because we have conscientiously taken them into account. This may be true if the principles are incontestably moral, but it still does not give us security, for men of good faith have made the most terrifying errors. Therefore, when we made this reservation before, we emphasized that the impact of the absolute must be experienced to prevent such errors.* Yet if morality is regarded as self-sufficient, as it often is, the impact of the absolute is excluded.

Even conscience, though the clearest manifestation of the good, can weaken the good by making us rebel against it, for we may experience what can be called 'undeserved guilt', namely a feeling of guilt caused by actions which we were unable to judge properly at the time or unable to avoid. By sheer accident, we may have been instrumental in bringing about a marriage which had disastrous consequences, welcoming it because we could not foresee the future, for we did not know all the circumstances or were blind to the true characters of the partners or of their relationship. An old woman may walk into the path of a car and be killed; the driver, though blameless, will nevertheless, if his conscience is awake, be unable to absolve himself completely. Both our own blindness (or lack of knowledge) and the inevitability of an event should be, but are not quite felt to be, valid excuses. Moreover we are members of a society, and all societies are bound to trespass against the moral law; society, however, conditions our lives to such an extent that many of our actions, through no fault of our own, are morally equivocal. Even if we try hard, we remain unable to extricate ourselves entirely, and it would even be wrong to isolate ourselves; but we still feel guilty because of the unavoidable element of wrong in some of our actions. Of course, we ourselves are also never wholly good, always more bad than good, but if we are good at all we reproach ourselves for being bad and feel responsible if we are influenced, even unconsciously, by our bad instincts. But why should we be held responsible? Neither society nor man has been fashioned according to our own designs.

The supreme example of this human predicament is presented in the story of Oedipus. When he marries, he does not and cannot possibly know that he is marrying his mother; he is merely receiving the reward promised to the man who saves Thebes

* See pp. 161–2.

10-2

from the Sphinx; but in the end he feels profoundly guilty and punishes himself in a terrifying way.* Here the problem is pushed to its uttermost extreme, but we understand his remorse and are unable to disapprove of his final action; any easy consolation would be utterly inconsistent. Thus conscience can appear too demanding or even destructive; at times it may seem necessary to fight against it to save one's sanity, and sanity, after all, is also a condition of being moral.

Nevertheless, goodness can be made the most certain value—which it fundamentally is—if we remember another characteristic of the absolute values, which is thus thrown into relief—that they are not only different, but also interconnected. If the dangers of a self-sufficient morality and the doubts threatening to undermine any ethical teaching are to be overcome, we have to interconnect goodness with truth. (Beauty is less relevant in this context.)

We have explained that statements containing 'ought', since they establish obligations, must ultimately be based on statements containing 'is'. As moral laws apply to actions and tell us only what we ought to do, they cannot themselves disclose what exists; but if the good is to be accepted unconditionally, it must be in agreement with what exists—that is, it must be true. To truth we have to listen; we have to be receptive so that it can convince us by 'shining in its own light', and this quality is also a condition of a full realization of goodness. Yet it cannot be established by rules alone which make sensitivity—the sense of value—superfluous, offering us instead clear-cut demands; rules blur the radiance of the good and reduce its power to appeal to us directly. Once we touch upon truth, however, we are bound to become entirely involved, with all our faculties, for it would undoubtedly distort our lives to choose to live by illusions. Truth also lessens the doubts which always accompany the trust that, if only we give due weight to all contradictory moral principles, we shall fulfil the demands of morality whichever choice we finally make. A conflict of loyalties can never be avoided, but when we confront

* We may feel differently today about his killing of an old man; it would appear wrong to us even if he had not been his father.

our decision with the truth by which we live—which, since the right context for truth is the world of free persons, is bound to be the conviction that we must not disregard man as an end in himself—errors, though not excluded, will no longer lead to merely destructive actions.

The significance of truth for goodness is illuminated by the problem of undeserved guilt. So long as goodness is isolated, responsibility for unavoidable actions tends to lead to despair, to hopeless accusations against an unjust fate. But when, at the same time, we experience a confrontation with truth, the feeling of responsibility can have a liberating effect; when we no longer insist upon our own innocence, we recognize that to feel responsible demands action, that we ought to do and possibly can do something, and this may, except in extreme cases, enable us to discover a different course of action or way of life. 'Go at once and seek suffering for yourself, as though you were yourself guilty of that wrong. Accept that suffering and bear it and your heart will find comfort, and you will understand that you too are guilty, for you might have been a light to the evil-doers . . . and you were not a light for them.'* Who of us has never given a bad example or failed to give a good one? Evidently, there are strokes of fate which break a man and leave him in complete despair. But, as Oedipus shows, even extreme cases may be susceptible of some relief if truth makes itself felt. Oedipus, because of his feeling of responsibility, discovers the truth, and thus the utterly cruel punishment which he inflicts upon himself for an undeserved, mysterious guilt has a liberating effect for the community—and in the end even for himself; the apparently hopeless tragedy *Oedipus the King* leads to reconciliation in *Oedipus at Colonus*. And again we are forced to admit that Sophocles has succeeded in making the extreme case reveal a generally valid truth.

Such conclusions may sound unrealistic or far too optimistic. But they are not, for they exclude neither great suffering nor despair; horrible events are not passed over nor their weight reduced by facile explanations, and the possibility of failure is

---

* Dostoevsky, *The Brothers Karamazov* (Everyman, vol. 1), p. 334.

admitted. As always in the sphere of essential knowledge, problems are neither removed nor solved; we are given a new insight, an additional knowledge. In fact, our conclusions are confirmed by important implications which the interconnection of goodness with truth also has for truth itself.

Truth as an absolute value must be lived and acted upon. This means that the divination and contemplation of truth, though required and most valuable, is not alone sufficient; truth also has to be tested by judgments referring to actions—that is, by goodness. We have said that we can find our way through the jungle of fascinating ideas and ideals only with the help of goodness. The good cannot be firmly established unless it is based on a knowledge given *a priori*—that is, on a meeting with the absolute; the truth on which the good is based—and thus truth itself—consists in the certainty that in the absolute values we grasp facets of the transcendental. Experience of the connection with truth makes goodness the most certain of the absolute values and confirms that the absolute is not only needed, but really met; we are led to accept it as truth. This, as we have said, is the crucial point, the point at which it is decided whether or not we should accept absolute values. The interaction between truth and goodness, once recognized, removes any doubt for both. If truth is tested by goodness, as it obviously must be, and if goodness is based on truth, which is equally necessary to give it the obligation we know it to have, we cannot but experience the existence of the transcendental.

3

Finally, distortion of the absolute values is prevented if they are, as we have said they ought to be, permeated by love. This is necessary because they are ends in themselves; thus to pursue them without love could lead to ruthlessness, the search for truth and beauty just as much as the enforcement of moral rules, for we have just mentioned that they carry with them their own temptations which, if successful, reduce them to relative values.

But how can this final condition of their correct application be safeguarded? We have not included love among the absolute values, so that their interconnection (which we found such a safeguard) does not apply here. It is true that love of one's neighbour—which in this context is the sense given to the concept 'love'—is demanded by goodness and thereby also connected with truth; yet the commandment itself is not sufficient, for unless it can evoke an experience of what we shall call 'fullness of love' (and shall go on to explain), the law can remain purely formal and its misapplication is by no means impossible; or love can deteriorate into sentimentality or a too great readiness to forgive all and every sin, and such a love will be too shallow and weak to resist stronger impulses of selfishness or hatred. It is true that, since the absolute values are entirely dependent on our inner participation, a complete disregard of man is precluded; but we can still disregard the individual when pursuing a purpose which seems to serve mankind, if we are only concerned with man in the abstract. Moreover, the experience of an impact of the absolute can be so overwhelming that we become entirely absorbed and forget everything else, including our neighbour and ourselves, as appears to be the case in some mystical experiences. But the difference between mysticism and ethics is precisely that, in ethics, this should not happen. We have to ask, therefore, how loving one's neighbour can produce that particular quality of love which ensures that we do full justice to goodness.

The problem is elucidated when we now come to consider the reasons which have led to our decision that love should not be made a further absolute value. Since love is undoubtedly of the highest value, it could seem more convincing to accept it as an absolute value. There is also another similarity which seems to support this claim. We have pointed out that the absolute values are starting points for any value-judgment which leads to their realization; they must be known *a priori*—that is, beforehand; and love is obviously a starting point too, for it must be given in experience to be known at all. But this similarity shows, in fact, their basic difference. In the sphere of values the meeting with the absolute is brought about as the result of a correct judgment; the values are given beforehand, but the impact of the absolute is experienced through their application or appreciation. Love, however, is not the result of any other activity or experience; to permeate the values it has to come to life independently of them and to be experienced directly; it does not open approaches to the absolute, but springs from it. Since love is rooted in the transcendental, it meets the absolute values, so to speak, from the other side. This can be recognized whether we look at love from the point of view of goodness or try to understand what fullness of love means.

One of the differences between external and internal reality which we have established is that only the subjective method enables us to understand the existential meaning of existence—that is, the meaning which makes sense in terms of experience.* This difference creates a gap between the two realities; we only grasp either external facts or inner meaning. It is true that internal reality has to be expressed by external objects, but external knowledge of these is not gained at the same time; it is presupposed.† Goodness closes this gap; since it leads to actions based on the good, we acquire both external knowledge of the actions and understanding of their meaning, so that we experience the oneness of the absolute. But we still grasp only single embodiments, single facets of the absolute; the experience of its oneness is never complete and cannot be translated into words; oneness, too, has to be experienced always anew and in many different ways. Thus, however, goodness confronts us with a serious difficulty. We are men among men and it is this fact which provides us with the most significant glimpse of the all-inclusive oneness of the absolute—by the experience that we are one with the others. But for this goodness alone is insufficient because it requires to be made real by value-judgments, and these, if they are negative, may cut us off from others by leading to accusations or contempt. Therefore goodness must be based on and include love. Yet how can love be reconciled with the need to make value-judgments?

* See pp. 72–3, 77.   † See p. 119.

To this contradiction between love and the absolute values we have already referred.* Love must not rest on an evaluation of persons; we have to love men whatever our judgment of them; the individual has to remain a value in himself. This demand creates the difficulty, for although love thus transcends the application of values, it would be constantly threatened if we were blind to the true character of those we love. Therefore love must not interfere with the judgments; it must be aware of them and yet transcend them. To ensure that love is more than mere indulgence, we have to love men despite their faults, shortcomings, and even wickedness. Here we are reminded of Kant: inclinations are not sufficient, we should also love people whom by natural inclination we dislike; and yet love will only become fully real if, against all odds, it becomes an inclination. Dostoevsky says: 'Everyone can love occasionally, even the wicked can.' Only 'love in action' is real love, and this love 'is a harsh and dreadful thing compared with love in dreams . . . is labour and fortitude.'† And he also emphasizes that it is easy to love 'mankind', which is bound to remain an abstract idea and does not force us to overcome our disinclinations; the true and difficult test is to love the particular individual who repels us. And Kierkegaard says: 'If you do not see your neighbour so close at hand that you see him . . . unconditionally in every man, then you do not see him at all.'‡

Yet can such a love—different from and yet inextricably interconnected with inclination—really be demanded? Can we force ourselves to love persons whom we dislike or know to be in the wrong? Should we even love a man who is brutal and vicious? Fullness of love obviously requires a feeling of solidarity with men, but this feeling hardly seems appropriate in such cases, any more than when we feel justified in rejecting the aims of a group of people or of the society in which we live. Love cannot be supported by those rational processes which are possible once we accept a value, and if we force ourselves to love those whom we do not naturally love or feel forced to reject, the attempt will more

* See p. 272. † *The Brothers Karamazov*, vol. 1, pp. 331 and 54.
‡ *Works of Love*, p. 66.

often than not carry its own revenge; our feelings will be distorted, remain artificial or sentimental or perhaps even turn into hatred. And yet love is demanded; to love one's neighbour is an unconditional commandment which 'shines in its own light' and clearly belongs to that essential knowledge which is only fortified by doubts.

This contradiction is the reason which leads Kierkegaard to claim that fullness of love is only possible if it springs from the transcendental—that the commandment, since it establishes obligation, also proves that the transcendental breaks into our existence. He claims that only a love which is greater than ours and embraces us all can demand that we love each other as ourselves. Kierkegaard bases his claim on Christian religion, but its justification can also be seen in ethical terms. Here once more Dostoevsky can help us.

We have discussed the problem of undeserved guilt and emphasized that acceptance of responsibility for it can have a liberating effect. Dostoevsky enlarges the scope of this responsibility when he says that everyone is really responsible for everyone and everything. He is aware that such a statement may seem outrageous; 'sometimes one is afraid to put it into words, for fear of being laughed at'; therefore he tries to understand it in a literal and not in a religious or mystical way, insisting 'that every one of us is undoubtedly responsible for all men and everything on earth, not merely through the general sinfulness of creation, but each one personally for all mankind and every individual man.' He tries again and again to prove that our responsibility is greater than we can possibly know. 'You pass by a little child . . . spiteful, with ugly words, with a wrathful heart; you may not have noticed the child, but he has seen you, and your image, unseemly and ignoble, may remain in his defenceless heart. You don't know it, but you may have sown an evil seed in him and it may grow.' We cannot escape: 'All is like an ocean, all is flowing and blending; a touch in one place sets up a movement at the other end of the earth.' This acceptance of responsibility is, for him, more realistic and stronger than all external means of combating evil:

'Loving humility is marvellously strong, the strongest of all things, and there is nothing else like it.'*

To appreciate what Dostoevsky means, we have to pay attention to the limitations—in this case the practical limitations—of our knowledge. In the sphere of human relationships we can never completely ascertain the connections between cause and effect; we can never hope fully to know or foresee how the fact that we exist affects others nor all the consequences of our actions. We should not, therefore, rest satisfied with accepting responsibility for the guilt we know, but remain aware of the possibility of an unknown guilt. Yet because of our limited knowledge even speculation about the scope of our guilt will be insufficient; such a quest will always be faced with unanswered questions and thus drive us on and on to ask further questions. This will easily lead to an evasive short cut—to accusing others or circumstances or fate for our misfortunes—because we are soon faced with undeserved guilt; and this will have a paralysing effect, for then we can do no more and will lose hope. Dostoevsky demands a different short cut; we should abandon speculation, see guilt as all-embracing and accept responsibility for it; and this short cut is both justified and liberating. It is justified because the absolute is one, so that all men must be included in it; and it is liberating because the solidarity of men which love demands is thus accepted, and through it love of the guilty, including ourselves (for we may hate ourselves because we are guilty), becomes possible. Restriction of responsibility to known causes and effects cuts us off from the oneness of both the absolute and the human sphere.

The liberating effect of such a decision is confirmed when we test it in the light of our actual experience. We are often unable, even in cases in which we clearly recognize our responsibility, to repair the damage done or to see what we could possibly do to counteract the bad consequences our action has had. However desperately we try, we cannot undo a wrong deed once done, and

---

* *The Brothers Karamazov*, vol. 1, pp. 302, 164, 331, 302. (Most of the passages quoted are statements of Father Zossima, but they obviously express Dostoevsky's own view.)

if it is due to an error rather than ill will, it does not even seem to call for atonement, yet it remains a burden on our mind. We are again paralysed. But the acceptance of complete responsibility does not force us to concentrate exclusively on the one particular guilt which we have incurred; we are faced with a more fundamental and comprehensive guilt; it demands the constant exercise of love and thus sets us free to act. It is true that this kind of responsibility can be misused, as when some people excuse their misdeeds by taking refuge in the fact that all of us are bound to be sinners; collective guilt can appear to make any specific injustice negligible. But if complete responsibility is accepted in the right way—that is, if it arises from our responsibility for an individual deed and is not used as an excuse—it is liberating because the realization that 'all is like an ocean' can give us the trust that an action springing from love will relieve guilt even if the two are not visibly connected with each other. 'A touch in one place sets up a movement at the other end of the earth.'

The acceptance of all-inclusive responsibility is only possible, however, when we feel supported by the oneness of the absolute; only if we also accept the transcendental without any reservation will love constantly be renewed from its source and not be destroyed by our inevitable shortcomings and failures or by an overpowering feeling of guilt. In moments when we suddenly find ourselves able to respond to the impact of the absolute, we shall experience that fullness of love which can face this responsibility. We can never hope for more than moments of complete fulfilment, but these will enable us to build up the required attitude. Yet this also means that our experience of love, though originating from the absolute, is not to be identified with it; since we always grasp mere facets of it, the absolute must have other facets too. It contains love, but only because it is more than love does it give us the strength we need if we are to love. A feeling cannot be its own source. The transcendental must transcend even love itself; it must have a reality of its own from which feeling can emanate; and we have to accept the absolute with all these implications.

But is it really necessary and legitimate to extend the sphere of ethics so far? Dostoevsky is right when he fears that this fullness of responsibility will usually be dismissed or ridiculed. Despite all we have said, weighty reasons can be adduced for rejecting all-inclusive responsibility as well as the absolute. This can be seen even from a purely ethical point of view.

For those who take ethics seriously today, ethics usually means concern with social problems and with establishing more humane relationships within society and also between nations; by them, the desirability of such a limited and practical kind of love is taken for granted. Even Christianity is often interpreted in this way, so that preoccupation with social problems tends to replace belief in God. What we have just said about the transcendental would imply that this interpretation of the Christian faith is wrong, but the preoccupation itself—whether Christian or not—is in agreement with ethics, and we are investigating ethics. How valuable, indeed, it would be if this kind of love were generally taken for granted! It is true that, to be humanitarian in this way, men hardly need to experience love, especially not that fullness of love which has been described, and this may lead to their relying on rules and institutions. Despite the possible bad effects of mere obedience to rules, however, it is hardly unreasonable to argue that it is better to implement love of one's neighbour in a way which is feasible and produces practical results, rather than to insist on a fullness of love which may in any case be utopian.

Of course, there is also a greater danger in such a purely humanist approach. We have discussed the insufficiency of ethics founded on humanism,* and this lack of an adequate foundation makes a love based on humanism alone always susceptible of deterioration into shallowness, sentimentality or a too sweeping forgiveness. The purely humanitarian attitude is beset with a basic uncertainty which often produces an unlimited permissiveness, and thus it does do great harm. It can demand, as we have seen, that criminals should not only be treated with leniency whenever advisable, but that they should be understood in a

* See ch. VI.

psychological way, which has the consequence that crimes are no longer acknowledged as crimes, but only as a reason for treatment or for pity. Such a demand abolishes the boundaries between crime and illness, between moral and immoral behaviour, and clearly the possible effects of such an attitude could ultimately lead to chaos. Yet to avoid even this danger would not necessarily involve looking beyond man; it could merely mean that we need a proper foundation for value-judgments, a firm knowledge of standards and values—namely the elaboration of relative and absolute values which have been outlined. We could agree that we have to have standards, without seeing any need to go further. Humanitarianism could ensure that man is not entirely disregarded, and the absolute values could ensure that humanitarianism does not give in to shallow, dubious, or even excessively humane inclinations. It would seem that undue permissiveness could be avoided. In some contexts the idea of mankind might be substituted for the individual, but is not all-inclusive responsibility, although it provokes much more concrete experiences than an idea, in the last resort also concerned with mankind?

The answer to all these questions is given by our findings concerning the absolute values themselves. We did not start from any desire to enhance love by making it impossibly exacting and thus appear supernatural, nor with any special religious or romantic yearning, and yet we have been forced to recognize as necessarily inseparable from the absolute values that fullness of love which is only made possible by the absolute. The absolute values can exercise their much-needed influence only if their real, that is to say their transcendental, nature is realized and accepted. If, therefore, we do accept these values it becomes of the first importance to accept them for what they are and not to cherish illusions concerning them. If the results of our investigation are correct, as I hope I have shown them to be, this means accepting the absolute as well, for rejection of it will in the end undermine moral values. Ethics may still go on functioning in favourable circumstances in a limited way, but not when it is most needed—namely when its cause seems hopeless, as it so frequently does.

This shows, however, that the contradiction which Kierke-gaard emphasized—that love is a spontaneous feeling and yet demanded—is in one respect still unresolved, for our argument does not say how we can be enabled to accept the absolute. No argument will ever convince us that the transcendental exists if we do not ourselves experience it, and even if we do experience its impact, we need not recognize it as such. Those who have had no such experience will find our demand meaningless and go on asking what use it is for them. Therefore a last step is required— to show how we can start from the absolute and thus safeguard a correct appreciation of the absolute values by meeting them 'from the other side'. It may be said that such a step leads beyond ethics, because it is no longer concerned with the good and with what we ought to do, but even if this were true, ethics remains incom-plete without it. We have to explore how such a step can be made.

The need for it can also be seen if we remember the difficulties which actually confront ethics. We have referred to the power of evil within man and the ever-present cruelty and ruthlessness throughout the history of mankind. We have not enlarged on these factors because our task has been to build up a positive ethical teaching, in the hope of making it strong enough to out-weigh the evidence supporting the attacks on it, so that, perhaps, we could adhere to it in the face of adversity.* Ethics will never fulfil this task, however, if it remains isolated, protected by idealistic illusions; it will only be secure if it can withstand con-stant confrontation with the actual situation. We shouldnot—and in fact we hardly can—ever forget that the good seems powerless, is defeated by evil again and again, and has exercised no definitive influence upon man's history. Thus doubts will always assail ethics; it will always appear more sensible to restrict morality to a private sphere, while relying on deliberate calculation, even on complete unscrupulousness, when striving for even the slightest outward success. But then morality is no longer what it ought to be—binding. Will anything less than the acceptance of the

* See p. 69.

transcendental enable us to meet this challenge—to accept the validity of unconditional moral obligations and act according to them, whatever the evidence which seems to disprove their relevance?

This necessary last step—the actual acceptance of the absolute—may, when seen from outside, seem to create further difficulties; but when it is experienced, much of what has appeared difficult so far becomes very natural indeed. Ethics becomes what it should be—self-evident and a matter of course.

CHAPTER XII

THE LEAP INTO CERTAINTY

The further step which we have to discuss has been called by Kierkegaard the 'leap into the unknown' or the 'jump into the abyss'. This leap is required both in the religious and in the ethical sphere, but has different implications according to whether we consider it in a religious context, as Kierkegaard does, or in the ethical context with which we are concerned. We shall nevertheless first explain his elaboration of it, because this can help us to understand what any such leap means.

Kierkegaard recognizes the need for a leap because we cannot force anybody to have faith, not even ourselves. A longing for faith may easily arise; we may feel impotence, frustration, despair, recognize that belief in God could solve our difficulties, and yet remain unable to believe; or the impact of the absolute which we have described may give us a glimmer of understanding of what faith is and we may yet be unable to accept it. In such moments we probably have a kind of faith, but it is fugitive and unreliable and superseded by doubt. In itself, the impact of the absolute is not sufficient because it remains dependent on fleeting experiences which, though powerful and arresting, lead only to moments of insight; faith, however, implies the constant awareness of a transcendental reality which can be relied upon always and unconditionally. In short, even if we genuinely desire faith and have some understanding of it, we may still remain unable to believe. Nor will the example of people whose faith we admire necessarily lead to more than a longing for faith. Yet Kierkegaard claims that we can nevertheless do something—namely take the risk of leaping into the unknown.

This leap means that we give up any ultimate reliance on those certainties—practical, rational, scientific—which we have been accustomed to trust and perform the action which is always basic to faith: surrender completely and unconditionally to God. This is a risk, and as we thus surrender before we have faith, we cannot be certain that it is a risk which is really worth taking; since we do not yet believe in God, we are acutely conscious that we may be mistaken and merely throwing away our trust in reason. But if we have no faith and yet want faith the risk has to be taken, because anything absolute or transcendental cannot be used or tried out as if it were a kind of scientific hypothesis; it cannot be understood unless we commit ourselves to it and are involved in it; our experience must first make us open to its impact by which alone it can become real. There is no other way to faith; we have to surrender to the absolute with nothing tangible to grasp; we must accept it merely in the hope that the ensuing experience will prove us right.*

The need for the commitment on which this demand for the leap is based is made clear by Paul Tillich when he says: 'There are objects for which the so-called "objective" approach is the least objective of all, because it is based on a misunderstanding of the nature of its object. This is especially true of religion. Unconcerned detachment in matters of religion (if it is more than a methodological self-restriction) implies an *a priori* rejection of the religious demand to be ultimately concerned. It denies the object which it is supposed to approach "objectively".'†

Thus, however, the leap confronts us with a danger—that we surrender to the irrational and destroy reason. Kierkegaard is very much aware of this danger. It is true that he has been criticized for being too irrational because he says: 'Faith begins precisely where thinking leaves off.'‡ But he is a passionate and incisive thinker nonetheless, and never gives up before discovering the exact point where thinking can no longer help, so as to ensure that the jump is not made too soon. And this point can be discovered.

The leap is required—and the longing for faith is natural—because we find ourselves in a paradoxical situation. We have said

* For a fuller elaboration see P. Roubiczek, *Existentialism—For and Against*, ch. 4.
† *The Protestant Era* (London, 1951), p. xxv.
‡ *Fear and Trembling*, p. 78.

that we are constantly confronted with the contradictory results of the two methods and cannot solve these contradictions; we are caught between the two realities, neither of which we fully understand, and thus we are suspended above an 'unfathomable depth'. It is true that at the same time this situation exposes us to the impact of the absolute and makes essential knowledge accessible to us, but the absolute still remains out of reach and essential knowledge does not solve any problems outside itself; so that, on the basis of a conscious effort of thinking, we can account neither for the absolute nor for essential knowledge. Yet it would be contrary to our experience to deny their existence.* At this point, therefore, there is no other solution but to make the leap of accepting the absolute, even though its existence cannot be proved, and essential knowledge, even though it cannot be derived from any other knowledge. The very nature of faith makes the leap necessary; it is the only way in which faith can be embraced without a falsifying rationalization (because we do not rely on thinking alone) and without the sacrifice of intellect (if we make sure that the leap is not made too soon). Once we have made the leap, reason can be employed again; it can—and ought to—contribute to a fuller understanding of the transcendental sphere and of Christianity. But there is a break in between; these two uses of reason (before and after the jump) are not continuous; if we rely on reason alone we are bound to reach a point where it can no longer help us.

We have to accept reality as it is given to us. Reality is not 'rational' or 'realistic' in the sense that everything which exists or happens is logical or necessary or explicable; most of it is surprising, fantastic, improbable. This is so obvious that it hardly needs elaboration; it can be seen whether we look at the expanding universe, the evolution of plants and animals, or think of earthquakes, floods, droughts and their disastrous consequences. Even more perplexing is man, whether we consider his history, the existence of nations or the amazing structure of his body and mind. Why are we born only to die? Fundamentally reality

* See pp. 120–2.

remains irrational in that we are never able to explain why it is as it is, and this irrational element has to be admitted when we face the foundations of existence.

But the irrational need not be destructive; it can become constructive. If it is experienced in the way we have tried to describe, the contradiction between the two realities, by exposing us to the impact of the absolute, discloses essential knowledge, and if we accept this challenge and risk the leap, the irrational is transformed and becomes the basis of a positive approach which enlarges the sphere of relevant and revealing experience. The leap can have this effect because it has the two aspects which we have just mentioned; it confirms essential knowledge which is needed for ethics, and transforms the impact of the absolute into the basis of faith which is required for religion. These two aspects, moreover, reveal differences which allow us to discriminate.

Religious concepts remain meaningless unless they are experienced and accepted; for those who have had no such experience even the word God will remain an empty word. We cannot assume that everybody must understand what it means, however much we explain it. But when using ethical concepts we can hope that we are appealing to potentialities which every man should recognize in himself; since he has an ethical self, he will probably be able to respond to such an appeal. The good is certainly more commonly understood than is God; hence the attempts to rescue Christianity by reducing its content to ethics. Even the sceptic will hardly deny that his conscience is sometimes troubled by the moral commandments; he knows that he should be concerned with them because they refer to his own behaviour, and that some of them may be justified. In fact, fundamental morality is fairly generally acknowledged, even if not generally acted upon, and love of one's neighbour, as we have said, is taken for granted by a significant minority.

Nevertheless, the main stumbling block even for those who would like to agree that ethics should be based on the results of our investigation is certainly still—despite all that has been said—the acceptance of the absolute. They may agree that, so long as we feel unable to start from the absolute, the leap into the unknown is the only way of accepting it open to them, but they may still feel reluctant to take this risk and doubt whether they really need to take it. Many prefer to remain uncommitted with regard to the absolute. Yet these doubts, which arguments alone cannot remove, immediately disappear once the leap itself is experienced, for the ensuing experience confirms that the decision has been right. This becomes particularly clear in the sphere of ethics because here the urge to make the leap is more pressing and its result more directly conclusive than in the religious sphere, even though, fundamentally, the act itself is the same.

The need to make the leap is urgent because, if the good is experienced at all—and we believe, as we have said, that it is a common experience—those who experience it are constantly brought into the vicinity of the absolute. The ethical self and its potentialities will, whenever touched upon, come into the open, and once they are actual they will make us accept moral commandments and principles and the love of one's neighbour—that is, the essential knowledge which impresses itself upon us as absolute. It is in this way that the subjective method opens approaches to the absolute. But since neither this method nor internal reality can actually include it, we shall be harassed by its claims and feel the need to start from it; by being driven to accept the absoluteness of ethical demands, we shall also be driven to make the jump into the abyss which separates us from the transcendental. In ethics, moreover, the results of the jump are more directly conclusive because, when we make and experience it, we realize immediately that our fear of it was mistaken. For here the leap into the unknown turns out to be a leap into the better known—into a sphere which we actually know better than any other.

Much of what we have said before explains why this is so. The good is familiar to us even if we meet it for the first time; essential knowledge is self-evident and only fortified by doubts. In fact, as soon as we accept the absolute as the source and basis of ethics and are thus enabled to accept ethics without hesitations and no longer question its foundation and justification, we experience that liberation which we have described when discussing all-inclusive responsibility, because we are enabled to move freely in a world in which we are completely at home. We actually know morality far better than anything which is known by the objective method, better than any object known only from outside, because we know it by inner experience. Even abstract ethical principles are more familiar and intelligible to us than any scientific or psychological theory, despite the difficulties of application, because they do not require any specialized knowledge; they embody and guide a generally accessible experience. We also know ethics better than we know ourselves, for our individuality, although known from inside, remains in parts mysterious to us. Ethical experience is not our only immediate experience, but it is that experience which is immediately understood. What could be more natural and self-explanatory than that we should not kill our neighbour, but love him and respect the humanity in him as well as in ourselves? We are set free to trust our innermost nature, to develop those potentialities which lead to self-fulfilment, and to build upon foundations which entirely conform to what we are. When the leap enables us to shed our doubts, we are liberated because we discover a world which is entirely our own.

The contrast between the leap into the unknown and the leap into the better known corresponds exactly to the difference between faith and ethics. In both cases, the leap is required because of the limitations of our knowledge; the difference lies in the way in which the absolute becomes real to us. Faith demands a clear conception of the absolute; we accept, in fact, not the abstract idea of something which is absolute or transcendental, but God and thereby a definitive statement about all existence. Ethics demands essential knowledge which springs from the absolute, but does not lead on to its exploration; it is immediately applied in action and thus leads back to our own world; it is concerned, therefore, with a more restricted experience than is faith. This experience, moreover, can be tested by action, while faith implies a much more complete surrender, for God must needs immensely transcend us

The leap into certainty

—God known is no God—so that it would be blasphemy to make our belief in God dependent on any test conducted by our limited knowledge. Ensuing experiences may again and again support faith, but we remain constantly dependent on them, for we are confronted with a reality entirely other than all we know, while ethics involves us in a world which we actually know most intimately.

In ethics, therefore, we can remain content with a simple acceptance of the absolute which needs no further elaboration; here the leap enables man to recognize and trust the absoluteness of ethics, so that he need no longer doubt that moral commandments are unconditional and binding. Thus he will move with confidence in that sphere for which he is best fitted and will act accordingly, and this is what ethics demands. But the fact that the leap is needed in both the ethical and the religious sphere and is yet different in each also allows conclusions to be drawn with regard to religion. These certainly lead beyond ethics, but they should not be omitted because they also throw light on it.

Formerly, ethics was understood as the outcome of religion; moral commandments were given by God and expressed His will. The attempts to rescue Christianity with the help of ethics show that this view is no longer generally convincing. For many today, belief in God seems impossible, but this is no proof that He does not exist. In any case, the question remains essential, for if He did not exist and we lived as if He did, or if He did exist and we lived as if He did not, all our endeavours would be falsified. We must therefore consider religion. Is it possible that ethics could now become a way towards the understanding of religion, even a way towards its acceptance? It probably could if it were not used to replace religion, but if the conclusion of our investigation—that ethics is only correctly understood when completed by the leap— were accepted. For then ethics provides us with evidence of the existence of the absolute which is generally accessible and can be tested by action; acceptance of the transcendental, therefore, could no longer appear dishonest, over-idealistic or absurd; and even though faith would still remain more exacting, the leap into the better known could prepare us for the complete surrender demanded by the leap into the unknown.

In fact, the reason why ethics cannot simply be considered a substitute for religion is because it points to this other leap. The absolute, as we have said, is given *a priori* and not deduced from other knowledge; the absolute values have confirmed that we must start from it.* In external reality, *a priori* concepts, such as the categories, remain purely formal; to acquire meaning, they ·have to be applied to what has been perceived.† Ethical principles have to be applied, too, but the *a priori* concepts in this sphere give us knowledge of a content because they give rise to actions based solely on them; the absolute is embodied in the absolute values. Certainly, these merely disclose facets of it, yet they indicate its content in a very definitive way—they have to be founded upon, and permeated by, love. The ethical leap is a surrender to love. Love, however, cannot be abstract and impersonal; it points the way to the leap which faith demands. We have been led to include the fullness of love to make ethics complete; if this fullness of love is experienced, the leap into the unknown has perhaps already been made.

This means that ethics, although not explicitly demanding the other leap, is actually safeguarded by it. So long as ethics is considered to be relative, it is constantly in danger of becoming shallow or sentimental or of being robbed of its very basis by psychology, sociology or humanism. Therefore the way towards religion should at least always be kept open. Ethics does not necessarily require a religious foundation, but it has nothing to lose and much to gain if the pressure to make the leap into the unknown is constantly felt and if, in the end, faith no longer appears either impossible or superfluous. The two kinds of leap are different and independent of each other, but they are complementary.

This connection between ethics and religion can be clarified by the concept of sin. Disobedience to moral commandments leads to failures, immoral actions and crimes, but it would be wrong to use

* See pp. 286–7. † See p. 184.

the concept 'sin' so long as we are moving within the sphere of
ethics. For sin implies not only trespassing against the absolute,
but also provoking the reaction of a higher authority, namely
judgment, and this presupposes that specific form of the absolute
which is established by religion. Yet can we really think of ethics
without considering sin? We actually do think of sin, not because
of traditional prejudice, but because of the impact of the absolute
to which ethics responds. Nevertheless, we leave the sphere of
ethics when we include sin. Kierkegaard says: 'An ethics which
disregards sin is a perfectly idle science; but if it asserts sin, it is *eo
ipso* beyond itself.'*

Despite this contradiction, however, the inclusion of sin is
essential because ethics without it still remains in one important
respect inconclusive. We have said that an action, once done,
cannot be undone; therefore, even when the acceptance of responsibility sets us free, an evil deed can remain a burden on our
mind and block the way to a complete reformation which, after
all, is the final aim of ethics. We may make the deed a spur to
better actions and even succeed in relieving suffering caused by it,
but the deed will still weigh us down because these actions are in
themselves no atonement. Our guilt and the attempts to relieve it
do not quite meet. If we experience our failures as sins, they are
aggravated, for they are then seen as doing damage to the transcendental, as hurting not only men, but also God. Experience of
sin involves us in a remorse which is perhaps more desperate than
any other; the deed is not undone, but lifted into a higher sphere,
and this increases its weight. We may once more rebel: why are
we born as sinners? Yet this very aggravation can be a relief, a
final liberation, because it touches upon the source, not only of
punishment, but also of forgiveness. The actual experience of sin
can make our attempts to atone for it a way towards reconciliation, for we have come, as the individuals we are, 'into an
absolute relationship with the absolute'.† The evil deed loses its
paralysing effect when we feel that we have been forgiven.

This does not mean, however, that ethics could ever be dis-

---

* *Fear and Trembling*, p. 151.   † *Ibid.* p. 152.

pensed with; it is needed because sin, if it were understood as purely transcendental, would become unreal. Sin must be experienced as a real deed in a real situation and as trespassing against moral laws, ethical principles and the absolute values, for only thus can we realize it with all its implications and consequences.

The leap into the unknown also sets at rest the doubts which we have expressed concerning the human situation, which come from the fact that men are never entirely good, but always also bad and often evil, and that cruelty and brutality persist in man's history throughout the ages. We can struggle for improvements and discern some limited success, but failure can never be avoided and will again and again overshadow success. The human situation, seen from the ethical point of view, does not change. But ethics also shows that the way to transcend all relative conditions always remains open. It is possible at any time and in any situation to break through all barriers, to risk the jump and thus find access to the absolute. Man may be driven to despair, but he is never lost; individuals have shown at all times that it is in fact possible to choose this way. The task of ethics and religion is to make this way known and to keep it open. This is important from whichever point of view we look at it, for 'all is like an ocean' so that we never know all the consequences of our decisions, and we have also seen that social morality depends on individual morality. In spite of all inevitable doubts we should therefore realize that, if we risk the ethical leap, we reach a world in which we are completely at home and that, if we risk the leap into the unknown, we can hope, as Kierkegaard does, that we shall not perish, but 'fall into the open arms of God'.

INDEX

315

Index

Index

Index

relativity, 21–2, 24, 32–3, 46–9, 54, 65, 83, 85, 133–6, 139–40, 148–9, 173; theory of, 22, 78, 227
religion, 33, 42–3, 49, 70, 111, 129, 139, 171, 181, 202–3, 306–8, 311–13, 314
Rembrandt, 93
repetition, 79, 84, 90–1
respect, 196, 205, 214, 256
responsibility, 7, 39, 53, 54–5, 62, 64, 68, 146–7, 152–3, 201, 225, 250–5, 293, 298–300
Rilke, 246 n
Russell, B., 174 n
Russell, W. Ritchie, 25

Sartre, J.-P., 122, 126, 147, 186
scepticism, 21–2, 30
Scheler, M., 219 n, 245
Schelling, 170
Schopenhauer, 170
science, 15, 18–19, 22–3, 25–6, 31, 33, 35–6, 53–4, 65, 74–85, 103–4, 108, 111, 149, 171, 173, 180, 185, 226–30, 248, 250–5, 258, 262, 277, 280 n
self, ethical, 17, 41, 91, 136, 144, 148, 153, 164, 202, 213, 238–9, 308
sentimentality, 205, 245, 259–60, 295
Sermon on the Mount, 99, 136, 155, 205
sin, 312–14
Smethurst, A. F., 171 n
society, 45, 51, 52–3, 55–7, 61–2, 64–5, 147, 291
sociology, 21, 22 n, 45–55, 63–5, 254–5
Socrates, 14, 57, 155, 193, 200, 201, 281–2
Sophocles, 293
space and time, 116, 178, 183–90, 223
Spencer, Herbert, 170
statements containing 'is' and 'ought', 15–17, 143–4, 164, 193, 214–15, 218, 239–40, 292

Stoker, H. G., 156 n
subject and object, *see* object and subject
substance, 182–3

Taoism, 156
theology, *see* religion
theories, scientific, 76–7, 94, 119, 200, 227
thinking, two ways of, 14–16, 18, 74, 102–5, 106–9, 112, 170–4, 191–2, 207, 209
Thomas Aquinas, 107
Tillich, P., 306
time, 155; *see also* space and time
truth, 10, 21–2, 24, 28–9, 33, 47, 225, 250, 252–3, 268, 273, 274–5, 276–85, 288, 289, 292–4

uncertainty principle, 53, 75, 179–80
unconscious, the, 34–8, 41
utilitarianism, 47, 198–9, 201, 258

values, absolute, 10, 32, 47, 235–6, 241, 250–3, 264–6, 267–94, 295–7, 302–3; discussion of term, 219–29, 239–40; hierarchy of, 228–9; moral, 221; positive and negative, 223–5; purely subjective, 220, 241–6, 249; relative, 241, 247–58, 260–1, 268–72, 278; scales of, 226–9, 231–6
virtues, 222, 247, 255–8, 277

Weber, M., 46, 48
Wenzl, A., 5 n
Whitehead, A. N., 184

Zahn, G. C., 64 n, 282 n
Zoroastrianism, 105